Economics and Decision Making for Environmental Quality

Economics and Decision Making for Environmental Quality

Edited by
J. Richard Conner
Edna Loehman

A University of Florida Book

The University Presses of Florida
1974

Library of Congress Cataloging in Publication Data

Conner, James Richard, 1942–

Economics and decision making for environmental quality.

"A University of Florida book."

"The papers . . . are the result of a series of technical seminars sponsored by the Food and Resource Economics Department of the University of Florida during the spring quarter, 1971."

Includes bibliographies.

1. Environmental policy—United States—Congresses.
2. Environmental law—United States—Congresses.
3. Pollution—Economic aspects—United States—Congresses. I. Loehman, E., joint ed. II. Florida. University, Gainesville. Food and Resources Economics Dept. III. Title.

HC110.E5C67 301.31'0973 74–6056
ISBN 0–8130–0385–7
ISBN 0–8130–0508–6 (pbk.)

PRINTED BY STORTER PRINTING COMPANY
GAINESVILLE, FLORIDA

Contents

Preface

The discussion of social choice problems and decision making has been of historic concern in economics. Such issues have been dealt with in economic literature dating back to John Stuart Mill and have received new interest with recent works of such well-known economists as Paul Samuelson, Kenneth Arrow, and James Buchanan. With our present concern for environmental quality, we are again encountering problems in social choice and decision making in trying to decide what environmental quality should be. Since social choices are ultimately made by legislative and other governmental bodies, questions of who is involved in making essential choices and how they are involved have also become of interest to economists.

Problems of public decision making have not been considered solely by economists. Other social scientists have studied the problems on a theoretical level and engineers and public officials have been involved on a practical level. Thus, papers included in this book are from the fields of political science, law, and engineering as well as economics. However, the emphasis throughout is on decision making for environmental quality.

The papers included in this volume are the result of a series of technical seminars sponsored by the Food and Resource Economics Department at the University of Florida during the spring quarter, 1971. The papers were solicited from social scientists and engineers.

The book is divided into four sections with an introductory chapter and a short introduction to each section written by the editors. For the reader new to the field of welfare economics and public decision making, the introductory chapter will provide helpful definitions and perspectives. The first section deals with the relation of social choice problems and economics to environmental quality decisions and with the problems of selecting and implementing pollution control mechanisms. The second section examines various proposals for obtaining information on and assessing the benefits and costs associated with resource development projects. The third section is concerned with legal mechanisms for achieving environmental quality objectives, and the last section is concerned with decision making and informational tools for the analysis of environmental problems.

The purpose of this book is to explore all aspects of environmental decision-making problems, from the theoretical social choice issues to the practical problems of measurement. This book is designed primarily for those in economics and related disciplines interested in the relationship of economics to environmental decision making and for those interested in the multidisciplinary approach to environmental problems.

The support of Dr. E. T. York, Jr., then Vice President for the Institute of Food and Agricultural Sciences, and Dr. K. R. Tefertiller, then Chairman of the Food and Resource Economics Department of the University of Florida, is greatly appreciated. We are grateful to the authors who were kind enough to divert their time from very busy schedules in order to participate in the seminar program which precipitated this book. In addition to the authors whose papers appear in this book, we offer our thanks to Dr. Leonid Hurwicz, Professor of Economics, University of Minnesota, and Dr. M. R. Langham, Professor of Economics and Food and Resource Economics, University of Florida, for contributing stimulating presentations in the seminar program. We should also note that the papers by Randall, and Levi and Colyer, were solicited by the editors for inclusion in the book although the authors did not participate in the seminar program.

We would like to acknowledge the help of all of the faculty members of the Food and Resource Economics Department with special thanks to Drs. R. D. Emerson, M. R. Langham, W. W. McPherson, F. J. Prochaska, and M. L. Upchurch for their guidance and assistance throughout the development of the seminar program and publication of this book.

J. Richard Conner and Edna Loehman

Contributors

SUZANNE E. BAYLEY, Assistant Professor, Environmental Engineering Department, University of Florida, Gainesville.

DALE K. COLYER, Professor and Agricultural Economist, Division of Resource Management, West Virginia University, Morgantown.

J. RICHARD CONNER, Assistant Professor, Food and Resource Economics Department, University of Florida, Gainesville.

JOHN H. CUMBERLAND, Professor of Economics, Bureau of Business and Economics Research, University of Maryland, College Park.

PAUL H. GERHARDT, Assistant to the Director, Implementation Research Division, Office of Research and Development, U.S. Environmental Protection Agency, Washington, D.C.

CHARLES J. GOETZ, Associate Professor, Economics Department, Virginia Polytechnic Institute, Blacksburg.

EDWIN T. HAEFELE, Senior Research Associate, Resources for the Future, Washington, D.C.

WILLIAM K. JOHNSON, Civil Engineer, Board of Engineers for Rivers and Harbors, U.S. Army Corps of Engineers, Washington, D.C.

DONALD R. LEVI, Associate Professor, Agricultural Economics and Rural Sociology Department, Texas A&M University, College Station.

JOSEPH W. LITTLE, Professor, College of Law, University of Florida, Gainesville.

EDNA LOEHMAN, Assistant Professor, Food and Resource Economics Department, University of Florida, Gainesville.

WILLIAM B. LORD, Representative, Resources for the Future, Ford Foundation, Mexico City.

HOWARD T. ODUM, Graduate Research Professor, Environmental Engineering Department, University of Florida, Gainesville.

DAVID E. PINGRY, Visiting Assistant Professor, Economics Department, Purdue University, Lafayette, Indiana.

ALAN RANDALL, Assistant Professor, Agricultural Economics Department, New Mexico State University, Las Cruces.

HARRY A. STEELE, Private Consultant, formerly Associate Director, U.S. Water Resources Council, Washington, D.C.

JOHN F. TIMMONS, Charles F. Curtiss Distinguished Professor, Department of Economics, Iowa State University, Ames.

ANDREW WHINSTON, Professor, Economics Department, Krannert Graduate School of Industrial Administration, Purdue University, Lafayette, Indiana.

Introduction
Economic Perspectives on Environmental Decisions

Edna Loehman and J. Richard Conner

Environmental quality problems arise from the use and misuse of natural resources by both private and governmental enterprises. There are many uses of natural resources, not formerly of concern, which are now recognized as causing environmental problems. A list of current environmental problem sources would have to include waste disposal from industrial and municipal operations, power generation, transportation, use of pesticides and other chemicals, mining, forestry practices, land and water development, and increasing use of all resources due to increasing population. The key element of the problem is scarcity: the ability of the environment to restore itself is limited and resources are limited. Any use of resources at an activity level higher than nature's capacity to restore itself can result in pollution of air, water, and/or land. Since the amounts of underdeveloped land and free-flowing streams are fixed, more land and water devoted to development uses means less is available in the natural state and for other uses.

The remedies proposed for solving environmental problems depend on whether the cause of a problem is the actions of private individuals or governmental groups. Air and bodies of water are considered to be public resources, although water laws may differ from state to state. Air and water pollution result primarily from private use of resources (although governmental actions are also a source). Thus, most suggested pollution remedies attempt to restrict private actions, in the public interest. Likewise, land development by private individuals may cause public problems in flood control, sewage treatment, etc., so that remedies such as zoning are controls on individual actions, in the public interest. On the other hand, water development projects are usually undertaken by governmental units due to the public nature of water supply and flood control. Therefore, remedies for problems caused by governmental development projects seek to make government more responsive to the public interest.

Clearly, remedies for both pollution and development problems necessitate defining what use of resources is in the public interest. For any use of resources, benefits accrue to some individuals and costs to others. A decision about what use is in the public interest implies a judgment of who should receive benefits and who should bear costs and in what amounts. Problems of making public decisions when there are groups or individuals with varying preferences for benefits and costs are classified as "social choice" problems. If there were no scarcity of resources, such social choice problems would not arise since everyone could then be satisfied at the same time.

Economists have studied social choice and resource allocation problems since the time of Adam Smith and John Stuart Mill. A body of theory has developed which is applicable to environmental quality issues, and many economists are now concerned with trying to develop policies to achieve the desired levels of environmental quality. The following discussion is a brief introduction to some of the relevant economic concepts and terms which are beginning to be heard more often as economists get more involved in environmental issues. Since a complete discussion of all types of environmental problems would be very lengthy, we limit ourselves here to some general considerations concerning pollution and development. In addition, the information requirements for resolving environmental issues will be considered.

Although economic concepts will be emphasized, we do not mean to suggest that economics is the only discipline which has something to offer for solutions to environmental problems. For instance, law and social science must certainly be studied to find ways to effect social changes. Physical and biological sciences are essential to tell us what the consequences of our actions on the environment will be. In fact, all disciplines pertinent to the study of man, nature, or their interrelationships are relevant.

Some Economic Concepts Relating to Environmental Quality

THE MARKET SYSTEM

All students of economics are familiar with the market system and how it determines prices and allocates resources through the forces of supply and demand. In the market system, consumers and producers act independently of one another, i.e., the system is decentralized. In response to prices, consumers purchase goods to maximize their satisfaction or "utility," and producers purchase inputs and produce goods to maximize profits. The primary concern of economists with the equilibrium of such a system is whether the system allocates resources properly. Figure 1 illustrates the equilibrium for a market system with two consumers having demand functions D_1 and D_2 and a producer with a supply function S. P_E denotes the equilibrium price and Q_1 and Q_2 denote equilibrium quantities for the two consumers.

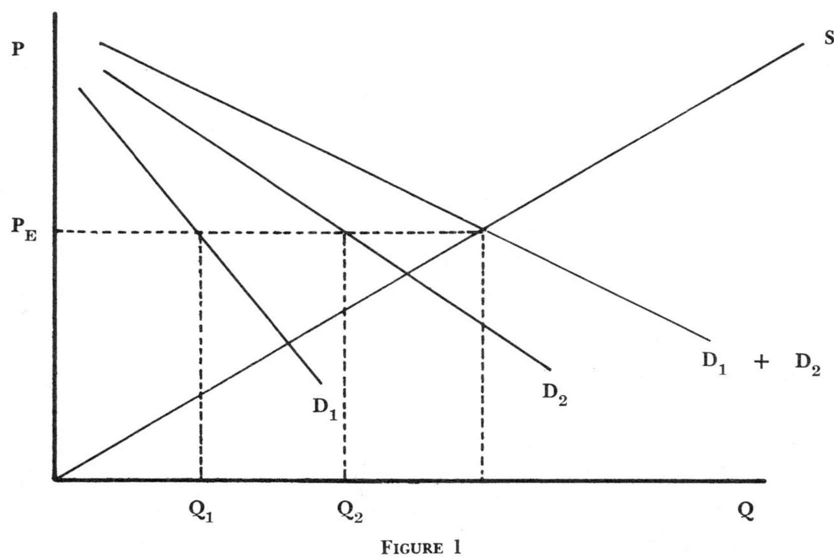

FIGURE 1

A main theorem of welfare economics (2, 20) states that for a given distribution of income, under assumptions of perfect competition such as decentralization of consumers and producers, and certain mathematical requirements on utility and production functions, a market equilibrium is a "Pareto-optimal" situation. (A "Pareto optimum" is a state where no one can be made better off without someone else being made worse off.) Thus, in this ideal situation, the market is a mechanism for achieving a socially optimal state. That is, decisions about resource use in the private interest are also in the public interest.

It is known that this theorem is not true when market imperfections such as monopoly violate the above assumptions. Then, decentralized decision making based on market prices no longer gives a Pareto optimum. In such situations economists look for modifications of the market mechanism or new mechanisms to achieve a social optimum.

EXTERNALITIES

Pollution is an example of a type of market imperfection known in economics as an "externality." An externality is a use of resources by a consumer (or producer) which has a direct effect on other consumers (or other producers). Restated, an externality is an activity by party A which either imposes costs on party B for which B is not compensated or gives benefits to B for which he does not pay. The concept of an externality thus recognizes that there are social costs and social benefits from use of resources apart from private benefits and costs.

An extensive literature has developed concerning optimal decision making when there are externalities (6, 10). The general conclusion in such cases is that decision making cannot be completely private or decentralized to achieve maximum social welfare. For example, a polluter's resource-use decisions should have to depend not only on his own satisfaction but also on how his pollution affects the welfare of other producers and consumers. Here, the usual market system does not give proper incentives for use of resources in the public interest.

ECONOMIC REMEDIES FOR POLLUTION

The literature on externalities is concerned with devising mechanisms to influence individual decisions to correspond to the public interest. Suggested mechanisms include: market-type solutions which involve defining new commodities and prices; mechanisms in which decision making is not completely private ("internalizing" externalities); taxation schemes; and setting limits and standards on resource use.

It is frequently said that pollution problems result because certain resources in their natural state, such as air and water, are "free" goods with a price of zero. A suggested remedy is to let a market allocate the use of air and water for waste disposal. However, economic theory tells us that resources which are not limited will have a zero price in a market. Thus, in order to have a market in which to allocate the use of air and water for waste disposal, limits will have to be placed on the amounts which can be used for such purposes. This, in effect, means defining air and water quality standards. Also, the rights of ownership would have to be well defined in order to have a market.

Bargaining among parties involved with and affected by pollution is a way of "internalizing" a pollution externality. In order for incentives for bargaining to occur, property rights and liability have to be well defined. If the polluter is held liable (i.e., citizens have rights to air and water quality), then he must bargain with and pay a tax to citizens to be able to pollute at a certain level. On the other hand, if the polluter is not liable, citizens have to bargain with the polluter and bribe him to limit his pollution. Coase (8) proposes that either taxes or bribes lead to the same final allocation of resources, i.e., how liability is defined does not matter. Some economists have begun to question this conclusion. For example, if the bribe required to limit the polluter is higher than citizens can afford, the outcome may be different than if the polluter must pay. Also, if citizens have to organize to bargain with the polluter, there may be extra costs of making transactions. The larger the number of citizens and interests involved, the higher the transaction costs. As Randall (chapter 2) shows, the nature of these transaction costs influences the outcome of the bargaining process. For a very large number of polluters and citizens, the bargaining situation merges with the market problems described above.

Government taxes levied on a polluter's use of resources is the third type of externality remedy. According to economic theory, the polluter would then reduce or change his use of inputs in the case of an input tax or reduce his output in the case of an output tax. The taxation solution for externalities dates back to Pigou (19). The Pigouvian tax simply sets a price on pollution in cases where ownership of resources is defined to be public rather than private and price is set by the government rather than being found in a market. The question is, what should be the amount of the tax? The common view is that the proper tax is the difference between private and social costs for an input or private and social benefits for an output (18). Since the definition of social costs and benefits requires an evaluation of the relative importance to society of the various groups experiencing losses and gains, the Pigouvian tax is not really as well defined as it might seem.

Iterative procedures for finding the correct tax have been suggested (3). These involve varying the tax until acceptable quality is achieved. Other types of taxes have also been suggested (26)—for instance, putting a tax on each productive use of resources based on the cost of the product.

The final suggestion is pollution standards. It must be noted that, at least theoretically, taxes and pollution standards are equivalent. (This is not to say that these measures will be the same in terms of ease of enforcement or revenues.) That is, a tax on air pollutants will limit the use of pollutants so that some standard of air quality is achieved; in turn, any given standard can be achieved through some tax. Thus, the problem for both taxes and standards is to determine at what level a standard should be set. Any quality level is experienced simultaneously by polluters, conservationists, and others so that to choose any standard requires social judgments about these interests.

The above discussion shows that all suggested economic remedies for pollution have related difficulties. Market solutions and bargaining both require definitions of property rights and liability which are not questions of economics but of social ethics. A market system also requires that a limitation, or standard, be defined on resource use. Taxation and standards are equivalent, and standards cannot be set without making social judgments outside the realm of economics.

PUBLIC GOODS AND ENVIRONMENTAL QUALITY

The concepts of private versus public decision making are closely related to the concepts of private versus public goods. Examples of private goods are the usual types of consumption items—shoes, bread, cars. A consumer's purchase of such private goods is a result of private decision making in response to prices where the price is the same for all consumers. Consumers use a private good in varying amounts, each according to his preferences; and an amount of a private good, once consumed, is not available to other consumers. In contrast, a public good is one which, if produced, may be consumed by all in the same amount; that is, its use by any one individual does not restrict the amount available to others. Frequently cited examples of such goods are national defense, cable TV, museums, and so on. Environmental quality is another example of a public good. Once a quality level is set, all citizens (polluters and conservationists alike) experience it simultaneously. Similarly, a hydroelectric dam is a public good since conservationists cannot choose to "consume" only part of the dam while power users "consume" the whole dam.

Samuelson (23, 24) is responsible for the development of many ideas in this area. He points out that, since all must consume the same amount of the public good, to determine an equilibrium quantity for a public good requires that consumer demand curves be added vertically instead of horizontally as in the case of private goods. The result is that it is not possible to find simultaneously an equilibrium market quantity and price. As Figure 2 illustrates, any quantity which sets market supply equal to market demand results in different prices for each consumer, and any price which is the same for both users results in different quantities. In the diagram, D_1 and D_2 represent the demand curves for two consumers

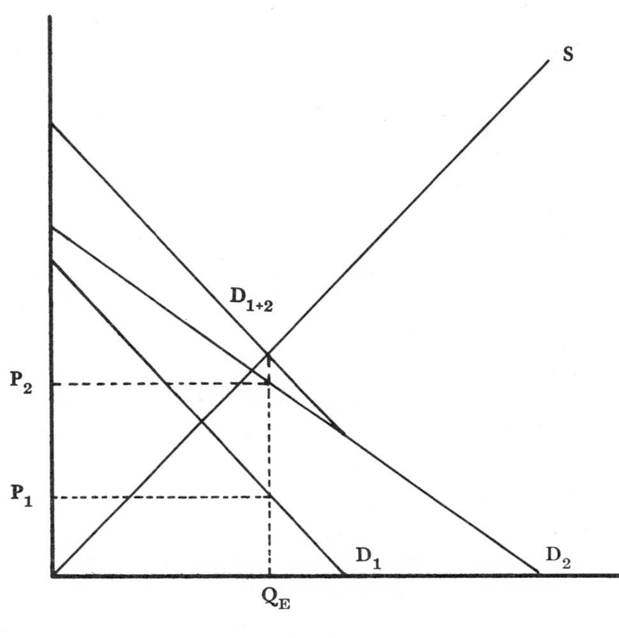

FIGURE 2

and S the supply curve; P denotes price and Q is quantity demanded. Q_E denotes the equilibrium quantity of the public good, but for this quantity consumer 1 would be willing to pay a price of P_1 while consumer 2 would be willing to pay P_2. This demonstrates that, in general, the usual market system with prices cannot be used to find the correct amount of public goods. Specifically, a market cannot be used to set pollution standards or to decide on the correct size of a dam.

PUBLIC DECISION-MAKING MECHANISMS AND THE SOCIAL WELFARE FUNCTION

The above discussion indicates that in both the cases of public goods and externalities, the laissez faire market system does not allocate resources correctly and public rather than private decision making is required. How then should public choices be made? The theory of public choice is not as well developed as some other branches of economics, perhaps because no definitive answers or rules about how to make such choices have been found. However, welfare economics does furnish some guidelines. A hypothesis introduced by Bergson (4) states that public choice should be based on individual preferences. The main question then is how these different preferences of different individuals are to be combined or aggregated.

One way to obtain social choices from individual preferences is with a system of ranking. If all individuals are no worse off in situation B than in A and some are better off in B, then B is said to be socially preferred to A according to the Pareto ranking system. However, it is impossible to say according to this ranking system which situation is better if some are better off in A and some are better off in B. In such a case, a social choice of one situation over the other requires the making of interpersonal comparisons, or social judgments about which individual interests are most important to society.

Another important idea first formulated by Bergson is that of a social welfare function which expresses the relation of social to individual preferences. Social welfare functions can be used to rank and choose among alternative situations. In comparing two situations, A and B, a decision can be reached as to whether A or B is socially preferred if relative weights are placed on the interests of the individuals better off in situation A compared to the individuals better off in B. This weighting combined with the individual preference functions defines a type of social welfare function. The problem then is to find the proper weights.

Arrow (1) has raised important questions regarding the possibility of obtaining a social welfare function if certain reasonable requirements are imposed. The requirements are that the function be responsive to changes in individual preferences, rational and consistent, and nondictatorial. He proved that such a function is impossible to obtain if the number of individuals with different preferences is too high. An implication of this result is that if no consensus can be found, any social choice mechanism will be imperfect in some way. This result has had a profound impact on social choice theory.

One other theoretical procedure for making social choices which attempts to circumvent the problem of making interpersonal comparisons is the compensation principle developed by Kaldor, Hicks, and Scitovosky (Mishan, 17). This principle asserts that for one state to be better than another, gainers should be able to compensate losers in going from one state to the other. Kaldor and Hicks did not require that compensation actually be paid. If the sum of monetary gains is greater than the sum of monetary losses, then gainers are able to compensate losers, and the conditions for use of the compensation principle are fulfilled. This provides the theoretical foundation for benefit-cost analysis which has been widely used for making public investment decisions.

Samuelson and others (17) have pointed out the fallacies in the compensation principle. Not only can this principle lead to contradictions, but it also cannot be used to judge which social state is better if compensation is not actually paid. That is, it is the *distribution* of gains and losses that is important and not just the *totals.* Again, social judgments are needed to rank situations in which distributions of benefits and costs vary.

DEVELOPMENT AND DECISION MAKING

Development is a very broad term which may refer to such diverse projects as dams, irrigation canals, or houses. Generally, development of a resource such as land or water involves transforming a resource from one state to another which requires a higher level of technology to maintain. As already mentioned, choosing the level of development is a public goods and social choice problem since all individuals have to experience the same level of development, but the incidence of benefits and costs varies among groups affected by development. All the problems of social choice mentioned above apply to making development decisions.

Many development projects in the United States, particularly in the area of water resources, have been constructed with public funds. Decision-making responsibility for such projects has primarily rested with government agencies such as the Army Corps of Engineers and Soil Conservation Service, which were directed by Congress (29) to evaluate such projects according to benefit-cost analysis.

The avowed purpose of the use of benefit-cost analysis is to achieve maximum national efficiency (maximum total national benefits over costs) in the allocation of public funds. The above discussion concerning the compensation principle points out that such analysis ignores the distributional issues of public policy. As Haveman (12) has shown by studying past projects, water development actually has been aimed at serving regional income distribution goals as well as national efficiency. New proposals for altering evaluation procedures for making decisions on development projects are based on making explicit such other concerns as environmental quality and income distribution rather than national efficiency alone.

All current proposals for improvement of decision-making procedures have some common features, which include: (a) for any given development problem, consideration of several development alternatives including the status quo; (b) for alternative projects, presentation of information relating to "trade-offs" among social objectives (usually in an account sheet format); (c) evaluation of trade-offs according to multiple social objectives; and (d) changing the structure of decision-making processes to include more public participation. However, as Steele (chapter 5) and Lord (chapter 6) indicate, there are disagreements about these matters. (In fact, Steele illustrates that there are decision-making problems encountered in establishing a decision-making mechanism for development projects.) For instance, there is disagreement about whether information on trade-offs should be in terms of broad national goals or in terms of specific effects on the well-being of individuals in various groups. (Well-being would include such factors as income and employment, health, education, recreation opportunities, and so on.)

Welfare economists in the tradition of Bergson would favor the latter approach since social choice should be based on factors which affect individual preferences. The social goal approach would require an additional step in the choice process of finding a social mechanism to define social goals. The Arrow Theorem limits the possibilities of finding a perfect mechanism to define social goals if there is no consensus on what these goals should be. While there are certainly some very broad, commonly held goals and beliefs in our society, it is difficult to define social goals very specifically. For instance, increasing personal income is a common goal, but increasing income to the poor would probably not be a goal of the middle class, especially if a reduction of middle-class income were required.

Economic theory gives some further guides for optimal allocation of scarce resources. First, a possibility frontier is required. This frontier relates, for a given level of any social output, the maximum amounts possible of other social outputs. Due to resource scarcity, the frontier is downward sloping. Alternative development plans would yield varying amounts of various social outputs and so would generate points along a possibilities frontier. This provides a theoretical basis for the need to consider several development alternatives.

The slopes of tangent lines along the frontier give possible trade-offs in social outputs. Thus, trade-off information for development projects is derived from consideration of alternatives on the possibilities frontier. However, resource allocation decisions cannot be based solely on the trade-off information. That is, trade-off information is necessary but not sufficient for social choices. A way is needed to pick the correct level of trade-offs.

As discussed above, one way to make social choices is with a social welfare function. From the welfare function, social indifference curves can be obtained which express the combinations of social outputs which yield the same welfare levels. Figure 3, for two social outputs X and Y, illustrates how the optimal resource allocation is found using the possibility frontier and the social indifference curves. A is the point of optimal resource allocation between X and Y since A yields the highest social welfare consistent with resource possibilities. At A, the trade-off possibility between X and Y is the same as the slope of the indifference curve. The slope of the indifference curve at A defines a set of relative social weights

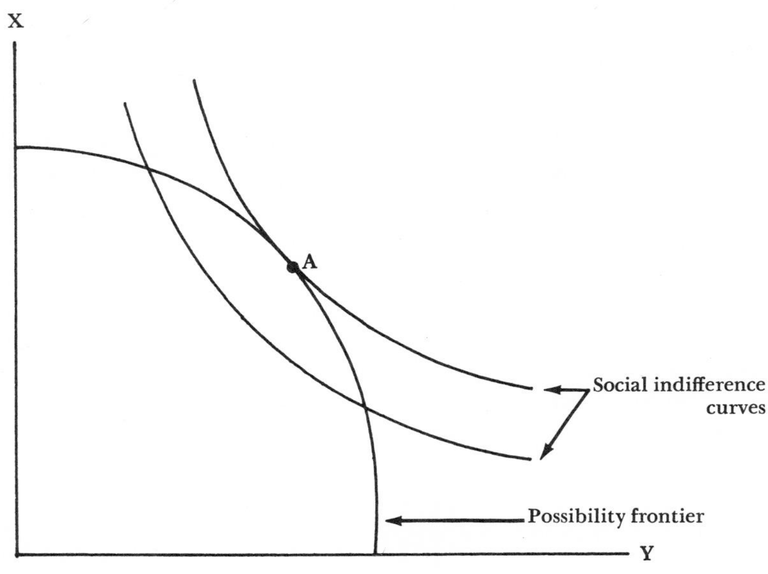

FIGURE 3

on X and Y. Further discussion of these points may be found in any welfare economics text (17, 18, 20).

Although the approach outlined above is conceptually useful, the Arrow Theorem limits the possibility of finding a social welfare function for making optimal choices. However, mechanisms other than the social welfare function approach exist. These may be imperfect for allocating resources optimally, but they may be useful in achieving acceptable decisions. The concept of "satisficing," or finding decisions agreeable to most interests, is replacing the concept of "optimizing" in public choice theory.

Voting has been one social choice method, first suggested for making public goods decisions by Bowen (5). Buchanan and Tullock (7) have also written a book in this area. The idea behind voting is that each citizen decides for himself how various alternatives affect him and then votes accordingly. Voting may be directly on the issues (as in bond issues) or based on representation in a governmental body; it thus provides a decentralized system of making choices based on individual evaluation of trade-off information. However, it has been shown that majority voting can sometimes lead to inconsistencies (1, 2), and it also may not adequately account for the interests of minorities.

Another way that decisions affecting the environment are made is through governmental agencies. The bureaucratic or agency decision-making structure also has its problems. (For discussion of these, see Wildavsky [30].) The tendency is for agencies to become too involved with a particular interest group. Agency decision making is a centralized process based on a bureaucrat's concept of the public interest in contrast to decentralized choice systems such as voting or the market. As Lord (chapter 6) puts it, agency decision making is "top down" rather than "bottom up." Of course, there is some public influence on agency decisions, but it is mainly indirect and comes through the budgetary process. One suggested reform of agency development decisions is to decentralize them more by having more direct public participation in decisions. Other than the suggestion itself, no formal mechanisms for public participation in agency decisions have been developed. The environmental impact statement as required under the National Environmental Policy Act illustrates the problem. Though it is required that all agencies file impact statements for development projects to obtain public reactions, they are in no way legally bound to respond to such reactions.

Clearly, there are many unanswered questions in the area of public choice and decision making for development projects. Economic analysis can help here to quantify trade-offs, benefits, and costs, and reveal requirements for decision making, but the basic social choice problem still remains. Such social choice issues can only be resolved through political and legal processes.

Law as a Social Choice Mechanism

Our legal system provides another mechanism for making social choices. The mechanism consists of interactions among citizens, legislative bodies which pass new laws, the executive branch which enforces and executes laws, and the court system which passes judgments on social behavior according to interpretation of current law. Levi and Colyer (chapter 8) describe the array of legal tools currently applicable for environmental problems.

The legal system can be viewed as a complement to economic solutions for environmental quality control. Legal definitions of property rights and liability are necessary before any mechanism based on economic incentives can work to improve the quality of the environment. Any proposed quality standard or taxation system must first be enacted into law to be of use in pollution control. Requirements for public participation and other new procedures for agency decision making must become a part of statutory law before they are operable.

The law as interpreted through the courts can also be viewed as an alternative to economic mechanisms. For instance, legal suits against polluters for damages can serve to internalize externalities. This procedure is presently not very effective due to limitations on who has the right of suit. (In any case, a system of economic incentives such as taxation may be a more efficient way of reducing pollution than legal suit against every polluter.) The present usefulness of the courts in solving environmental problems is also limited because suits often have to be based on peripheral legalities rather than basic issues. This is due not so much to failures in the court system as to failure of statutory law to keep up with the social complexities involved in environmental issues.

Little (chapter 9) illustrates that the law is a dynamic and evolving process for deciding social choice issues in correspondence with changing concepts of the public interest. Sax (25) points out that the most useful role for the courts in environmental matters lies in this area. He proposes that the role of the courts in such matters should be expanded to serve as a catalyst for the legislative process: "Environmental litigation does not ask of a judge that he devise national policy nor that he repeal any settled statutory policy in contravention of explicit legislative desires. Rather, by inquiring into the effects of such policies in individual instances, it asks the courts to help promote the sort of continuous review and reevaluation that any large scale program needs and that legislatures often find themselves without time or adequate incentives to undertake. . . ." That is, in presiding over legal suits against polluters and government agencies, courts can bring into focus conflicts of public versus private rights and thrust upon legislative bodies the obligation to redefine and clarify these rights.

Just as the court does not replace the legislative process in making social choices, it also does not replace the planning responsibilities and expertise of government agencies; the aim is only to ensure that all public interests are properly considered. Though the judge may not be a technical expert, he is expert in perceiving and balancing public interests and values in the environmental area as he does in other areas of social concern. As stated in several papers in this book, Sax says that it is necessary to revive and strengthen the legal theory of public trust to provide a basis for this broader view of environmental litigation. This would give wider access to the decision-making process to ordinary citizens whose only status is that of victims of environmental disruption.

Sax's concept of the interactions and roles of the citizen agencies, legislative bodies, and courts in effect defines a new mechanism for making social choices in the environmental area. This mechanism is not decentralized since it includes judges and agency decision makers, but it does have elements of decentralization with increased citizen participation in the courts. This mechanism would increase the social costs of decision making due to increases in court case loads, but these costs would hopefully be offset by obtaining decisions in the environmental area more acceptable to all citizens and more in keeping with public interests.

In this new view of the legal process, the complementary nature of legal and economic concepts is even more apparent. If environmental issues are to be decided by balancing conflicting public and private interests, measurements of social and private benefits and costs are essential.

Information Needs for Environmental Decision Making

Regardless of how decisions about use of the environment are to be made, information on benefits, costs, and trade-offs is required for decisions. The type of information needed, however, depends on what basis the decisions are to be made. In general, the more centralized the decision process, the greater the need for a decision maker to have complete information about how various components of a problem interact and are affected by alternative policies.

Information requirements for policy formation in the environmental area include ecological, sociological, and economic effects of alternative resource uses. The types of information that the decision maker needs are: (a) what alternative courses of action are available, (b) what circumstances or events (sometimes called "states of nature") are relevant to the problem or controversy, but beyond the decision maker's control, and (c) what consequences or outcomes are associated with each set of alternative actions that the decision maker might decide to take (21). Since social, economic, and ecological systems and their interrelationships are so complex, it is often difficult a priori to predict these effects.

To provide the decision maker with this type of information, a method of analyzing real-world problem situations is needed. Such a procedure is found in a technique called systems modeling.

Modeling may be undertaken on several levels of sophistication. A systems model can consist simply of a diagram with arrows indicating the direction of causality, or interrelations can be described by equations. These equations can be of several levels of complexity also: linear, nonlinear, differential, etc. Models may be based on concepts of equilibrium (as in many economic models such as the supply and demand model of the market system), or they may be dynamic to express the adjustment process of a system toward equilibrium in response to some exogenous stimulus. "Simulation" is a term used for models which describe dynamic processes. A different sort of model is based on "optimization": an optimization model includes an objective function to rank the outcomes associated with alternative courses of action and states of nature.

In addition, models may be on a "micro" or "macro" level. A micro model describes in some detail the behavior of a relatively small system. A macro model is a large-scale representation in which only gross features of subsystems and their interactions are included. Models can also be classified according to two other types: deterministic or probabilistic. In deterministic models, it is hypothesized that outcomes can be predicted with certainty. Probabilistic models allow predictions of outcomes in terms of some probability distribution.

Economists have made greater use of these different types of models for analyzing environmental problems than have other social scientists concerned with decision making. Some typical models used in economic analysis include finding waste treatment arrangements to minimize costs of achieving given quality levels (chapter 11), predicting social costs of pollution (22), and predicting what pollution levels will result from changes in consumption through use of input-output analysis (15). These analyses have required the cooperation of physical scientists and engineers. To evaluate further the effects of environmental degradation on humans and human systems, other social scientists must also join in this modeling effort.

Since there are obviously many types of models, only a few could be included in this book. The first example, by Loehman, Pingry, and Whinston (chapter 11), is an optimization model which includes modeling of pollution in a river. This is the most micro of the three papers. On a more macro level is the model presented by Cumberland (chapter 12), which seeks to describe the whole economy and the relation of pollution to output. The Odum and Bayley paper (chapter 13) is the most macro, since their modeling technique can be used to relate the whole world to its ecological and economic systems. The three papers are also examples, respectively, of optimization, equilibrium, and simulation models.

This discussion is a brief and probably incomplete description of the different types of models. It should be remembered that all but the most micro of models are necessarily only approximations of reality. This is because some less important relationships are deleted from models and because mathematical expressions of interrelationships are themselves usually just approximations of true relations. (Otherwise, models would become unworkable due to complexity.) Thus, information on effects obtained from such models may be just an approximation of actual effects. Generally, the more macro the model, the less precise predictions about micro features will be.

Environmental impact studies require knowledge on a micro level, such as what may happen to a particular species of animals or plants, what may happen to a particular stream, and so on. Since modeling of environmental systems and effects must often be on a macro level for reasons of practicality, one might wonder what use can be made of information from such models if it is inaccurate. In fact, knowledge of *relative* magnitudes of effects is sufficient for decision makers to rank and choose among alternative policies or resource uses. Macro models including gross relationships between environmental, economic, and social systems can be used for such comparisons.

A final important point about information and decision making concerns the costs of obtaining information. To collect information obviously involves some costs, since sources of information are dispersed. In addition, in the area of pollution information, there may be some reluctance on the part of polluters to divulge necessary information for fear of legal suit. Not to be slighted are costs in terms of computer time and salaries of experts for building sophisticated systems models. Information for use in the decision process can be made as accurate as desired, given enough money and time—factors that are often lacking, especially when pressures for quick decisions are brought to bear on decision makers.

Conclusion

This discussion has indicated some of the theoretical and practical difficulties associated with remedies suggested for solving environmental quality problems. We have tried to make the point that no remedy presented so far is perfect. This does not mean that we should settle for the status quo in regard to environmental quality. It does mean, however, that we need not reject a suggested remedy on the basis of possible imperfections, but that we should consider each remedy in terms of how it can help to solve environmental problems compared to other alternatives. No one approach may be found to be completely adequate: for example, taxes may be most useful in some areas and legal suits in others; some matters may be best handled through agencies and some through representative bodies.

The selection of a social choice mechanism or policy is then a social choice problem on a higher level. Again, the Arrow Theorem limits the possibility of making perfect choices. The theory of the Second Best (11, 16) is a developing area of economics dealing with how to make social choices when the best situation is not attainable. Second Best approaches may prove far more helpful for making environmental choices than approaches based on finding optimal solutions.

Obviously, criteria will be needed to choose among alternative (imperfect) policies and choice mechanisms. Tullock (28) has observed that sometimes a given method of correcting a problem may cause social costs in excess of the costs caused by the problem itself. Thus social costs are created by the need for increased information and enforcement as well as by pollution itself. One obvious criterion then would be that the social costs of implementing some policy should be less than the social costs caused by the problem. Hurwicz (13) has suggested four other criteria which are satisfied by the market system under perfect competition assumptions. These are: decentralization in information requirements (information costs are minimized); unbiasedness (any Pareto optimum can be achieved after some redistribution of income); nonwastefulness (choices result in efficient use of resources); and incentive compatibility (enforcement costs are minimized).

It seems that social scientists should devote more attention than they have to issues such as developing general criteria for choice of policies. As Klasson (14) states, "policy formulation has been superficially treated by social scientists since it entailed largely unstructured, open-ended and value laden decision problems." He further points out the need for a general theory of policy science. If the current problems of our society are considered, it is clear that there are many issues besides achievement of environmental quality that present the same social choice difficulties in finding solutions. Environmental issues are notable mainly because the results of pollution and development are so pervasive. The reemergence of interest in theories of social choice and externality among economists may be due in great measure to the direct experience of environmental degradation.

As the papers in this book and this introduction demonstrate, the main difficulties in achieving environmental quality are not so much technical as they are involved with decision making and politics. In the case of a market mechanism, how should property rights be decided and prices determined? If standards are to be used, how should quality standards be decided? In the case of taxes, who should have to pay and what manner of taxation should be used? How are agency and legal decision processes to be structured? Ultimately, who decides what are the proper choices of mechanisms and policy for environmental quality decisions? Any of these questions require that problems of social versus private values, rights, and responsibilities be resolved. To make these social choices, adequate information must be available. Hopefully, this book provides insights to various aspects of environmental decision problems and suggests some methods for obtaining information on which to base such decisions.

References

1. Arrow, Kenneth J. *Social Choice and Individual Values*. Cowles Foundation Monograph 12. New Haven: Yale University Press, 1963.
2. Arrow, Kenneth J. "The Organization of Economic Activity: Issues Pertinent to the Choice of Market Versus Nonmarket Allocation." In *The Analysis and Evaluation of Public Expenditure: The P.P.B. System*. Joint Economic Committee of Congress. Washington, D.C.: Government Printing Office, 1969.
3. Baumol, William J., and Oates, Wallace E. "The Use of Standards and Prices for Protection of the Environment." *Swedish Journal of Economics* 73 (1971):42–51.
4. Bergson, Abram. "A Reformulation of Certain Aspects of Welfare Economics." *Quarterly Journal of Economics* 52 (1938):310–34.
5. Bowen, Howard R. "The Interpretation of Voting in the Allocation of Economic Resources." *Quarterly Journal of Economics* 58 (1943):27–48.
6. Buchanan, James M., and Stubblebine, William Craig. "Externality." *Economica NS.* 29 (1962):371–84.
7. Buchanan, James M., and Tullock, Gordon. *The Calculus of Consent*. Ann Arbor: University of Michigan Press, 1962.
8. Coase, R. H. "The Problem of Social Cost." *Journal of Law and Economics* 3 (1960): 1–44.
9. Davis, Otto A., and Kamien, Morton I. "Externalities, Information and Alternative Collective Action." In *The Analysis and Evaluation of Public Expenditure: The P.P.B. System*. Joint Economic Committee of Congress. Washington, D.C.: Government Printing Office, 1969.
10. Davis, Otto A., and Whinston, Andrew. "Externalities, Welfare, and the Theory of Games." *Journal of Political Economy* 70 (1962):241–62.
11. Davis, Otto A., and Whinston, Andrew. "Welfare Economics and the Theory of the Second Best." *Review of Economic Studies* 32 (1965):1–14.
12. Haveman, Robert H. *Water Resource Investment and the Public Interest*. Nashville, Tenn.: Vanderbilt University Press, 1965.
13. Hurwicz, Leonid. "Optimality and Informational Efficiency in Resource Allocation Processes." In *Mathematical Methods in the Social Sciences*, edited by K. J. Arrow, S. Karlin, and P. Suppes, pp 27–46. Stanford, Calif.: Stanford University Press, 1960.
14. Klasson, Charles R. "Theoretical and Empirical Foundations of Policy Sciences." Paper read at the nineteenth meeting of the Institute of Management Sciences, Houston, Tex., 1972.
15. Laurent, E. A., and Hite, J. C. *Economic-Ecologic Analysis in the Charleston Metropolitan Region: An Input-Output Study*. Water Resources Research, Report No. 19, Clemson University, Clemson, S.C., April 1971.
16. Lipsey, R. G., and Lancaster, Kelvin. "The General Theory of Second Best." *Review of Economic Studies* 24 (1957):11–32.
17. Mishan, Ezra J. *Welfare Economics: Ten Introductory Essays*. New York: Random House, 1969.
18. Nath, S. K. *A Reappraisal of Welfare Economics*. New York: Kelley, 1969.
19. Pigou, A. C. *The Economics of Welfare*. 4th ed. London: Macmillan, 1932.
20. Quirk, James, and Suposnik, Rubin. *Introduction to General Equilibrium and Welfare Economics*. New York: McGraw-Hill, 1968.
21. Richmond, S. B. *Operations Research for Management Decisions*. New York: Roland Press, 1968.
22. Ridker, Ronald G. *Economic Costs of Air Pollution*. New York: Praeger, 1967.
23. Samuelson, Paul A. "The Pure Theory of Public Expenditures." *Review of Economics and Statistics* 36 (1954):386–89.

24. Samuelson, Paul A. "Diagrammatic Exposition of a Theory of Public Expenditure." *Review of Economics and Statistics* 37 (1955) :350–56.
25. Sax, Joseph L. *Defending the Environment: A Strategy for Citizen Action*. New York: Alfred A. Knopf, 1971.
26. Solow, Robert M. "The Economists' Approach to Pollution and Its Control." *Science* 173 (1971):498–503.
27. Steiner, Peter. "The Public Sector and the Public Interest." In *The Analysis and Evaluation of Public Expenditure: The P.P.B. System*. Joint Economic Committee of Congress. Washington, D.C.: Government Printing Office, 1969.
28. Tullock, Gordon. "The Social Costs of Reducing Social Cost." Paper read at the nineteenth meeting of the Institute of Management Sciences, Houston, Tex., 1972.
29. U.S., Congress, Senate. *Policies, Standards, and Procedures in the Formulation, Evaluation, and Review of Plans for Use and Development of Water and Related Land Resources*. Prepared under the direction of the President's Water Resources Council. 87th Cong., 2d sess. Washington, D.C.: Government Printing Office, May 1962.
30. Wildavsky, Aaron. *The Politics of the Budgetary Process*. Boston: Little, Brown, and Co., 1964.

Social Choice Problems and Economic Mechanisms for Pollution Control

Edwin Haefele (chapter 1) examines the social choice problem in relation to setting water quality standards. He discusses how a standard can be chosen through the political process. The outcome of this political process depends on institutional arrangements, that is, who is to be represented in the process, and what is to be the voting or social choice mechanism. In this context, Haefele investigates several different institutional arrangements for establishing and controlling water quality standards.

Alan Randall (chapter 2) discusses three broad classes of solutions to externality problems: market solutions, systems of charges, and systems of standards. Market solutions are emphasized. He examines the question of how resource allocation varies with the definition of liability and concludes that full liability of polluters will result in higher pollution abatement and fewer and higher-priced commodities than with zero liability.

Charles Goetz (chapter 3) emphasizes the public goods aspects of the pollution problem. He introduces the idea of pollution as a public "bad." That is, whatever level of pollution is decided to be tolerable to society is the level which each individual will have to experience. Since the market system does not serve to allocate public goods or bads, he addresses the question of what sort of solution for pollution and pollution price (i.e., tax) is achievable through the political system.

Chapter 4, by Paul Gerhardt, focuses on the problems of designing and administering governmental programs for achieving environmental quality. He summarizes current national and state regulations on air quality and compares the economic costs of air pollution with the costs of control under the Clean Air Act. The point is made that the standards-setting and regulatory approach to air pollution control requires a complex process of research on standards as well as establishment of control agencies and enforcement procedures relying heavily on court action. He suggests that costs of pollution control could be lowered if market-type economic incentives were to replace some of these administrative remedies.

I

Social Choices and Individual Preferences Is There a Connecting Mechanism?

Edwin T. Haefele

It may be useful to start by calling attention to the difference between two kinds of problems: a determinate problem and an indeterminate problem; the former has a solution or range of solutions, while the latter has no solution.

An example may illuminate the distinction. It is a determinate problem to ask what is the most profitable use of a piece of land given agricultural prices, input costs, and technical production possibilities. It is an indeterminate problem to ask what publicly imposed restraints should be put on the uses of that same piece of land. The latter problem is indeterminate not because there is more uncertainty, but because the goal is unspecified and unspecifiable except by a collective choice process.

It has long been recognized that we must use social choice processes to resolve indeterminate problems. It is beginning to be recognized that we must use social choice processes to solve determinate problems when those solutions have strong distributional effects. All of our traditional benefit-cost studies, for example, are posed and solved as determinate problems in the aggregate. Costs are summed; benefits are summed. The incidence of the costs and benefits has been, until recently, ignored. It was that kind of calculus which put highways through ghetto neighborhoods and through public parks. In an aggregate benefit-cost sense, that was the efficient place to put them. But when the question of incidence was raised—why are you benefiting well-to-do suburbanites and pushing the disruption costs on poor blacks?—then the problem rapidly became an indeterminate one requiring social choice resolution.

We make social choices about our environment because we cannot differentiate the environment down to the individual level. If that were possible, we could allow each person to purchase as much (or little) environmental quality as he wished and as his income would allow.

Since the decisions are forced into the collective choice mechanisms, it is not surprising that the decisions are colored by other decisions that are also in the process of being made. We are, collectively, concerned about welfare, and hence we may use decisions about environmental quality to advance a particular income redistribution scheme, such as improving water quality in a stream because poor blacks use it for swimming and fishing. We are, collectively, concerned about regional economic "balance" and may use decisions about environmental quality to advance a particular region, such as tying a flood control project in with a water navigation scheme to bring "low-cost" water transport to an area previously served only by rail, air, and road.

When we mix our motives for public investment we are often subject to the apt criticism that our instruments are inefficient for the purposes. Perhaps swimming pools and food stamps can produce equal benefits to poor blacks at less cost than improving water quality. No doubt rail rates can be forced down administratively more cheaply than by digging what are, in effect, canals for barges. Much of the criticism is well founded, on efficiency grounds, but we must not allow the criticism to obscure the necessity for the collective choice on environmental goods, even if we ignore income redistribution and equity considerations. Environmental quality partakes of the characteristics of a public good, particularly in its nondivisibility aspects, so that we cannot escape making collective choices about it.

How are we to decide how much environmental quality we are to have? In an economics discussion such as this the obvious answer is: as much as we are willing to pay for. But how are we to determine that amount if we cannot divide it up and price it in individual, separate packages? Moreover, since many different bundles of environmental quality might cost the same but have far different patterns in the distribution of the costs and benefits, how are we to distinguish one bundle from another? And if you view motorboating as recreation and I view it as noise pollution, how are we going to determine simple inclusion and exclusion in our definition of environmental quality?

Perhaps we can agree that both economic and political beliefs have their roots in personal utility and use that assumption as the foundation of our analysis. Then we will be able to think about my disutility and your utility associated with motorboats. How do we combine the two? We have known since Bergson that we cannot sum utilities across individuals. We are beginning to discover that we cannot sum benefits across individuals (except by ignoring welfare implications). How are we to relate personal utilities (preferences) to the social choices we make about the environment?

In this paper I will examine the ways by which we attempt to make the connection between personal preferences and social choices. To make the discussion concrete I will investigate four specific situations involving water quality—two actual cases, the Delaware and the Ruhr; and two hypothetical cases, the Dorfman-Jacoby model of river basin management, and my own work. (Needless to say, this introduces a certain bias in the discussion which the reader must guard against.) I shall be concerned specifically with the setting of standards, or levels, of water quality and thus will be neglecting a whole host of technical issues. In particular, the implementation features in each case will be neglected. Although the focus will be on *how* the decision to adopt a certain goal is made, I will not emphasize how the goal is to be achieved except when this is intertwined with the setting of the goal itself (as it is in cost-sharing arguments). I will simply record, however, that I am a devoted believer in the use of effluent charges as an efficient means of achieving whatever water quality goals are decided upon.

Four Water-Quality Models

CHOICE OF WATER QUALITY IN THE DELAWARE ESTUARY

A detailed and critical review of the steps leading to the formation of the Delaware River Basin Commission (DRBC) is not warranted here. We will rely on Kneese and Bower's (7) analysis of the studies made on the water quality of the Delaware River.

The social choice about water quality in the Delaware estuary was directly related to preferences by three mechanisms. In point of time the first of these was the system of advisory committees that were set up as a part of the Delaware Estuary Comprehensive Study (DECS) undertaken by the Public Health Service at the request of the concerned states and interstate agencies before the commission was established. In the words of the director of the DRBC: "The Delaware Estuary Comprehensive Study selected various technical committees which would permit the voice of the estuary community in the development of recommended judgments. The committee on water use included four groups—one represented recreation, encompassing conservation interests in fish and wildlife; another was representative of the general public; a third represented industry; while the fourth was made up of representatives of local governments and planning agencies."

The study was a notable technical advance over earlier studies of water quality and included the development of a model for looking systematically at the interrelationships among reaches of the river and for arriving at cost-minimizing solutions under different sets of assumptions.

One of the outputs of the DECS was the identification of "five 'objective sets' each representing a different package and spatial distribution of water quality characteristics, with the level of quality increasing from set 5 (representing 1964 water quality) to set 1" (7, p. 226). Total and incremental costs associated with each set were estimated, and benefits associated with moving from one set to another were estimated. Table 1 summarizes these costs and benefits.

TABLE 1
COSTS AND BENEFITS OF WATER QUALITY IMPROVEMENT IN THE DELAWARE ESTUARY AREA[a]
(MILLIONS OF DOLLARS)

Objective Set	Estimated Total Cost	Estimated Recreation Benefits	Estimated Incremental Cost		Estimated Incremental Benefits	
			minimum[b]	maximum[c]	minimum[b]	maximum[c]
1	460	160–350				
			245	145	20	30
2	215–315	140–320				
			130	160	10	10
3	85–155	130–310				
			20	25	10	30
4	65–130	120–280				

SOURCE: Kneese and Bower (7, p. 233).
a. All costs and benefits are present values calculated with 3 percent discount rate and 20-year time horizon. Data for set 5 are not included in this table.
b. Difference between adjacent minima.
c. Difference between adjacent maxima.

The water use advisory committee recommended adoption of objective set 3, indicating an agreement with the incremental costs and benefits estimated by DECS. The incremental benefits relate chiefly to recreation benefits, specifically swimming, boating, and sport fishing, since there are no benefits of any magnitude to industry and municipalities. Indeed industry might be expected to suffer negative benefits (higher costs) due to corrosion stemming from higher oxygen levels in objective sets 3, 2, and 1.

The second mechanism that related preferences to the social choice under consideration was the series of public hearings held by the DRBC prior to commission adoption of quality standards. Hearings were held in Delaware, Pennsylvania, and New Jersey, the last being the most extensive in terms of testimony. Kneese and Bower (7, p. 233) note that "nearly all discussion related to objective sets 2 and 3; the other sets were recognized by almost everyone as not being in the public interest." Although I agree with that statement, I also note for the record the statement at the beginning of the hearing by the alternative commissioner for New Jersey: ". . . New Jersey advocated and the Commission adopted that the public hearing on these water quality standards . . . be presented in the form of two alternatives representing the two depictive sets deemed feasible for consideration at this time—objective sets 2 and 3" (10).

The pattern of testimony at the hearings found most industries willing to support objective set 3 while carefully pointing out that no advantages accrued to them by this choice (they would be happy with set 4, which would cost less); the representatives of governments supported either set 3 or set 2, depending mainly on whether they were elected or appointed. The appointed (executive) official was more apt, of course, to be concerned with the costs of responding to the higher quality level while the elected official clearly saw votes in the advocacy of "clean" water. Conservation groups supported set 2 while carefully pointing out that it was sinful not to go for objective set 1, which they really preferred.

The water use committee established under DECS testified, as did its individual subcommittees, and continued to support set 3. The fish and wildlife subcommittee surprisingly advocated set 2 in the Delaware state hearings.

The third mechanism for relating preferences to the social choice was the act of choosing by the commission. The commission chose standards falling between set 3 and set 2. As an agency set up by interstate compact, the state commissioners vote as sovereigns, i.e., each state has one vote. The federal government, for the first time a party to an interstate compact, also has one vote. Presumably there is a connection between these votes and people's preferences. Clearly there is a connection between the votes and executive agency preferences.

The questions raised by the process of decision making in the Delaware case are threefold: (a) Is the benefit-estimating technique valid in this context? (b) What purpose is served by using representatives of interest groups, including one "representing" the general public, to advise in the formation of public policy? (c) How does the one state–one vote tradition of interstate compacts affect outcomes on social choice issues? These questions will be discussed later.

WATER QUALITY IN THE RUHR

The German Genossenschaften are justly famous for their long and distinguished record for management of basin-wide water systems, a record that includes both technical and economic innovations of a high order.[1] In Fair's words: "One of the river-basin authorities, the Emschergenossenschaft, has been in action, almost without constitutional change, for over half a century, under no less than four sovereignties: a constitutional but authoritarian monarchy, a strongly centralized federalist republic, a ruthless dictatorship, and a decentralized federal republic. Survival has, patently, been through strength" (2).

The Ruhrverband, the Genossenschaft responsible for water quality in the Ruhr, is described by Kneese and Bower (7, p. 261): "The basic political power in the Ruhrverband lies in the governing board which is made up of: (1) the owners of business and industrial establishments and other facilities that lie in the Ruhrverband area and that contribute to water quality deterioration in the Ruhr or its tributaries, and those who benefit from the activities of the Ruhrverband to the extent that they make a specified minimum financial contribution to its activities; (2) communities within the Ruhrverband area; and (3) the Ruhrtalsperrenverein as a representative of the waterworks and other water withdrawal facilities.

"The political organs are the assemblies and the board of directors. The assembly members (about 1,500) elect the board of directors, approve or disapprove the plan for water quality management, approve or disapprove the assessment of charges, and decide upon the basic method for calculating the level of charges. The assembly reaches its conclusions on the basis of absolute majority with the number of votes cast by each member being dependent upon the amount of financial contribution."

Since the assessments levied by the Ruhrverband have the legal force of taxes, and the level of assessments relates directly to the water quality goals agreed upon, we obviously have a social choice issue at hand but a mechanism somewhat different from those in the Delaware case. In some respects, the mechanism resembles a mixture of a private corporation and a cooperative. The voting basis has much of the Wicksellian theme of tying specific expenditures directly to specific taxation. Fair (2, p. 152) notes that "both the cost of pollution abatement and the value of direct, as well as indirect, benefits derived by a member . . . are assessable" in some of the Genossenschaften. Thus, the incidence of benefits as well as

1. I have relied on Fair (2) and Kneese and Bower (7) for my understanding of the Ruhr water management system.

costs can be calculated and used as an element in the assessment of members.

It is hard to assess this German mechanism without getting entangled in differences between cultures. For instance, would the charges levied by such a body against a municipality (which would be a member) and hence passed on to taxpayers stand against a "due process" argument in this country?

However, ignoring the questions of direct transferability of the mechanism, and viewing it only as a mechanism for relating social choice to preferences, the following questions arise: (a) Is it possible that some pay for "benefits" they do not want? Or is there a bias for underproduction of benefits? (b) Are there "interests" in addition to those represented? (c) How would a shift in public tastes toward water quality be reflected by the Ruhrverband? These questions will be taken up later.

THE DORFMAN-JACOBY MODEL OF RIVER BASIN MANAGEMENT

Robert Dorfman has recently outlined a conceptual model "within which the political, economic, and technological aspects of regional water management can be brought together." With Henry Jacoby, Dorfman then constructed a hypothetical river valley and an authority (the Bow Valley Water Pollution Control Commission) in order to test the model (1). In the account which follows, I intend to discuss only the political aspects of the Dorfman model. (The discussion should *not* be relied upon for an understanding of the Dorfman-Jacoby work.)

Dorfman views a river basin authority as a "synthesizer of the goals and objectives of other groups and agencies" and thus directly faces the question of translating preferences into social choices. His model accepts willingness to pay as a measure of benefit, while recognizing the difficulties of application. Assuming that reasonable estimates exist, Dorfman then defines a class of feasible decisions as Pareto-admissible decisions, as follows: "A decision Y is said to be Pareto admissible if it is feasible (i.e., if it satisfies all pertinent constraints) and if there does not exist any alternative feasible decision X for which NB^i (X) $\geqq$ NB^i (Y) for all participants i, with strict inequality holding for at least one participant. (NB = net benefits.)" The purpose of the model is first to determine the set of Pareto-admissible decisions under any given set of constraints. Some of these constraints may be the powers (and lack thereof) of a river basin authority. Thus, some idea of how changes in the constitution of the authority affect the set of admissible decisions may be gained.

Functioning of the model involves, of course, an aggregation of benefits and costs. This creates problems, not only of estimation but of interpersonal comparisons of utility. (Dorfman's discussion is clear on these issues and is highly recommended.) His solution is the traditional one of assigning weights, w_i for each participant (municipality, industry, etc.) whose costs and benefits are at issue. These weights he calls political weights, and they are used to form the objective function

$$W = \sum_{i} w_i \; NB^i \; (X)$$

that is to be maximized with respect to X, assuming X is a feasible solution. Each choice of a set of w_i's will produce a new Pareto-admissible decision. Since there is an infinite number of w_i sets, Dorfman's procedure at this point is to solve for "a number of widely different sets of political weights."

For any specified economic and technical constraints, and with a specified set of political weights, the feasible and Pareto-admissible decision is generated. By changing weights, a number of admissible decisions are generated. A priori there is nothing known about whether or not different assumed weights will give widely different decisions or the same decision. Dorfman is well aware that the political weights must be based on judgment (that they are not known), but suggests that reasonable guesses may be made. Moreover, he suggests that if the range of decisions proves to be fairly narrow, i.e., not sensitive to the choice of weights, then the model's predictive powers may indeed be strong.[2]

The latter point is the main point of the application of the model to a hypothetical case by Dorfman and Jacoby. The illustration affords an excellent explication of the whole model, but I will again confine my discussion to the political (translating preferences to choices) aspects of the illustrative case.

The hypothesized Bow River Valley (see Figure 1) contains an industry, two cities, and one recreation facility. The water quality parameter subject to control is dissolved oxygen, and a minimum level (3.5 ppm) is required at the state line. The control commission may choose this level or any feasible level above this minimum and may implement its decision by regulating the level of treatment required at each source of pollution—the cannery and the two municipalities. The water quality problem hypothesized is an upstream-downstream conflict. The stream becomes anaerobic beyond Bowville (due to the discharges from the town and from the cannery), hence improved treatment by them benefits Plympton. Various constraints are imposed dealing with politically feasible tax increases in the two towns, the amount of improved treatment

2. The usefulness of the model in excluding non-Pareto-admissible decisions is also claimed, but this "usefulness" depends on whether or not the weights have been "correctly" judged.

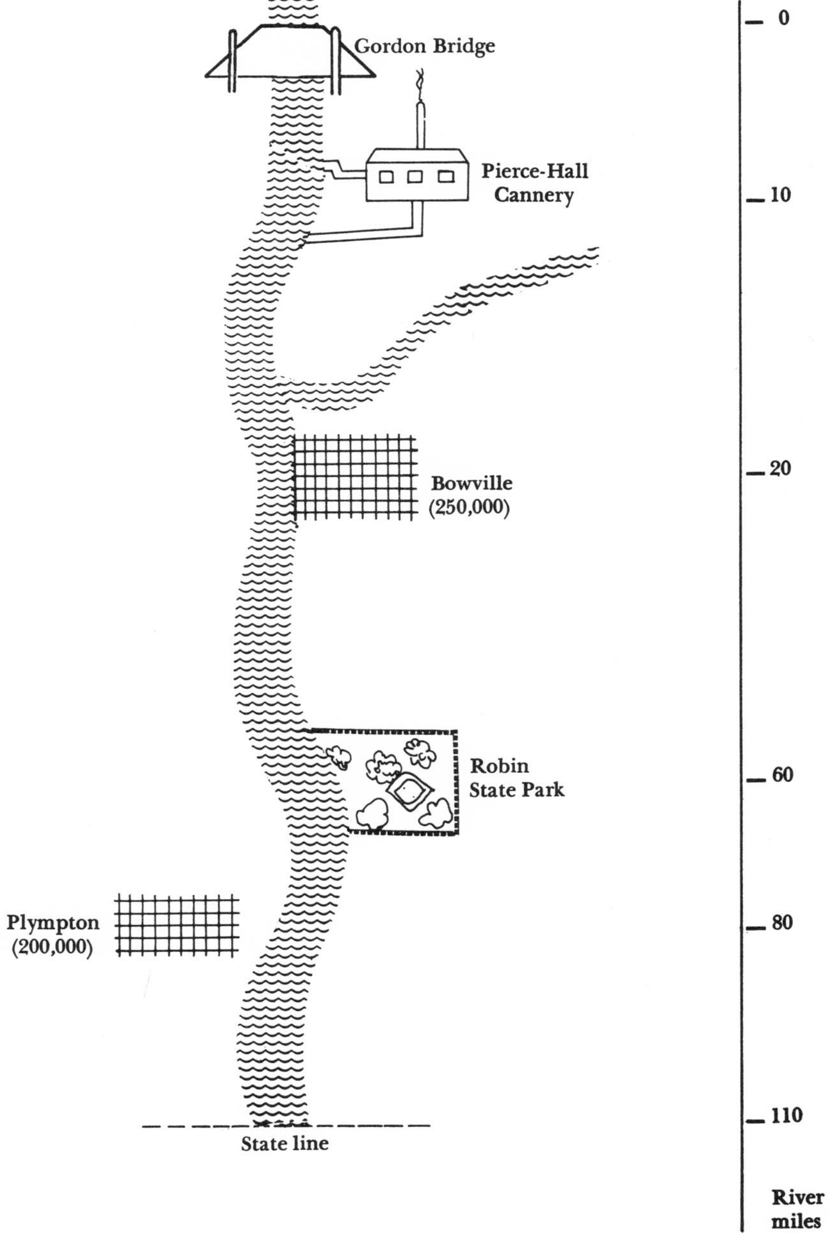

FIGURE 1. Main features of the Bow River Valley. Source: Dorfman, Jacoby, and Thomas (1).

the cannery can bear without going out of business, public interest in improving the river, and so forth.

A schedule of quality standards similar to the objective sets in the Delaware case is supplied—classes A through D in terms of decreasing DO levels.

The Bow Valley Water Pollution Control Commission is composed of members from the city councils of both cities and the deputy state commissioner of parks and recreation; it is chaired by the crusading editor of the *Bow Valley News*. Precise numbers or decision rules are not specified.

The model was solved for seventeen different weight allocations (see Table 2) and three quality minima (B through D). In order to give a

TABLE 2
WEIGHT ALLOCATIONS USED TO EXPLORE POSSIBLE DECISIONS

Relative Weight Assigned to			
Pierce-Hall w_1	Bowville w_2	Plympton w_3	FWQA w_4
0	0	0	1
3	1	3	3
3	3	1	3
3	3	3	1
1	3	3	3
4	1	4	1
1	4	1	4
4	4	1	1
1	1	4	4
1	4	4	1
1	5	3	1
1	3	5	1
1	6	2	1
1	2	6	1
1	1	7	1
1	7	1	1
7	1	1	1

SOURCE: Dorfman, Jacoby, and Thomas (1).

measure of national interest, weights were assigned to the Federal Water Quality Administration (FWQA). For example, the first weight allocation (0, 0, 0, 1) gives exclusive emphasis to national, as opposed to local, interests in the traditional cost-benefit sense. In addition, least-cost (aggregate) solutions were calculated for each of the B through D standards. These solutions appear as decisions 3, 7, and 11.

The total number of Pareto-admissible solutions generated by the 17 x 3 trials was fourteen. These are displayed in Table 3.

TABLE 3
DECISIONS RECOMMENDED BY THE ANALYSIS

Decision Number	Quality Class Achieved	Treatment Level in Terms of Percentage BOD Removal by		
		Cannery	Bowville	Plympton
1	D	95	50	67
2	D	90	52	67
3	D	80	55	67
4	C	95	65	61
5	D	90	66	61
6	C	90	67	61
7	C	80	70	60
8	B	95	80	54
9	B	94	80	54
10	C	90	80	55
11	B	90	81	54
12	C	80	80	56
13	B	80	85	54
14	B	90	90	51

SOURCE: Dorfman, Jacoby, and Thomas (1).

Tables 4, 5, and 6 display costs and benefits associated with the achievement of water quality minima. Net costs refer to the outlays required to meet the treatment levels specified in Table 3. The net benefits refer to the difference in benefit between any decision and decision 3, the least-cost plan to achieve class D water. Note that the seventeen weighting schemes converge on a substantially smaller number of admissible decisions in each table.[3]

Some of the questions that are raised by the Dorfman model include: (a) What is political about his political weights? (b) What are the limitations on his definition of Pareto admissibility? (c) What is the predictive value of this model? These questions will be discussed later.

A UTILITY MODEL FOR AGGREGATING PREFERENCES

My own work has been concerned with the direct confrontation of the aggregation problem of individual preferences to social choices. Thus, I have had to contend with the General Possibility Theorem as restated by Kenneth Arrow in his landmark work, *Social Choice and Individual Values.* In another paper (4) I attempted to show that a two-party system could, under majority rule, produce decisions on issues that were identical to the decisions which would be produced if all individuals

3. Nine solutions using class D as a minimum; eight solutions using class C; five solutions using class B. Some solutions appear in more than one class minimum.

TABLE 4

DECISIONS CORRESPONDING TO SPECIFIED WEIGHT ALLOCATIONS UNDER A MINIMUM QUALITY CLASSIFICATION OF D

Weight Allocation	Decision Number	Quality Class Achieved	Net Cost (Thousands of Dollars/Year)				Net Benefits (Thousands of Dollars/Year)			
			Pierce-Hall	Bowville	Plympton	FWPCA	Pierce-Hall	Bowville	Plympton	FWPCA
1711, 1621	1	D	95	201	302	829	−87	72	−3	−61
4411	2	D	35	217	302	750	−27	48	−2	10
L.C.	3	D	8	250	301	746	0	0	0	0
3313, 1531, 1414	5	D	35	349	255	863	−27	−38	160	101
1441, 0001, 3133, 1144, 1351, 1333, 3331	10	C	35	491	204	985	−27	−131	282	147
1261	11	B	35	512	199	1,007	−27	−148	292	139
7111	12	C	8	491	214	953	0	−158	255	125
4141	13	B	8	568	198	1,034	0	−219	294	97
1171	14	B	35	659	169	1,162	−27	−279	348	36

SOURCE: Dorfman, Jacoby, and Thomas (1).

TABLE 5

DECISIONS CORRESPONDING TO SPECIFIED WEIGHT ALLOCATIONS UNDER A MINIMUM QUALITY CLASSIFICATION OF C

Weight Allocation	Decision Number	Quality Class Achieved	Net Cost (Thousands of Dollars/Year)				Net Benefits (Thousands of Dollars/Year)			
			Pierce-Hall	Bowville	Plympton	FWPCA	Pierce-Hall	Bowville	Plympton	FWPCA
1711, 1621	4	C	95	344	251	952	−87	−21	169	34
4411, 3313, 1414, 1531	6	C	35	360	251	873	−27	−45	170	105
L.C.	7	C	8	393	249	869	0	−94	171	94
1441, 0001, 3133, 1144, 1351, 1333, 3331	10	C	35	491	204	985	−27	−131	282	147
1261	11	B	35	512	199	1,007	−27	−148	292	139
7111	12	C	8	491	214	953	0	−158	255	125
4141	13	B	8	568	198	1,034	0	−219	294	97
1171	14	B	35	659	169	1,162	−27	−279	348	36

SOURCE: Dorfman, Jacoby, and Thomas (1).

TABLE 6
Decisions Corresponding to Specified Weight Allocations Under a Minimum Quality Classification of B

Weight Allocation	Decision Number	Quality Class Achieved	Net Cost (Thousands of Dollars/Year) Pierce-Hall	Bowville	Plympton	FWPCA	Net Benefits (Thousands of Dollars/Year) Pierce-Hall	Bowville	Plympton	FWPCA
1711, 1621	8	B	95	487	200	1,074	–87	–115	292	80
1441, 1531	9	B	81	491	200	1,056	–73	–121	292	96
4411, 3313, 0001, 3133, 1144, 1351, 1333, 3331, 1261 (also L.C. solution)	11	B	35	512	199	1,007	–27	–148	292	139
7111, 4141	13	B	8	568	198	1,034	0	–219	294	97
1171	14	B	35	659	169	1,162	–27	–279	348	36

Source: Dorfman, Jacoby, and Thomas (1).
Note: N.B. 1414 not listed.

could take advantage of vote-trading. This result uses Arrow's neglected Possibility Theorem for Two Alternatives and provides a set of rules for choosing the two alternatives. The rules turn out to be a simulation of a perfectly functioning two-party system.

The basic building block of the utility model is a vector of preferences related to a given set of independent issues, e.g.,

$$\begin{bmatrix} Y_2 \\ N_1 \\ Y_3 \end{bmatrix}$$

which combines yes-no voting stances with an ordinal ranking of the importance of the issues to any individual. Thus, in the example above, the individual is for the first issue, against the second, and for the third. The second is most important to him, the first next, and the third issue least important. A display of three such vectors (a three-man committee) might give us:

$$\begin{array}{ccccc} Y_2 & N_1 & Y_1 & - & \text{Pass} \\ N_1 & Y_3 & Y_3 & - & \text{Pass} \\ Y_3 & Y_2 & Y_2 & - & \text{Pass} \end{array}$$

in which case, if we sum the vote across rows, all three issues would be passed by the committee (assuming majority rule). However, note that the first two men can trade votes on the top two issues:

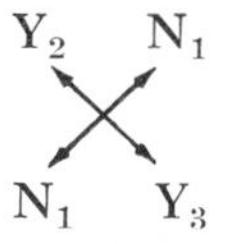

$$\begin{array}{cc} Y_2 & N_1 \\ \multicolumn{2}{c}{\times} \\ N_1 & Y_3 \end{array} \quad \text{giving} \quad \begin{array}{ccccc} \enclose{circle}{N_2} & N_1 & Y_1 & - & \text{Fail} \\ N_1 & \enclose{circle}{N_3} & Y_3 & - & \text{Fail} \\ Y_3 & Y_2 & Y_2 & - & \text{Pass} \end{array}$$

making both better off. The outcome on the three issues now is that the first two fail and the third passes. The two men have improved their positions (both are better off) at the expense of the third, who is now worse off. Clearly we are not dealing with Pareto states here but with an exchange mechanism that has third-party effects. (In larger matrices, some nontraders gain and others lose.)

Let us look again at the vectors:

$$\begin{array}{ccccc} \enclose{circle}{N_2} & N_1 & Y_1 & - & F \\ N_1 & \enclose{circle}{N_3} & \enclose{circle}{Y_3} & - & F \\ Y_3 & Y_2 & Y_2 & - & P \end{array}$$

The third man will find it to his advantage to offer to change his vote on the middle issue if the first man will *not* trade off his vote on the first issue. Then the vote will go:

$$\begin{matrix} Y_2 & N_1 & Y_1 & - & P \\ N_1 & Y_3 & \textcircled{N_3} & - & F \\ Y_3 & Y_2 & Y_2 & - & P \end{matrix}$$

If we analyze the results of the trades in terms of payoff for each person, we may display the outcomes as follows:

	$\begin{bmatrix} P \\ P \\ P \end{bmatrix}$	$\begin{bmatrix} F \\ F \\ P \end{bmatrix}$	$\begin{bmatrix} P \\ F \\ P \end{bmatrix}$
1st man win	2d 3d choices	1st 3d choices	1st 2d 3d choices
2d man win	2d 3d choices	1st 2d choices	2d choice
3d man win	1st 2d 3d choices	2d choice	1st 2d choices

The last solution [P, F, P] is stable[4] and cannot be overturned by additional trades, given the issues. It must be emphasized that the significance of the result is not that it is the Pareto-optimal solution, but that it is the unique Pareto-admissible solution which results when each participant tries to achieve more of his own objectives by trading off things that interest him less. Pareto-admissible solutions in this mechanism are generated in the issue formation process, where there is incentive to draw the provisions of each issue as close as possible to its supporters' preferences so that it achieves as high a place on their ordinal ranking as is consistent with their underlying interest in the issue; and where there is a recognition that if it is drawn too strongly against the interests of those opposing it, the issue may be more vulnerable to defeat through vote-trading.

In another article (3) I explored how the probability of vote-trading increases as a function of the number of independent issues. Thus, it was suggested that a legislative body (the body set up to provide an orderly and efficient market for vote-trading) should have a number of independent issues come before it for resolution. This happens in governments of general jurisdiction but occurs less in special-purpose authorities,

4. Under the assumption that an offer from man 2 to man 3 to return to [P, P, P], making both better off than they are at [P. F, P], will not be accepted as trustworthy.

such as river basin commissions, where the issues are apt to be highly interrelated.

It may be, and the possibility is currently being explored, that an environmental agency with authority over regional residuals management (air, water, and landfill) would have a sufficient number of interrelated issues (e.g., trade-offs between air quality and water quality) to enable a vote-trading approach to work. The exploration involves taking a region (the lower Delaware), constructing preference vectors for various districts[5] in the region that reflect hypothesized preferences relative to air quality, water quality, landfill, tax rates, and the like, and using these vectors to estimate what quality standards and environmental policies are likely to be successful. One output of the process is to explore, as does the Dorfman model, whether changes in the constitution of the agency change probable outcomes.

Questions raised by this approach include: (a) What is the measure of the "best" outcome? (b) What criteria determine which political boundaries are used for decision making? (c) How reliable need the estimates of the preference vectors be? These will be discussed in the following section.

Connecting Mechanisms between Preferences and Social Choices

Perhaps the first statement in a critique about actual operating agencies, the Delaware Commission and the Ruhrverband, is to acknowledge that they work. Such an acknowledgment does not take us very far analytically but it is useful nonetheless, for we will focus only on the connecting mechanism between preferences and social choices. This focus illuminates only a portion of an agency, or a model, and is not intended to provide light to judge the whole. With that caveat, let us consider the questions asked in the first section, under several general headings.

Benefit Estimation

Both the Delaware Commission and the Ruhrverband use estimates of benefits to decide upon objectives and means of achieving them. In each case the benefits to A are estimated by someone other than A. This neatly escapes the revealed preferences problem in public goods provision but does so by a father-knows-best principle. As a senior civil servant said recently in describing the Budget Bureau, "They know what you want, and by God, you better want it."

5. Municipalities, congressional districts, counties, equal population districts, etc.

The estimation procedure in the Delaware case was a willingness-to-pay measure. The usual criticisms of this approach are that it neglects "merit" needs and income effects and that the estimation may be faulty. In order to get to the heart of the problem, I shall ignore those criticisms (any one of which may be telling in a particular case), and deal instead with a different issue, the appropriateness of willingness to pay as a benefit measure above a project level. The point is that as long as all publicly provided goods are not provided on the basis of specific willingness-to-pay estimates (as they cannot be), then the use of such a measure in one case must inevitably be faulty. What I am willing to pay for water quality is surely related to what I already pay for other publicly provided goods, some of which I do not want. My political activity may consist of trying to shift a portion of my taxes to uses I prefer. Indeed, the whole debate on reordering of priorities is of this character. Analysis which assumes that the selection of a quality standard represents a marginal adjustment, other things changing only at the margin, cannot be squared with the reality of the interdependence of publicly provided goods. What such analysis does is to disguise the interdependencies, often with the active cooperation of politicians who do not want to be forced to make social choices. If the politician is willing to make the choice, then willingness-to-pay data *on one good* are of no help to him. In order to choose and construct his own preference vector, he must loosen all of the *ceteris paribus* assumptions which this measure uses, solve in his mind all the issues simultaneously, then see how he can improve his lot through vote-trading.

INTEREST REPRESENTATION

While the Dorfman model and my own work assume that "interests" are reflected as pressures on elected representatives,[6] in the Delaware and Ruhr cases "interests" are either officially or unofficially directly represented in the choice mechanism. The advantage of such "representation" is clear. Technical options can be explored informally. Cooperation of affected parties can be achieved with a minimum of delay and misunderstanding. In the give and take of committee work, the possibility of workable compromise is enhanced. As long as such technical committees and "representation" are advisory, much good can be accomplished. When, however, the advisors become the policy makers (as in the Ruhr case) or when they are used to give the appearance of "public" participation in the decision process (as in the Delaware case), a different issue arises.

6. I gather that Dorfman is not concerned particularly with whether the representative is elected or appointed; it is central to my work.

One must be clear on this issue, particularly since we depend very much, as a practical matter, on interest lobbying before representative bodies as a means of clarifying arguments and bringing out opposing points of view. The legislature, while it uses advocacy testimony to sharpen issues, is not a court, and it responds to voters. Replacing voter-elected representatives with industry and/or municipally appointed representatives interrupts the link between voters and their representatives. We tolerate the break in greater or lesser amounts depending upon the politicization of the issues under review. At one time we were content to establish the Port of New York Authority as a way of achieving a fiscally solvent management. Now people in the area are in revolt against it because the issues of transportation and land use have become hot political issues.

Similarly, as environmental quality rapidly becomes a political issue,[7] it is less likely that interest representation will be allowed to dominate the decision process and less likely that appointed representatives will be allowed to make basic policy decisions about environmental quality.[8] Ironically, it has been the misreading of political theory and the neglect of political history by the academic political scientist that has fostered interest representation in this country. In that misreading, Arthur Bentley's book *The Process of Government* played a large role.

THE CHOICE OF A VOTING RULE

The one state–one vote rule, used in traditional interstate compacts, and the vote that is proportional to financial contribution (the territory vote and the dollar vote) are both devices for weighting preferences and defining boundaries. Both are seriously deficient as means of translating preferences into social choices. In the one state–one vote case there are two distortions. The first occurs whenever the whole state is not affected by the decisions being taken (whenever the river basin covers less than the state) . The second occurs because a person in a populous state counts for less than a person in a less populous state. The legal defense for both distortions is quite clear and unexceptionable, but as questions of environmental quality become more political these distortions are apt to be under increasing political attack.

The dollar vote is of obvious usefulness in corporate management and similar concerns where dollars are at risk. When lives, tastes, and wills are at issue, the dollar vote has little to recommend it. Moreover, unless the

7. See, for example, the survey by Hill (6) .

8. In Germany the pressures for direct representation are probably not so great, as cultural tradition is not so attuned to representative government.

Wicksellian feature of voting simultaneously on program and budget were a uniform feature of the governmental sector, the dollar vote, as in the Ruhr case, would remain an anomaly which works probably because there is no political issue at hand (largely homogeneous goals) or there is no tradition of self-selection of goals.

THE USE OF POLITICAL WEIGHTS FOR ANALYTICAL PURPOSES

A different kind of weighting is proposed in the Dorfman model. Dorfman does not advocate any weighted voting scheme. Although he is not explicit about whether he envisions a one jurisdiction–one vote scheme or a vote pattern that follows population, his discussion seems to favor population. However, he proposes the use of a reasonable range of political weights for the actors (representatives on a commission, for example) for the analytical purpose of specifying the range of politically acceptable solutions. There are two objections to their use, only one of which Dorfman acknowledges. Dorfman recognizes that the choice of the set of reasonable weights is judgmental and that this creates a problem for the analyst. The more important objection, which Dorfman ignores, is that while one may take a decision and, by working backwards, assign a set of weights which allows that decision, there is no justification for working through the process the other way.

A political process works because intensities of preference exist. These intensities allow trade-offs to occur. The results of these trade-offs determine the solution. The "weights" that produce the same solution exist, no doubt, but they exist in the same sense that Stimson's constant is a constant, i.e., it is always the number you need to get from where you are to the answer. The weights have no political significance at all.

There is even a way, for example, for a political process to work in the Bow Valley model constructed by Dorfman and Jacoby. It is difficult, because the commission really has one decision to make, i.e., what water quality by what distribution of costs? Since the elements are interrelated, trade-offs are limited severely, but the decision can be cast in an issue-formation framework.[9] In issue formation, trades are used to achieve a more acceptable version of one issue, e.g., blocking versions neither you nor I like as well.

Preference vectors can be constructed for each of the four parties (cannery, Bowville, Plympton, and FWQA), and we may be as vague as Dorfman as to how these are reflected in the commission. Assuming they are, and ignoring the possibility that there are more politically acceptable decisions than the fourteen generated by the weights used, we may con-

9. See Section IV of Haefele (4).

struct an issue-formation matrix as follows (excluding D-level solutions).

First, rank the top three decision choices of each:

	Cannery	Bowville	Plympton	FWQA
1st	12, 13, 7	4	14	10
2d	6, 11, 14, 10	6	8, 9, 11, 13	11
3d	9	7	10	12

Next, drop all decisions that do not appear in at least three columns. This is done on the plausible assumption that if anything is to be passed, it will have to be something that a majority of the actors favor over the other alternatives. Rearrange the remaining decisions by rows (Y's are indicated since we have assumed passage of something and are simply finding out which one):

	Cannery	Bowville	Plympton	FWQA
Decision 10	Y (Ind.)	Y_1	Y_2	Y_1
Decision 11	Y (Ind.)	Y_2	Y_1	Y_2

Decision 10 will be chosen unless trade-offs outside the issue of water quality take place. The indifference of the cannery is unlikely to be a source of bargaining strength, since none of the cannery's more preferred positions can win over 10 and 11.

This result does not depend upon the assignment of "political" weights to anybody, although the decisions were generated originally by the use of weights. The politically feasible solution space could have been calculated directly from the given cost and benefit functions, and preference vectors constructed within that space to define the trade-offs. The solution from that process would not necessarily be any of the fourteen decisions accepted by the Dorfman model.

Whether or not the analyst has any business estimating political feasibility is another question and one which each person must answer for himself. He should know, however, that he is acting as a price setter when he does so, and analysts who can correctly calculate equilibrium prices in actual markets are rare.

It may be useful, before leaving the discussion of political weights, to make a more general point. A critique of benefit-cost analysis made by Maass (8) in 1966 called attention to the political necessity for consideration of goals other than that of economic efficiency in public investments. His suggestion, however, was that the political process assigned weights to various goals and hence solved such investment decisions. It was a most unfortunate figure of speech, if that was what it was; if meant in a more precise sense, it was clearly wrong. Mera (9), among others, has shown that to solve any such trade-off between an efficiency and nonefficiency goal, both the total transformation curve (production possibility curve) and the social welfare function must simultaneously be known for an optimum trade-off to be specified. This may be represented by a diagram which plots percentage of efficiency gain as independent of some nonefficiency gain (Figure 2).

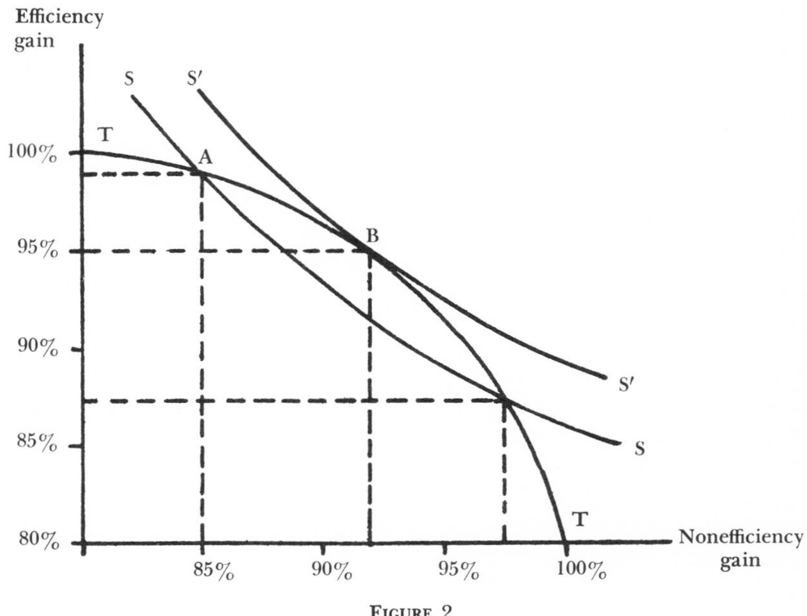

FIGURE 2

Given TT as the transformation curve between efficiency gain and some nonefficiency gain, and SS and S′S′ as social welfare curves encompassing these two goals, then optimum point B (95 percent efficiency gain and 92 percent nonefficiency gain) can be identified. Any economic analysis which simply identifies the 100 percent efficiency point and, say, point A, would not be providing sufficient information for any policy body or legislature to choose between the two. The trade-off ratio at A (99 over 85) would tell the economic analyst even less about the shape of the social welfare function. Hence, it is as useless to ask a legislature to specify *a* trade-off ratio (or constraint) as it is to ask the analyst to guess that point on the transformation curve which is relevant. If the analyst could supply the whole transformation curve, presumably the relevant policy-making body could supply the welfare curve which relates to it. That welfare curve cannot be inferred from past actions and will not result from a political consideration of *just* that transformation curve.

The criticism of using "political" weights is not therefore confined to the reasonableness of the weights chosen but refers also to the conceptual problem that goes back to Samuelson's statement about the need for simultaneously solving the income distribution questions and the public goods decisions. That is what an ideal political process does. Ex post, one could calculate "weights" which would have given the same result, but the politician cannot specify those weights as he goes along. They "all depend" on all the others, in a very real sense. When one gets an "it all depends" answer from a politician, it is not always an evasion; it may be a literal translation of Samuelson's theory of public expenditures.

THE BOUNDARY PROBLEM

Present in all four case discussions has been an unresolved problem of where to draw the boundaries of political jurisdictions over these social choices. What people should be included? When the country was new and politicians were more skilled in the conscious formation of social choice mechanisms, two principles were relevant to the drawing of political boundaries: they had to be (a) large enough to encompass a heterogeneous mixture of people and problems so as to avoid the tyranny of the majority (Madison's defense of the American republic against Montesquieu's criticism of large republics is based on this principle), and (b) small enough to insure that most of the problems were of concern to most people. This principle was an attempt to guard against the possibility that many would have "free money" to make political deals, i.e., many issues would concern them not at all and they would be free to sell their votes to the highest bidder.

In modern times we find that the application of these two rules does not allow us to converge on any set of governmental institutions, and some economists in the Tiebout tradition can construct almost as many governments as people while others end up putting everything at the national level. I know of no good theoretical work on these questions. Elsewhere (5) I have argued that the combination of technical interdependence of residuals plus these two rules makes a strong case for regional governments of general jurisdiction in many areas of the country.

If that proposition is accepted, then districts within the overall jurisdiction must, on legal grounds and on utility grounds, be drawn in terms of equal population. Beyond that we have few guidelines. The size of districts will not, within some limits, make much difference except for two cases: (a) if the population is heterogeneous and the heterogeneity is, as is usual, reflected in the settlement pattern, then the districts must be small enough to reflect that, and (b) if the issues are likely to vary significantly from one area to another, then the districts must be small enough to allow those issues to be captured in the electoral process.

References

1. Dorfman, Robert, and Jacoby, Henry D. "A Model of Public Decisions Illustrated by a Water Pollution Policy." In *The Analysis and Evaluation of Public Expenditures: The P.P.B. System.* Vol. 1. Joint Economic Committee, 91st Cong. Washington, D.C.: Government Printing Office, 1969.
2. Fair, Gordon. "Pollution Abatement in the Ruhr District." In *Comparisons in Resource Management,* edited by Henry Jarrett. Baltimore, Md.: Johns Hopkins University Press, 1961.
3. Haefele, E. T. "Coalitions, Minority Representation and Vote Trading Probabilities." *Public Choice,* Spring 1970.
4. Haefele, E. T. "A Utility Theory of Representative Government." *American Economic Review* 61 (June 1971):350–67.
5. Haefele, E. T. "Residuals Managements and Metropolitan Governance." Resources for the Future, Washington, D.C. Mimeographed.
6. Hill, Gladwin. "Polluters Sit on Anti-Pollution Boards," p. 1. *New York Times,* 7 December 1970.
7. Kneese, Allen V., and Bower, Blair T. *Managing Water Quality: Economics, Technology, Institutions.* Baltimore, Md.: Johns Hopkins University Press, 1968.
8. Maass, Arthur. "Benefit-Cost Analysis: Its Relevance to Public Investment Decisions." *Quarterly Journal of Economics* 80 (May 1966).
9. Mera, Koichi. "Income Distribution in Benefit-Cost Analysis." Discussion Paper 33, Program in Regional and Urban Economics. Cambridge, Mass.: Harvard University, May 1968.
10. Water Quality Hearings, Delaware River Basin Commission, pp. 13–14. Trenton, N.J., 26 January 1967.

2

Can We Trust the Market to Solve Externality Problems?

Alan Randall

Many of today's environmental quality problems result from the deposition of residuals into natural resources. The party who has created an unpleasant residual gets rid of it, often simply by dumping it elsewhere. If dumping it elsewhere happens to adversely affect other people, directly or indirectly, we have a potential environmental quality problem.

An externality is said to exist wherever the utility of one or more individuals is dependent upon, among other things, one or more activities which are under the control of someone else. Buchanan and Stubblebine (2) have defined a Pareto-relevant externality as one which may be modified in such a way as to make the externally affected party better off without making the acting party worse off. A Pareto-relevant externality is characterized by the existence of potential gains from trade between the affected and acting parties. In what follows, the term "externality" may be taken to mean Pareto-relevant externality. An external diseconomy is an externality in which the affected party is made worse off by the activities of the acting party.

Where environmental quality problems are the result of external diseconomies, improvement of environmental quality requires a modification of the behavior of acting parties who produce these external diseconomies.[1]

The Theory of Market Solution of Externality Problems

The theory of economic policy is based on the premise that if one wishes to modify the behavior of an economic unit, one must modify the incentives facing that unit so that the preferred behavior becomes more appealing to it (i.e., more pleasant, more profitable, or both). There are three broad classes of methods of solving environmental externality problems, each intended to change incentives so that creation of Pareto-relevant external diseconomies becomes less profitable to acting parties. They are: (a) market solutions, following establishment of a liability rule to serve as a starting point for negotiations; (b) systems of per unit taxes, charges, fines, or subsidies; and (c) systems of standards, enforced by the threat of fines or jail sentences. While (a) relies on private negotiation and (b) and (c) on government intervention, the three classes represent a clear progression from more to less reliance on market forces to determine the equilibrium output of externality.

Market solution allows both price and quantity of externality to be determined by the market. Systems of per unit fines or subsidies allow the market to determine the quantity of externality in response to a price set by a government agency. Systems of standards allow the market an even smaller role. A government agency sets the price of an externality and a quantity (the standard); if the allowable quantity is not exceeded, the price does not apply. Market forces find expression only in the polluter's decision of whether to meet the standard or pay the penalty. Given adequate information, of course, the final equilibrium quantity of externality may be similar for each method of solution.

The logical underpinnings of the suggestion that the market may be relied upon to achieve solutions to externality problems are as follows. A Pareto-relevant externality is, by definition, characterized by the existence of potential gains from trade between the acting and affected parties. Surely, then, we can rely on self-interest to ensure the realization of these potential gains through exchange between the involved parties. As always, efficient exchange requires precisely defined, rigidly enforced, and transferable property rights. In the case of external diseconomies, these property rights include some specification of the laws of liability for damages associated with the diseconomy. If liability rules are trans-

1. The adverse effects of a degraded environment on people may in some cases be minimized by evasive action taken by affected parties. However, this type of solution would not strictly improve environmental quality.

ferable—i.e., if they allow a specified amount of externality to be created with impunity and that amount to be exceeded only if the affected party is willing to agree—they serve as the starting point for negotiations to realize the potential gains from trade. The two extreme examples of such liability rules are the zero liability rule, L^z, and the full liability rule, L^f; an infinite number of intermediate rules could be conceived. L^z specifies that external diseconomies in any amount may be created with impunity; under such a rule, the affected party would have an incentive to offer a bribe to induce the acting party to reduce his output of external diseconomy. L^f specifies that absolutely no externality may be created without the consent of the affected party; under such a rule, the acting party would have an incentive to offer compensation to induce the affected party to accept a positive amount of externality.

Coase (5) perceived that, regardless of which liability rule is in operation, one or another party has an incentive to modify a Pareto-relevant externality. Given perfect competition and zero transactions costs,[2] negotiations will continue until all gains from trade have been exhausted. Coase argued that all gains from trade will be exhausted at the same Pareto-efficient outcome, regardless of which liability rule is in operation. In other words, the market solution to a particular externality problem is allocatively neutral with respect to the assignment of liability. The specification of liability influences the final distribution of income at the completion of the exchange, since an L^z rule would result in the affected party making payments to the acting party and an L^f rule would result in the opposite flow of payments. But, income distribution is the only variable influenced, Coase claimed.

It is understandable that such an approach to externalities would be attractive to academic economists. It relies upon the market to establish the price of an externality. All the society has to do is to establish a liability rule, and it does not matter too much what that rule is since any rule will result in the same Pareto-efficient equilibrium solution. Market solutions, it seems, offer an efficient solution to externality problems, requiring little information and minimizing the risk of bureaucratic mistakes. If the society is concerned with income distribution, it may attempt

2. It is worthwhile to define transactions costs carefully, since they play an important part in the analysis to follow. Transactions costs are the costs of making and enforcing decisions. Included are the costs of obtaining information, establishing one's bargaining position, bargaining and arriving at a group decision, and enforcing the decision made. Any method of modifying externalities will involve some transactions costs. The size of the transactions costs and the type of transactions services used are likely to vary with the use of different types of solution methods and with the actual solution obtained. Transactions costs may be so large that they become a major factor in the selection of an efficient method of solution of any particular externality problem.

to choose a liability rule which will lead to a satisfactory distribution of income, or it may use any other income redistribution method to attempt to restore a situation of equity.

Of the three broad groups of methods of solving externality problems listed above, it is noticeable that academic economists usually prefer market solutions or systems of per unit fines, charges, taxes, or subsidies. There is a group of academic economists who are fervent supporters of the market solution method. However, politicians, administrators, and the general public seem to have more faith in systems of standards. This divergence of opinion between academic economists on the one hand, and the public and its representatives on the other, motivated the preparation of this paper, which focuses on market solutions in theory and practice and offers some speculations on their applicability.

The Coasian analysis of externality was rapidly incorporated into the tool kits of laissez faire economists. Whereas Coase's analysis concentrated entirely on the case in which both the acting and the affected parties were single firms engaged in production, Davis and Whinston (7) in 1965 considered the case in which both parties were single consumers. Their results duplicated those of Coase in all respects, including the finding of allocative neutrality of liability rules. Calabresi (4) spoke for the proponents of market solutions in 1968: all externalities[3] can be internalized and all misallocations can be remedied by the market except to the extent that transactions cost money.[4]

Beginning in 1966, the Coasian analysis came under attack from at least two quarters: one group claimed that Coase's assumptions were so far removed from the real world that his analysis was irrelevant for prescriptive purposes; and another group accepted Coase's static perfect-competition assumptions for the sake of argument, but even so were able to demolish Coase's claim of allocative neutrality of liability rules. In the second group, Dolbear (9), Randall (13, 14), and Mishan (11), using static perfect-competition analysis of two-party cases, have made varying

3. Calabresi's claim that "all externalities" can be internalized by the market is incorrect, as not all externalities are Pareto relevant. For example, inframarginal externalities, while not Pareto relevant, may cause environmental problems.

4. This line of reasoning culminated in Demsetz's (8) argument that where a market for an external diseconomy does not exist it should not exist, since the benefits from such a market clearly cannot exceed the costs of its operation. The absence of an observable market is, in itself, a market solution. This argument would seem to lead to the conclusion that any externalities which are observed to exist unmodified should not be modified, since transactions costs must therefore be so high that modification is unprofitable. However, the fallacy is obvious. The unprofitability of market solution does not prove that solution by any other method must also be unprofitable. If some other method of solution involves lower transactions costs, solution by that method may be preferable to no solution at all.

degrees of progress toward circumscribing the claimed generality of Coase's allocative neutrality doctrine. Here, I will summarize the treatment in Randall (14), in which the following propositions are proven mathematically.

First, let us consider an external diseconomy situation where both the acting and affected parties are consumers. A change in liability rules will change the budget constraints faced by both parties. Under the L^z rule, the affected party would offer the acting party a bribe. Under the L^f rule, the acting party would offer compensation to the affected party. The relevant budget constraints are:

under L^z, for the affected party,

$$\overline{Y}_1 - \overline{p}_1 q_{11} - \ldots - \overline{p}_m q_{m1} - p_n^* (q_{n2}^\circ - q_{n2}) = 0 \quad [1]$$

and for the acting party,

$$\overline{Y}_2 - \overline{p}_1 q_{12} - \ldots - \overline{p}_m q_{m2} - \overline{p}_n q_{n2} + p_n^* (q_{n2}^\circ - q_{n2}) = 0; \quad [2]$$

under L^f, for the affected party,

$$\overline{Y}_1 - \overline{p}_1 q_{11} - \ldots - \overline{p}_m q_{m1} + p_n^* q_{n2}^\circ - p_n^* (q_{n2}^\circ - q_{n2}) = 0 \quad [3]$$

and for the acting party,

$$\overline{Y}_2 - \overline{p}_1 q_{12} - \ldots - \overline{p}_m q_{m2} - \overline{p}_n q_{n2} - p_n^* q_{n2}^\circ + p_n^* (q_{n2}^\circ - q_{n2}) = 0; \quad [4]$$

where the affected party suffers an external diseconomy from the acting party's consumption of the good n, m denotes the number of externality-free goods, $\overline{Y}_j$ is the income of Mr. j, q_{ij} is the consumption of the good i by Mr. j, $\overline{p}_i$ is the competitive market price of the good i, p_n^* is the unit bribe or compensation price, and q_{n2}° is the amount of the good n which would be consumed by the acting party if $p_n^* = 0$.

These changes in budget constraints associated with changes in liability rules are sufficient to induce shifts in the resultant demand and supply curves for abatement of the external diseconomy. This is true for all cases, except the very special case where the affected party has an income elasticity of demand for abatement equal to zero and the acting party has a zero income elasticity of demand for the commodity associated with the externality. Figure 1 shows the situation. The L^f rule results in a greater level of abatement of an external diseconomy than does the L^z rule. Where any consumers are involved in an externality situation, the demand or supply curves of abatement associated with those consumers will shift

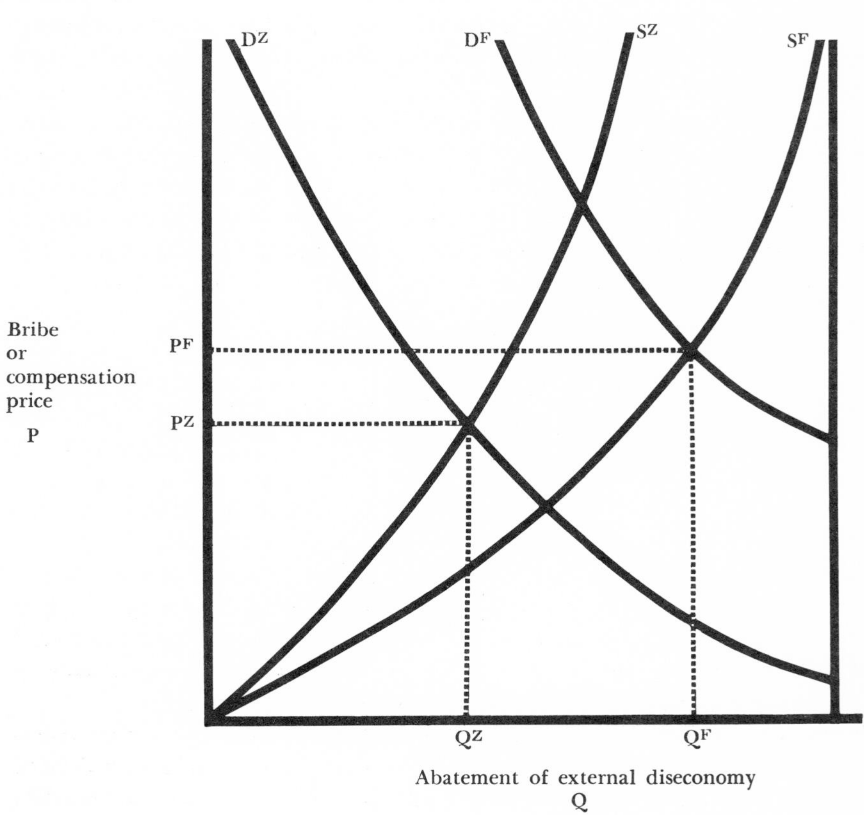

FIGURE 1. Market solutions to externality in consumption. Superscripts: Z = zero liability status quo. F = full liability status quo. Source: Randall (13, 14).

with a change in liability rules, resulting in different equilibrium levels of abatement.

In the case where all involved parties are producers, a change in liability rules will result in a change in equilibrium output of externality, whenever (a) there is an inflexible capital constraint or (b) the use of capital has a positive price. The analysis is similar to that for externality in consumption: a change in liability rules changes the capital constraints affecting both parties. Again, an L^f rule will result in a greater level of abatement than an L^z rule.

Where transactions costs are greater than zero, the party who is less favored by the operative liability rule makes an offer. However, the party who receives payment receives only the amount remaining after transactions costs have been subtracted. The existence of positive transactions costs reduces the effective value of any offer. When the affected party must pay, the existence of positive transactions costs shifts the demand curve for abatement downward (and to the left). When the acting party pays, the existence of positive transactions costs shifts the supply curve for abatement downward (and to the right). As a change in liability rules from L^z to L^f results in the former payer becoming the receiver of payment and vice versa, the assignment of liability affects the equilibrium output of externality when transactions costs are positive. In fairness, it must be noted that Coase (5) recognized that the claim of allocative neutrality is predicated upon zero transactions costs.

Figure 2 shows the effect of positive transactions costs on the equilibrium output of externality in consumption under the L^z and L^f rules. The existence of transactions costs increases the disparity between the equilibrium solutions under different liability rules. The disparity between the equilibrium solutions under different liability rules increases as unit transactions costs increase, as illustrated in Figure 3. It is conceivable, as in cases (c) and (f) of Figure 3, that transactions costs may be so great that movements away from the starting point defined by the liability law may be impossible. In such cases, an L^z law results in zero abatement while an L^f law results in complete abatement of an external diseconomy. An educated guess would suggest that transactions costs of this magnitude may not be unusual, in practice.

Buchanan and Tullock (3) and Olson (12) have argued that transactions costs are likely to be larger when negotiations must be initiated by a large and diffuse group of individuals, rather than by a much smaller group of individuals who are more vitally interested in a particular issue. This hypothesis is relevant to cases of environmental pollution from industrial sources, where the affected party is usually a diffuse group of citizens and the acting party is a much smaller group of entrepreneurs whose incomes are directly related to pollution levels. It follows, then, that in cases of industrial pollution an L^z rule is more likely than an L^f rule to result in transactions costs too high for the achievement of a solution other than the status quo.

In summary, allocative neutrality with respect to liability rules can be accepted only in situations where all of the involved parties are producers, the use of capital is a free good, and transactions costs are zero. In cases other than these (i.e., in almost every significant externality problem), an L^f rule will result in a market solution specifying a higher degree of abatement of external diseconomies than will an L^z rule.

Mishan (11) makes one further observation which seems plausible: the incentives for strategies to reduce the effects of external diseconomies

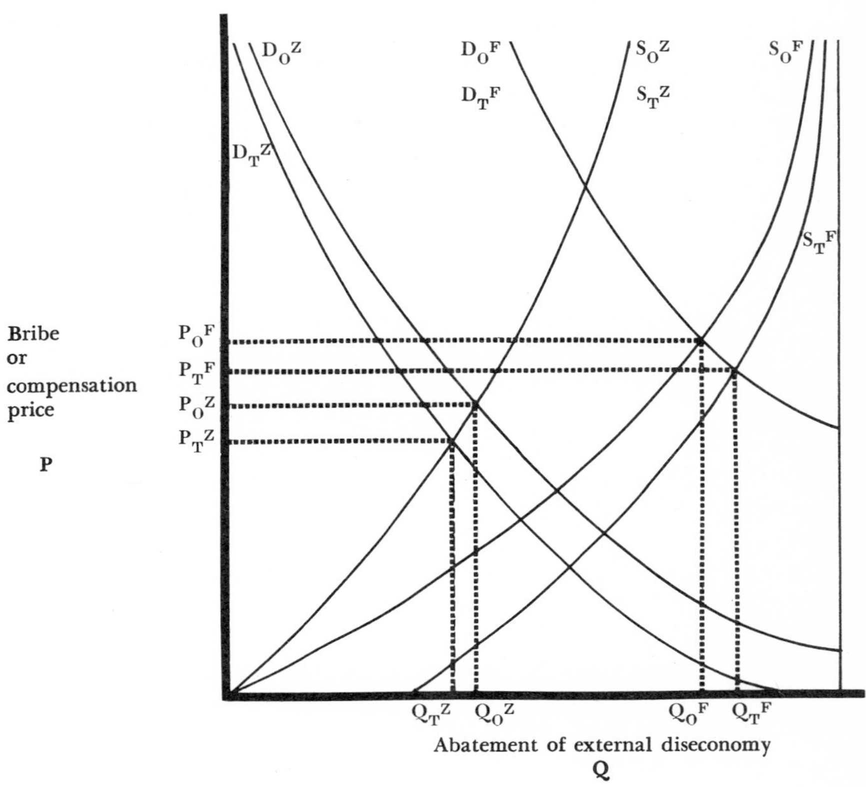

FIGURE 2. Market solutions to externality in consumption: the effect of transactions costs. Superscripts: Z = zero liability status quo. F = full liability status quo. Subscripts: O = transactions costs = O. T = variable transactions costs = T per unit. Source: Randall (13, 14).

are greater under a full liability law. The effects of pollution, for example, can be reduced by emission-reducing technological improvements, or by location of the externality-producing business in an out-of-the-way place, or by various other means. Mishan also argues for a full liability rule on the grounds of equity. He argues that if polluters are likely to be more prosperous than the affected parties, a full liability rule would be more equitable than a zero liability rule.

The current situation in the theory of market solutions to externality problems can be summarized as follows. A Pareto-relevant externality, being characterized by potential gains from trade, will generate incentives for one or another of the involved parties to initiate negotiations aimed at modifying that externality. A solution different from the status quo

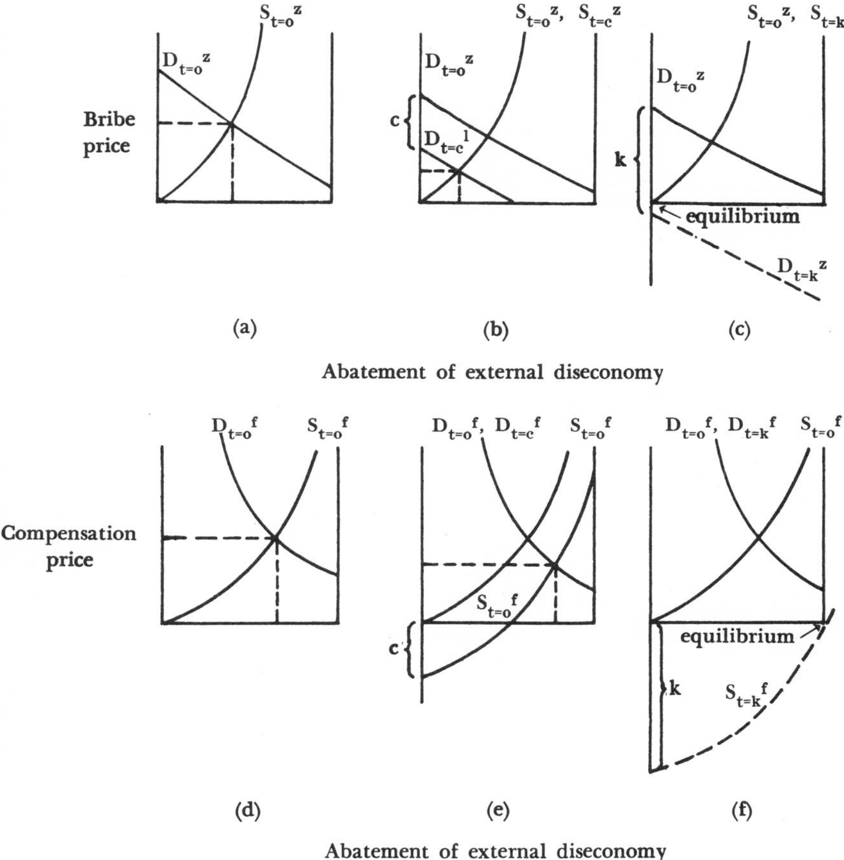

FIGURE 3. Externality in consumption, under two different liability rules and three different assumptions about the level of transactions costs.

situation may be achieved and, if perfect competition prevails in all relevant industries including the transactions industry, that solution may be Pareto efficient. However, the resource allocation and income distribution characteristics of the solution achieved are not neutral to the choice of liability rules. In comparison with a zero liability rule, a full liability rule will result in: (a) a higher degree of abatement of an external diseconomy such as pollution, (b) a reallocation of resources toward pollution control and production of commodities which can be produced by low-pollution processes, and (c) an income redistribution in favor of the affected party. The effective demolition of the doctrine of allocative neutrality of liability rules removes one of the prime advantages which has been claimed for market solutions to externality problems. The role of the body politic and the bureaucracy in setting the operative liability rule is now known to include the power to affect allocation of resources in production and allocation of budgets in consumption. In a macroeconomic sense, if externalities are as pervasive as is now believed, the power to set liability rules therefore implies the power to affect resource allocation in the whole economy, aggregate production and consumption, and relative and aggregate prices. Surely, then, the assignment of liability requires that the government body so empowered have at its disposal much more information than was formerly believed necessary. Resorting to market solution does not eliminate the possibility of bureaucratic mistakes.

Economic Analyses of Observed Market Solutions

Unfortunately, economic analyses of market solutions to externality in practice seem mostly confined to casual empiricism. As noted above, Demsetz (8) found several externality situations where no market transactions were observed. He attributed this to transactions costs so high that the operation of a market in externalities was unprofitable. Alexander (1) mentions cases involving aluminum-refining industries, where the threat of legal action against pollution encouraged the polluters to compensate affected parties. In some cases market solutions have occurred in which the aluminum industry has paid compensation to agriculturalists and orchardists on farms nearby. In other cases, the aluminum industry has purchased the land affected by its emissions, creating a merger between acting and affected parties. However, parties less directly affected (e.g., citizens who may suffer some unpleasantness but no loss of agricultural productivity, or future generations who may lose the assimilative power of the environment) may not feel that these externalities have been fully internalized.

Crocker (6), in a notable exception to this trend of casual empiricism, conducted a careful regression analysis of market solutions to one specific environmental externality problem over a time period in which the liability rule was effectively changed. He examined a situation in which inorganic fertilizers are produced from locally mined phosphate rock in Polk County, Florida. Air pollution was a by-product of the fertilizer production process. Damage to local citrus and beef cattle industries was observed over an area of about 400 square miles around the fertilizer plants. Prior to 1957, the liability situation approximated the L^z rule of our theories. Government institutions offered insignificant assistance to affected parties, who could suffer in silence, attempt to arrive at a market solution by bribing the polluters to desist, or initiate civil suit for damages. In civil damages suits, the burden of proof that damage is occurring and is due to the activities of the defendant lies with the plaintiff. This burden of proof has been extremely onerous and no plaintiff had been successful in recovering any damages from the polluting fertilizer companies. In 1957, an Air Pollution Control District was established. Fertilizer companies were in effect advised to buy the affected land or face the prospect of imposition of emission standards. This changed the liability rule from something approaching L^z to an intermediate liability rule more nearly, but not completely, approaching L^f.

Crocker obtained and analyzed land sales data for a period of about twenty years, about ten years before and after this change in the operative liability rule. In the earlier period there was a downward trend in land prices, correlated with the decreasing agricultural productivity of the land. However, after the establishment of the Air Pollution Control District, land prices began to rise as the fertilizer companies bought up land in order to avoid the imposition of emission standards. Along with a rise in prices of affected land, and a gradual but continuous increase in the amount of agricultural land owned by phosphate companies, the output of polluting emissions by the fertilizer companies was reduced gradually and consistently over the years. Crocker interprets this reduction in emissions as the result of internalization of the externalities. When the companies owned most of the affected land, their optimum economic strategy was to maximize total returns from both the use of the land and the production of phosphate. No longer could they regard the land and the air above it as a cost-free waste disposal resource. The empirical result of Crocker's analysis was that the change in liability rules changed resource allocation in the phosphate fertilizer, citrus, and beef industries. Income distribution between the fertilizer and agricultural industries was also changed.

Transactions costs of market solution were very much higher in the period when the liability situation was essentially L^z than in the later period when the fertilizer companies faced the threat of emissions standards. The change in liability rules shifted the burden of initiating negotiations from the affected party to the acting party. The acting party had fewer members, each vitally concerned with the level of pollution, which was a major variable in the profit function. The affected party was no longer forced to rely on bribery or civil suit. Crocker was able to correlate a change in resource allocation with a change in liability rules and a concurrent change in transactions costs.[5]

5. Crocker interprets this change in output of pollutants and resource allocation with the change in liability rules as being entirely attributable to the change in transactions costs. The theoretical work discussed above would suggest that the change in

Significantly, the only detailed empirical study of market solutions to external diseconomies currently available is entirely consistent with the theoretical work discussed above. A change in liability rules changes resource allocation, the output of polluting emissions, and the distribution of income between the acting and affected parties.

Market Solutions in Practice

What can we say, then, about market solutions to externality problems in practice? Market solutions are not allocatively neutral with respect to liability rules. Rather, an L^z rule is more likely than any positive liability rule to result in zero or low levels of abatement of external diseconomies. This may provide some explanation for what has been the major practical objection to market solutions: they are seldom observed in practice. In the past, laws with respect to externalities such as environmental pollution have been lenient, seldom and ineffectively enforced, or both. Something approaching a zero liability law has been in operation. If market solutions are to be used effectively to ensure environmental quality, the task seems to be that of converting our liability laws to L^f or to some intermediate position, while maintaining transferability.[6] Now, we will consider the operation of market solutions under a full liability rule.

Kneese (10) argues vigorously against reliance upon market solutions on the grounds that market solutions are best adapted (or are adaptable only) to the two-party case, while most significant pollution problems arise from the disposal of wastes into common property resources. One or a relatively small number of acting parties dumps wastes into a common property resource (e.g., air or water), reducing the welfare of many affected parties. Clearly, an L^z rule would minimize the likelihood of pollution abatement in such cases. Pollution in common property resources is a public "bad," and its abatement a public good. Exclusion of freeloaders from participation in the benefits of abatement would be almost impossible in the case of air pollution and difficult in the case of water pollution. Unanimous action on the part of affected citizens would avoid the freeloader problem, but would likely entail prohibitive transactions costs. Let us consider whether a general conversion to the full liability rule would reduce these problems sufficiently to make

liability rules would result in a different solution with respect to pollution emissions and resource allocation even if transactions costs were unchanged. But this is a relatively minor quibble.

6. A system of standards, for example, places some liability on polluters but also limits transferability. In the case of standards enforced by a governmental agency, transferability exists only in the range between complete abatement and the standard.

market solution a credible alternative method of solving environmental externality problems.

The process of negotiating and enforcing a market solution can be divided into three major steps. It is possible to identify a number of alternative ways these steps can be carried out. Since it is anticipated that the organization of the affected parties would provide the greatest difficulties, greater attention is paid to the affected parties.

1. The first step is enforcement of recognition of the status quo established by an L^f rule. Firms polluting without having obtained the permission of the affected parties must be made either to cease or to obtain that permission. This could be done in several ways.

1A: A public agency could ascertain that some emissions are being released[7] and

$1A_1$: directly impose a very high penalty on the offender unless he ceases polluting or demonstrates he has obtained permission from the affected party, or

$1A_2$: ask a court to do the same.

1B: The affected parties could initiate litigation to prove that emissions are being released, and seek court enforcement of the L^f rule. Organization could occur by means of

$1B_1$: unanimous action by the affected parties, or

$1B_2$: "unanimous" action by a leader or committee, after a majority vote of the affected parties, or

$1B_3$: a class action initiated by one individual on behalf of the affected parties,[8] or

$1B_4$: a series of individual actions by affected parties.

2. For the second step, the acting party now has an incentive to initiate negotiations to induce the affected parties to accept a certain amount of emissions in exchange for compensation. The affected parties must be organized in some way in order to conduct their side of the negotiations. Possibilities are:

2A: A public agency could bargain on behalf of the affected parties, or

2B: the affected parties could bargain by

$2B_1$: unanimous action by the affected parties, or

$2B_2$: taking a "unanimous" position and appointing a representative or committee to bargain, following a majority vote, or

7. A full liability rule requires proof only that emissions are being released. This is a much simpler matter than proving that (a) damage is occurring and (b) the defendant is responsible.

8. It would be necessary to change the law in most states to allow this.

$2B_3$: each affected individual dealing separately with the acting party.

3. The third step is the policing and enforcement of the agreement. Compensation payments must be made as agreed and the agreed emission limit must not be exceeded. The possible types of organization of the affected party for this purpose parallel those in 1 (above).

It seems reasonable that these different methods of organization of the affected parties may lead to solutions involving different amounts of transactions costs, different resource allocation *ceteris paribus* transactions costs, and different emissions levels. The following paragraphs are devoted to speculation about these differences.

(a) The $1B_1-2B_1-3B_1$ procedure is most unlikely to occur widely, since it relies on unanimity. Buchanan and Tullock (3) and Olson (12) caution us that procedures requiring unanimity may result in high transactions costs. Transactions costs to achieve unanimity probably increase quite rapidly as the number of people involved in the decision increases.

(b) At the opposite end of the range, decision procedures relying on $2B_3$, a series of bargains between acting and affected parties one-by-one, do not seem promising either. The public-good nature of pollution abatement makes a series of individual bargains almost impossible. Because the resource into which the waste products are dumped is a common property resource, it is physically essential that a unique amount of pollution exist in any one place at any one time. But different affected parties most likely have different demand curves for abatement, while the firm has a single supply curve. The result of individual bargains would probably be a series of individual agreements calling for different amounts of abatement, a clear physical impossibility. So extensive contracting and recontracting would be required to arrive at agreements with all parties allowing the same amount of emissions.

If the law allowed any one affected individual to demand adherence to the L^f law, acting parties would be obliged to conclude individual agreements with all affected parties. The "holdout problem" familiar to urbanologists may assume significant proportions. One or more affected citizens may steadfastly refuse to conclude bargains, hoping to obtain exorbitant compensation (i.e., to obtain a large proportion of the total economic surplus for themselves).

Everything considered, the prospect is for extremely high transactions costs and possible failure to obtain any solution other than the starting point defined by the L^f law. The problem here is not one of too little abatement but rather of too much. Complete abatement of pollution may disrupt the production of commodities, employment, wages, and prices to an extent intolerable to citizens of the affluent society.

The situation could conceivably be improved by a modification of the L^f rule so that once, say, 60 percent of the affected individuals had agreed upon a particular permissible amount of emissions and a unit compensation rate, the remainder must accept that agreement or forfeit compensation.

(c) The use of $1B_3$ and $3B_3$, class action suits, is currently limited by difficult legal problems. There is strong resistance in some quarters to any move to liberalize the laws restricting this type of suit. True class action suits, as distinct from suits initiated by one individual with legal powers to act for all affected parties, may be limited in use simply because there is a limited number of philanthropists willing to go to personal expense to obtain abatement, a public good.

(d) The 1A–2A–3A procedure is very similar to the system of emissions charges advocated by Kneese (10). A system of charges operated on a pollution-shed basis, allowing local public agencies to bargain with polluters to determine the local unit compensation price (i.e., unit charge) and to distribute the income from charges among the affected citizens, would closely approximate a market solution. Increasing bureaucratization would tend to increase the disparity between market solutions and charge systems. For example, the similarity of market solutions and charge systems becomes more tenuous as we move from problem-shed charges to state or nationwide charges, or from distribution of charge income among affected parties to spending it on their behalf (e.g., in environmental projects) to simply using it as government income to meet general government expenses.

(e) The $1B_2$–$2B_2$–$3B_2$ procedure would seem likely to involve lower transactions costs than the other procedures, which rely on direct bargaining among the involved parties without the help of a governmental agency. These procedures reduce transactions costs because they allow the affected party to make decisions on the basis of less than unanimous consent. We know too little about transactions costs to venture a guess on the relative costs of these kinds of direct bargaining methods versus bargaining by a public agency on behalf of the affected parties.

As pointed out in (d) above, the use of bargaining committees tends to blur any distinction between market solutions under L^f and systems of unit emissions charges. Nevertheless, important choices can be made concerning the optimal level of bureaucratization. Where pollution sheds can be easily defined on the basis of physical criteria and where there are relatively few sources of pollution, I suspect that market solutions negotiated by local committees may be appropriate. In cases of pollution in urban areas where there are many sources of pollution, each affecting different but overlapping geographical areas, reliance on $2B_2$ may require a huge number of committees to be set up, each dealing with a single polluter. Alternatively, one committee would bargain with all polluters. If this latter alternative were chosen, the amount of expertise required of committee members and the amount of their time used would tend to grow so large that the committee would take on the characteristics of a public agency.

The optimal level of bureaucratization must depend upon, among other things, transactions costs. The desirability of distributing compensation or charge income among the affected citizens may be somewhat offset by the additional transactions costs of identifying damaged parties and determining the extent of damage suffered. However, it may well be possible to develop rules of thumb for distribution which, while imperfect, are better than agency or committee expenditure of the income.

(f) It seems worthwhile to point out that any market solution relying on the help of a public or governmental agency (i.e., the 1A–2A–3A procedure) or on less than unanimous action by the affected parties, voluntarily organized for that purpose (i.e., the $1B_2$–$2B_2$–$3B_2$ procedure) would result in a unique amount of waste being dumped into a common property resource and a unique amount of compensation. This solution will not be optimal for all of the individuals and firms involved in an externality situation. (If it were optimal for all, unanimous agreement would have been reached.) So, some parties may regard the group agreement as simply a new starting point for further negotiations aimed at exhausting all possible gains from trade.

If this occurred, the group agreement would not be sabotaged. Further negotiations could not result in individual agreements to allow the quantity of emissions specified in the group agreement to be exceeded. Enforcement procedures for the group agreement would be adequate to prevent this. On the other hand, there may be some members of the affected party who feel so strongly about improvement of environmental quality that they would offer bribes to induce polluters to reduce emissions even more. I fail to see any harm in such private agreements, resulting, as they would, in reduced total emissions into the common property resource. On the other hand, the theory of common property resources does not lead me to expect such agreements to occur frequently.

From my sketchy examination of the various decision and enforcement procedures which could conceivably be used to facilitate market solutions, it seems that procedures other than those which use 2A or $2B_2$

(i.e., public agencies or committees) to facilitate the second step (the negotiations) have severe practical limitations.

In summary, it seems that market solutions could in many cases achieve substantial improvement in environmental quality[9] if the liability rules were changed to L^f or something approaching it and if the affected parties were legally required either to set up their own bargaining committee to make *binding* bargains or to accept the help of a governmental agency which would do it for them.

In the absence of institutional changes of this nature, it seems that market solutions to externality problems are limited in practice.[10] However, market solutions based on the suggested institutional changes seem to me to deserve serious consideration and empirical analysis, if only because market solutions promise less institutional rigidity and inefficiency than, say, a system of nationwide emissions standards.

Conclusion

This article has attempted to examine market solutions to externality in theory and practice. It has not attempted to rigorously compare (a) market solutions with (b) systems of per unit fines, charges, taxes, or subsidies, and (c) standards enforced by the threat of penalty. It is clear, nevertheless, that transactions costs are a crucial variable in the selection of suitable institutional mechanisms for the modification of externality. Unless ways can be found to reduce the transactions costs associated with market solutions, such solutions—even if under an L^f rule—will remain the plaything of academic economists, largely ignored by policy makers and the voting public.

Standards, inevitably inefficient but not necessarily very inefficient, are simple decision rules at least partially enforceable at low cost. Market

9. The allocative effects of a change to L^f have not received detailed consideration in this paper. In industrial pollution situations, a change to L^f would result in lower production of higher-priced commodities and lower industrial employment in a first-step adjustment. After the first stage of adjustment, a longer-term adjustment could result in lower wages. Unless the practice were forbidden, some less sensitive people would move into the affected area to gain compensation; this could also drive wages down. A reduction in wages would lead to some lowering of costs of production. The final situation would lie somewhere between the initial situation and the first-stage adjustment.

10. Crocker's (6) paper suggests one workable method of market solution in some externality situations: a full liability rule (or something similar) and the purchase of affected property by the acting party. But such a procedure is limited to external diseconomies from a few point sources and affecting a fairly small number of individuals in a well-defined geographic area. This "merger" solution is more likely to take place under a full liability rule.

solutions will be preferable to standards, for example, only if the gains in efficiency (*ceteris paribus* transactions costs) exceed the additional transactions costs of using the market solution method. The onus to develop ways in which market solutions can be made to work lies squarely on the shoulders of academic supporters of market solutions. An essential step is to generate institutional forms which minimize transactions costs.

References

1. Alexander, R. M. "Social Aspects of Environmental Pollution." *Agricultural Science Review* 9 (1971):9–18.
2. Buchanan, J. M., and Stubblebine, W. C. "Externality." *Economica* 29 (1962):371–84.
3. Buchanan, J. M., and Tullock, G. *The Calculus of Consent.* Ann Arbor: University of Michigan Press, 1962.
4. Calabresi, G. "Transactions Costs, Resource Allocation and Liability Rules." *Journal of Law and Economics* 11 (1968):66–73.
5. Coase, R. H. "The Problem of Social Cost." *Journal of Law and Economics* 3 (1960): 1–44.
6. Crocker, T. D. "Externalities, Property Rights and Transactions Costs: An Empirical Study." *Journal of Law and Economics* 14 (1971):451–64.
7. Davis, O. A., and Whinston, A. B. "Some Notes on Equating Private and Social Cost." *Southern Economic Journal* 32 (1965):113–25.
8. Demsetz, H. "The Exchange and Enforcement of Property Rights." *Journal of Law and Economics* 7 (1964):11–26.
9. Dolbear, F. T. "On the Theory of Optimum Externality." *American Economic Review* 57 (1967):90–103.
10. Kneese, A. V. "Environmental Pollution: Economics and Policy." *American Economic Review* 61 (1971):153–68.
11. Mishan, E. J. "The Post-War Literature on Externalities: An Interpretive Essay." *Journal of Economic Literature* 9 (1971):1–28.
12. Olson, M. *The Logic of Collective Action.* Cambridge, Mass.: Harvard University Press, 1965.
13. Randall, A. "Liability Rules, Transactions Costs and Optimum Externality." Ph.D. dissertation, Oregon State University, Corvallis, 1971.
14. Randall, A. "On the Theory of Market Solutions to Externality Problems." Special Report No. 351, Oregon Agricultural Experiment Station, Corvallis, 1972.

3
Political Equilibrium vs. Economic Efficiency in Effluent Pricing

Charles J. Goetz

The "invisible hand" of decentralized individual maximization behavior has errant fingers when it operates in the area of environmental quality control. This proposition is familiar and almost universally accepted among economists. Indeed, professional economists have played a prominent role in defining objective criteria of optimal environmental quality, establishing the manner in which such criteria tend to be violated by individual behavior, and suggesting forms of regulatory control designed to promote the achievement of appropriate levels of environmental quality. As might be expected, economists define the necessary conditions for efficient levels of environmental quality with reference to the normatively "weak" criterion of Pareto optimality. Also to be expected is the general nature of the economist's remedial prescription, that of corrective pricing imposed under governmental authority.

In sum, economists have identified the market-generated environmental state as not being Pareto optimal and have suggested that there is some politically achievable equilibrium state consistent with a pricing scheme which does satisfy the conditions of Pareto efficiency. McKean (6) has, however, explicitly called our attention to the existence of a political "invisible hand" which, like its counterpart in the market, is also based upon the maximizing behavior of individuals.[1] Does, then, the "anatomy of market failure" have an analogous "anatomy of political failure" when allocative decisions about the environment are made in a voting model? This paper uses simple economic-type models of individual political behavior to describe the nature of equilibrium political decisions about environmental pricing systems. The resultant analysis suggests certain extremely simple but generally overlooked difficulties of securing allocatively efficient environmental decisions via government intervention.

The discussion developed below employs the word "pollution" as a general proxy term for activities which adversely affect the environment. Broadly understood, therefore, it encompasses noise, congestion, and other phenomena not generally referred to as pollution. A basic notion is that pollution is actually of positive value for some individual decision makers, otherwise it would not exist at all. Moreover, if a pollution *regulation* problem exists, this implies that pollution is also a *net* social good over some range. Otherwise, it should simply be prohibited entirely. In this paper, consideration is restricted to regulation by corrective pricing. Specifically, it is assumed that a political unit is empowered to impose effluent charges and dispose of the resultant revenue according to majority decision. We abstract from the distributional problem of choosing among alternative Pareto-efficient points, thus focusing on only the necessary conditions for Pareto optimality in the context of whatever income distribution preexists.[2]

The concept of a Pareto-optimal pollution level, and its implied environmental control policy, can be derived from Figure 1. Let the curve labeled D be a curve of marginal pollution values. Most commonly, this curve is based on the marginal value product of the pollutant as an input in one or more production processes. The curve D is a *horizontal* summation of individual marginal valuation curves, thus indicating that, in its aspects as an economic *good*, pollution is purely private, possessing no "jointness" in use.[3] Also, D can be understood as a market demand

1. Of course, the classic path-breaking conceptualization of the political process as a market analogue is Downs (4).

2. The methodological inconsistency between Paretian efficiency criteria and a social welfare function has been noted by Buchanan (3). In even simpler terms, however, if one is willing to define a social welfare function over the choice space, the individualistic utility functions from which the Pareto conditions are derived, analytically speaking, appear to be mere excess baggage or, at most, limitations on the functional form of the social welfare function.

3. The graphic examples given in this paper implicitly assume that the inframarginal or "income feedback" effects of any pollution pricing scheme are negligible. This greatly simplifies the exposition without affecting the basic conclusions to any significant extent.

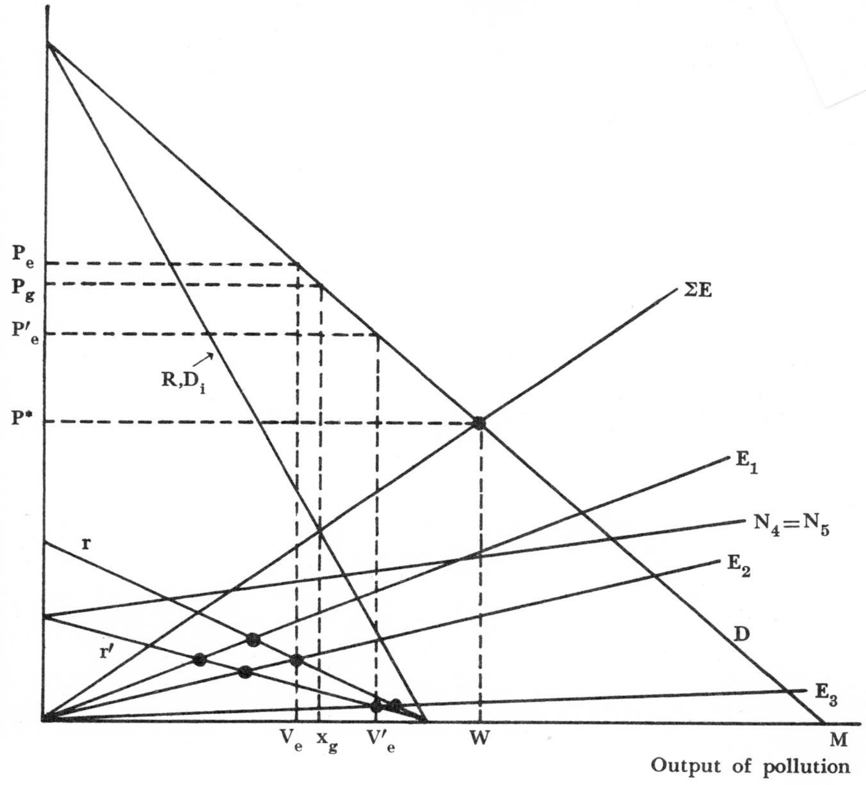

FIGURE 1

curve for pollution as an input. The marginal social cost of pollution is represented by ΣE, another aggregation from individual marginal evaluation curves. However, in arriving at ΣE, the (negative) marginal values of pollution are summed *vertically* over individuals because environmental quality is normally a Samuelson-type public good, i.e., one with perfect jointness in consumption. Thus ΣE is the vertical sum of E_1, E_2, E_3, the marginal evaluations by the three representative individuals of declines in environmental quality.[4] Alternatively, ΣE may be read from right to left as analogous to a market demand curve for environmental quality.

4. The convenient concept of "marginal evaluation" as the marginal rate of substitution between a particular good and a *numeraire*, money, was popularized by Hicks (5). Note that only the assumption in footnote 3 makes the diagrammatic depiction of

If, as is currently common practice, the use of pollution as an input is unpriced, the equilibrium market solution is at M where the private marginal product of pollution as an input reaches zero. The Pareto-optimal solution occurs at W, where the marginal cost of pollution equals its marginal value.[5] An economist would therefore prescribe that the price of p* be set by a government agency in order to maintain the Pareto-efficient environmental quality. But is p* the price that will emerge in a political equilibrium?

Equilibrium Political Choices of Environmental Regulation

A simple political equilibrium analysis may now be based on Figure 1. Assume that the input demands for pollution underlying D are by firms, while the consumption demands for environmental quality underlying ΣE are by three individuals. These individuals—1, 2, and 3—constitute the electorate unit which "owns" an aspect of environmental quality, whether it be a water source, air mass, etc.[6] We will first assume that the pollution price is set by direct referendum, then extend the case to representative government.

It is apparent that the potential "benefits" to voters in our model political unit come from effluent charges collected. The standard expectation is that the effluent charges are uniform over quantity and over economic units; i.e., there is no price discrimination engaged in by the political rate.[7] Therefore, D in Figure 1 is the curve of average revenue for the political unit. The marginal tax revenue curve is R. Maximization of benefits to the political unit calls for price p_g and environmental quality x_g, this solution being determined by the intersection of R, rather than D, with the marginal cost curve ΣE. Thus, completely efficient benefit maximization by the political unit would always result in what is from the economic efficiency standpoint an excessively high level of environmental quality.

Maximization of group benefits is not, however, a relevant considera-

such price-dependent "schedules" strictly correct. However, a mathematical formulation is not limited by this restriction, and the results remain fundamentally unchanged albeit somewhat more complex.

5. The marginal conditions here bear notable relationship to those derived by "public goods" by Samuelson (7). Pollution is, of course, a "public bad."

6. The simplest possible majority-rule political model is being used here, but the same general considerations can be applied to a voting model with any size of the electorate.

7. A price-discrimination model would, of course, alter the results presented below in certain aspects. However, the argument is easily adapted to this context, and the essential problems described in the text remain basically the same.

tion in determining the actual political equilibrium price. Like the market, a democratic political process is based on individualistic decisions. The individual voter will, after all, consider his own *personal* costs and returns.[8] An assumption is necessary, then, as to the disposition of the revenues from effluent charges. There are an infinite number of possible distribution schemes, constrained only by the requirement that the sum of the marginal compensation payments must exactly exhaust the marginal revenues from the effluent tax collections. One possible assumption is that revenues are returned on a pro rata basis to each voter. In this case, the marginal revenue curve to any individual is R/n where n is the number of voters involved. For the three-man case in Figure 1 the relevant individual marginal returns function is r. The three voters have their respective optima where r cuts E_1, E_2, and E_3. The preferences of the voters over the various environmental states will normally be single-peaked, and the median preference theorem of Duncan Black can thus be applied to predict the political equilibrium as occurring at E_2's optimum, an environmental state V_e and a price p_e.[9] This solution is stable since it will command a majority (two votes) over any other alternative.

The outcome at V_e is inefficient in economic terms because pollution is still a *net* good in that range. The marginal value product of pollution is an opportunity cost to society which the voters, quite rationally in individual terms, do not "properly" impute into their decisions.

It may be argued that this occurs principally because the demanders of pollution have been assumed to be firms and therefore nonvoters; a set of affected units is not being allowed to have an input into the political process. Assume, then, that the pollution in question is consumer-connected, such as noise or automobile exhaust. The curve D may then be thought of as the horizontal sum of identical demands by two additional voters, each of whom places some value on the pollutant and, for simplicity, is unaffected by it personally. This, of course, does not change the Pareto-optimal allocation W, but the political equilibrium will be altered. The individual marginal effluent charge returns function for five voters becomes R/5, shown in Figure 1 as a shift from r to r′. For the new voters, 4 and 5, the all-inclusive marginal returns function is the vertical sum of D/2 and r′ minus R/2, the latter being their own marginal tax *pay-*

8. This does not mean that we exclude altruism completely in arriving at the individual cost functions underlying ΣE. If it is worth something to me to prevent others from suffering the effects of pollution, this sum may quite properly be included in the construction of E.

9. The highest "peak" is obviously at the individual's global optimum where his net benefits are maximized. Under reasonable assumptions about the shapes of the E and r functions, there should be no additional local optima in the net benefits function which is, accordingly, "single-peaked." On the median voter theorem, see Black (2).

ments.[10] The net returns function for voters 4 and 5 has been mapped onto Figure 1 as curve N. Since N is positive until it becomes discontinuous where market demand becomes zero, these voters have their optima at M. For the original voters—1, 2, 3—their optima now lie at the lower pollution levels where r′ cuts E_1, E_2, and E_3. The median preference becomes voter 3's optimum at V'_e.

In the illustrative Figure 1 case, the new political solution does move closer to the efficient allocation at W. However, it is perfectly possible to derive the opposite, seemingly paradoxical, solution. Thus, Figure 2 is identical to Figure 1 except that the cost curves of individuals 1, 2, and 3 are identical. Under these circumstances, the original (unanimously chosen) political equilibrium is V_e and the new equilibrium V'_e actually departs further from W, lying to the left of V_e. If D is made the horizontal summation of demands by four or more voters, the outcome actually shifts back to the "market" solution of unpriced pollution. In this position, a majority of the voters simply exploits the minority on whom the pollution costs are imposed.

The particular equilibria derived above are obviously products of how the relevant functions have been drawn and no special case is made for their empirical content. On the other hand, the specific examples do illustrate general types of decision-making inefficiency which arises when effluent pricing is determined in a simple political model which, although abstract, does reflect important aspects of the real world.

Although the results presented thus far have been developed in terms of a simple "direct democracy" model wherein the appropriate pollution price is decided by referendum, no important modifications are entailed in extending the analysis to representative government, provided a winning candidate is required to achieve a majority vote. Under the customary American two-party competition, alternative policies are, in effect, always decided dually. In these circumstances, plurality rule implicitly becomes majority rule and the median-preference models indicate the "platform" toward which competition will force the opposing candidates. The competitive conditions for systems of more than two parties have been discussed by Downs (4). Such models require highly particular assumptions about the distribution of preferences among individuals. Consequently, the present discussion is limited to the more tractable two-

10. It may be worthwhile to clarify why D and R are divided by two. Social output of pollution X is on the abcissa of the figures whereas the individual's position is affected only by his own consumption x_i. The marginal values of D and R, which are evaluated with respect to x_i, must therefore be multiplied by $\partial x_i/\partial X(\frac{1}{2})$ for individuals 4 and 5.

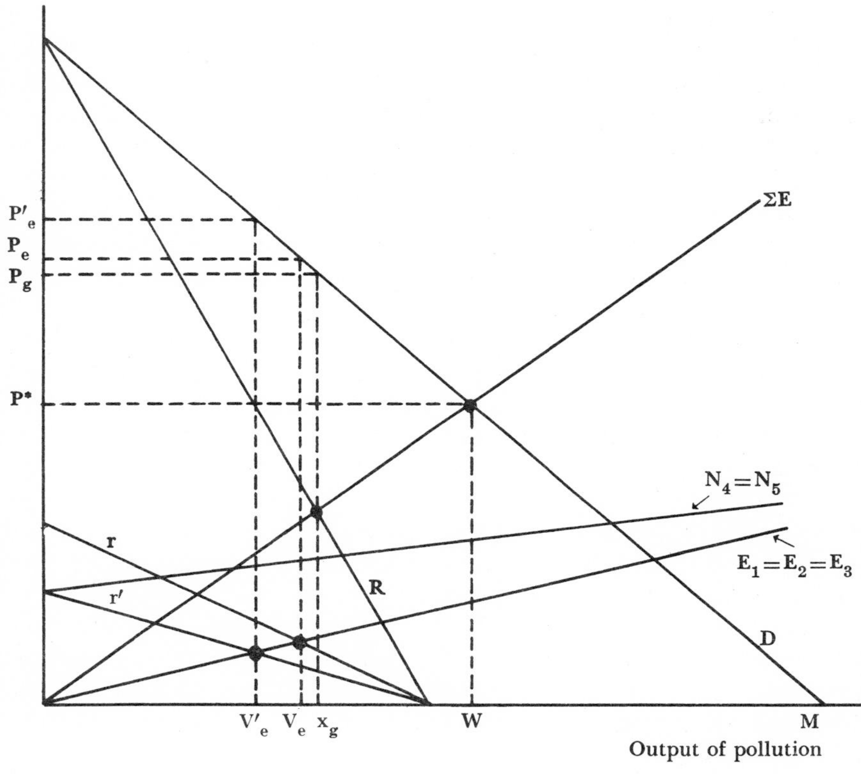

FIGURE 2

party case which, fortunately, seems to be more descriptive of U.S. experience.

IMPLICATIONS OF EQUILIBRIUM CONDITIONS

The above analysis has, for expository purposes, been couched in terms of specific examples whose verisimilitude is certainly open to question. However, a more generalized conclusion may now be suggested. For consistency of political equilibrium with the Pareto-optimal result, it is necessary that, for the pivotal median voter, the marginal personal benefits from the effluent charge revenues must precisely equal the marginal personal damages imposed by the environmental pollutant. This would be the case if the implicit "compensation payments" made out of effluent charge revenues were distributed to members of a majority voting bloc in strict equality with the marginal evaluation that each voter places on changes in environmental quality.[11] In general, there is no reason to expect that the political process will produce such a system of payments. In some cases, in fact, we can prove that the optimal result is actually impossible.

At first glance, it may seem that effective pressures toward an allocatively "efficient" distribution of the charge revenues will exist. If the result is not Pareto optimal, there are, after all, mutual gains from trade which are achievable by making adjustments in the solution. However, consider the original three-man model of Figure 1. Even in a world of zero political bargaining costs among the three voters, the tendency would be toward the "monopolistic" group maximum at x_g rather than toward the Pareto optimum at W. In fact, the original Figure 1 case is one wherein satisfaction of the individual marginal conditions for a political equilibrium is impossible to envision, since the marginal revenue curve R becomes negative at a lower level of pollution (higher level of environmental quality) than the Pareto-efficient allocation W. Under these circumstances, there exists *no* distribution of marginal effluent charges among the voters which will induce a majority equilibrium at the economically "correct" solution.

The five-voter version of the Figure 1 situation appears more hopeful in the zero bargaining-cost context. If, as is the case in the example given, *all* affected economic units are in the set of political decision makers, then it is clear that the group maximum also qualifies as a Pareto optimum for society. Closer inspection nevertheless reveals some problems even in this extreme case of highly favorable, albeit highly unrealistic, assumptions. Although it is quite true that the Pareto-efficient outcome W might be reached, it cannot be reached exclusively through governmentally imposed pricing schemes of the type that most economists have envisioned. The insufficiency of any such charge scheme will arise when, as in Figure 1, marginal effluent charge revenues reach zero at a lower pollution output than the Pareto-optimal one. These charges, after all, constitute the total side-payments fund available to the community via the political process. If these are the *only* side-payments made, the Pareto optimum cannot be reached because marginal side-payments become zero and no incentives exist for further moves. For instance, achievement of the solution W in the Figure 1 example would require that the demanders of pollution underlying curve D offer compensatory payments above and beyond the effluent charges imposed by law.

11. This problem is analogous to the one faced in determining marginal tax prices to individuals in a democratic model of public goods provision. An extensive discussion may be found in Buchanan (3).

In dealing with the zero bargaining-cost cases at all, we are of course really only indulging in a pedagogical exercise. If the world were really a zero-cost bargaining game, then the economically efficient "contract curve," or Pareto frontier, would always be reached by voluntary action. The existence of politically imposed environmental regulation would have no economic rationale in such a context.

In actual fact, the political process necessarily produces decisions on environmental regulation under substantial ignorance about components of the cost and benefit relations represented in Figure 1. The pollution demand curve D is, for all practical purposes, a "normal" market demand curve if our assumption about the "privateness" of pollution benefits is thought to be plausible. The shapes of both D and R are, therefore, observable with reasonable accuracy from standard market-type experiments. However, the individual cost-curves or demands for environmental quality are quite another matter. The joint-consumption and nonexcludability aspects of environmental quality introduce all the preference-falsification problems traditionally associated with the public goods problem. The fact that the bargaining now takes place through the political mechanism does not mitigate the motivation of individuals to falsify their degree of concern with environmental quality. For instance, it is rational for individual voters to overstate their marginal pollution costs if this may be expected to influence the distribution of compensation payments made out of effluent charge revenues.

We have very little empirical evidence on which to base any speculation about the distribution of individual returns out of effluent charge revenues. The equal-shares assumption used above was a simple expository device and does not seem at all likely as a real-world political outcome. In fact, one would not even necessarily expect the question of distributing effluent charge revenues to be raised in explicit form. It is more probable that these revenues simply enter the general fund and are used to supplement and/or supplant tax revenues from more orthodox sources. Viewed in this light, effluent charge collections may, *ceteris paribus*, be viewed as equivalent to reductions in the rate charged on the marginal tax medium. "Marginal tax medium" here means the tax form through which a political unit would normally make its revenue adjustments.

For local governments, therefore, effluent charge collections might plausibly be regarded as equivalent to reductions in the property tax rate. For state and federal governments, the collections might be interpreted as reductions in sales taxes or income taxes. Almost any reasonable conjecture would, however, tend to indicate that marginal individual payments out of effluent charge revenues will be directly related to income.

From the efficiency standpoint, the desirability of this correlation with income depends on whether or not the costs of pollution are also correlated with income. At least a weak general argument may be made in favor of a relation between individual income and the costs suffered from pollution. If environmental quality is a "normal" good, then its positive income elasticity implies that rich people put a higher value on environmental quality than poor people, *ceteris paribus.* We are, of course, using the standard of *money* cost; as measured in noneconomic terms of injury to health, discomfort, etc., the impact on rich and poor may be identical. Acceptance of this translation of "human costs" into monetary costs is nonetheless implied if one wishes to employ the Pareto-optimality efficiency benchmark so commonly applied by economists. On the other hand, the *ceteris*—to fracture some Latin—may not be so *paribus*; i.e., because of their general circumstances of life, prominently including residential factors, the poor may systematically be exposed to far more pollution than the rich. In the latter case, notwithstanding the income effects on individuals' evaluations of environmental quality, the structure of individual returns from effluent pricing may be just the reverse of what is called for in efficiency terms.

In sum, the choice of economically efficient environmental controls through the political process calls for a majority of voters to be confronted by the "right" payoff functions. Yet, there are no very convincing reasons to believe that political competition and bargaining will produce an individual payoff structure which leads to any reasonable approximation of Pareto-optimal allocation.

Internalization vs. Monopolistic Incentive

Ample reference has already been made above to the incentives for a political unit composed of rational voters to make monopolistic-type calculations in determining what is essentially equivalent in economic terms to its pricing policy in the marketing of pollution rights. In this, as in more familiar market analysis, the scope of monopolistic distortion is limited by the elasticity of demand for the thing being sold. The demand for the right to pollute in any particular unit is obviously a function of the available substitutes, among which is prominently numbered the opportunity to pollute in some *other* political unit. A unit is limited by the extent of what are essentially the locational advantages that demanders perceive in polluting within its borders rather than somewhere else. This suggests that monopolistic behavior can play no very important part in the determination of environmental pricing by very small political units.

At this point, it may be recognized that the economic arguments for "internalization" of pollution effects by spatially extensive units present certain problems. On the one hand, the problem of spill-over effects cannot be regulated unless the site where the pollution is emitted is brought within the regulatory jurisdiction of the unit that suffers the pollution's effects. This factor clearly dictates very large geographic extensions of political borders. On the other hand, such extension will almost inevitably result in a highly inelastic demand curve for pollution rights. Thus, we have a final example of how the economic efficiency *potential* of an institutional arrangement should not be endowed too cavalierly with correspondence to a plausible political equilibrium state.

Conclusion

The formal analysis presented above has necessarily been sketchy and is certainly subject to qualification on numerous points. Nevertheless, the specific conclusions may be rejected without invalidating the basic message. Economists have performed a great deal of commendable work in deducing the frequently inefficient or antisocial results of individual maximizing behavior in market models. In suggesting corrective measures to be imposed by the state, the same economists have then been curiously remiss not only in attempting to deduce but even in recognizing the possible effect of individual maximizing behavior in the political process. This analysis of political allocation is, moreover, relatively susceptible to adaptations of economic-type models.[12]

If our policy prescriptions are to have maximum relevance, then the anatomy of potential political failure is the logical concomitant of the anatomy of market failure. The world is, after all, mainly a choice of the least among all possible evils.

References

1. Black, Duncan. "The Unity of Political and Economic Science." *Economic Journal* 60 (September 1950):506–14.
2. Black, Duncan. *The Theory of Committees and Elections*, pp. 14–24. Cambridge, England: Cambridge University Press, 1958.
3. Buchanan, James. *The Demand and Supply of Public Goods*, pp. 194–96. Chicago: Rand McNally, 1968.
4. Downs, Anthony. *An Economic Theory of Democracy*. New York: Harper and Row, 1957.

12. An excellent essay on this point is provided by Black (1).

5. Hicks, J. R. "The Four Consumer Surpluses." *Review of Economic Studies* 2 (November 1943):31–42.
6. McKean, Roland. "The Unseen Hand in Government." *American Economic Review* 55 (June 1965):496–506.
7. Samuelson, Paul. "The Pure Theory of Public Expenditure." *Review of Economics and Statistics* 36 (November 1954):387–89.

4
Improving Air Quality—Some Strategy Alternatives

Paul H. Gerhardt

The pollution control programs of federal, state, and local governments rely almost exclusively on standards, direct regulations, and enforcement by court actions with fines and other penalties. Proponents of standards and regulation claim that the process has been at least moderately successful and that further refinements will make it even more capable of dealing with the pollution problem.

To be successful, any approach to pollution control requires scientific, technical, economic, political, and financial support. Scientific and technical support is needed to understand the mechanics of pollution production and the effects of pollution on health and welfare, and to reveal its potential danger and the needs and various mechanisms for control. Economic analysis is necessary to evaluate prospective costs and benefits of alternatives and to point the way to those approaches that promise the most in terms of economic efficiency. Political support is necessary to develop and enact legislative programs. Financial support comes first from the general taxpayer for the support of government programs and ultimately from the customers, suppliers, and equity holders of polluting activities to pay for private programs.

Action to control air pollution must ultimately be taken at the source of its production. Because there is little or no financial or economic incentive toward the expansion of control programs by individual polluters, some system of inducements is needed to stimulate control. This paper attempts to outline the potential role of economic incentives as one element in a system of inducements for the control of air pollution.[1] It deals primarily with market-type incentives as distinct from fines, threats of shutdowns, jail sentences, subsidies, and other conventional accouterments of standards enforcement. It shows why subsidies may constitute no incentive at all and begins by recognizing that as a practical matter economic incentives as such must be viewed as supplemental to regulation rather than as alternatives to regulation.

Potential Damage Costs

The American economy produces roughly a trillion dollars worth of goods and services a year. In terms of air pollution alone, it may also be producing over 300 million tons of pollutants and from $15 to 20 billion worth of economic losses. It may be worth noting that conventional measures of the value of our economic output seldom include the value of improving environmental quality.[2]

The principal U.S. air pollutants are carbon monoxide (CO), hydrocarbons (HC), nitrogen oxides (NO_x), particulate matter, and sulfur oxides (SO_x). National emissions of these pollutants totaled about 214 million tons in 1968. Forty-two percent of the principal air pollutants came from transportation sources, including automobiles, trucks, buses, trains, and aircraft; 21 percent came from fuel combustion in stationary sources such as public utility and industrial power plants, commercial and residential. The remainder was from industrial processes, solid waste disposal, and miscellaneous sources, such as open burning and forest fires (see Table 1). To a large extent, the production of pollution is a function of the fuels we burn and the production of our goods and services.

About thirty-six studies dealing in one way or another with the economic effects of air pollution have been undertaken. Of these, about one-third have been published, another third have been completed but have not been published, and a third are still in progress.[3] The studies share a common goal—to develop a better understanding of the effects of air pollutants on human, plant, and animal health, physical materials, property values, soiling, and aesthetics. An attempt is being made to in-

1. For an earlier summary by the same author, see Gerhardt (8).

2. Since GNP measures the final output of goods and services at market prices, it includes the value of products and services devoted to cleanup and control of pollution. Public and private costs are included, but many of the social costs are not. A system of social account would allow such costs to be considered.

3. See, for example, Crocker (4) and Lave and Seskin (12).

TABLE 1
ESTIMATES OF NATIONWIDE EMISSIONS, 1968
(10^6 TONS/YEAR)

Source	CO	Particulates	SO_x	HC	NO_x
Transportation	63.8	1.2	0.8	16.6	8.1
Fuel combustion in stationary sources	1.9	8.9	24.4	0.7	10.0
Industrial processes	9.7	7.5	7.3	4.6	0.2
Solid waste disposal	7.8	1.1	0.1	1.6	0.6
Miscellaneous	16.9	9.6	0.6	8.5	1.7
Total	100.1	28.3	33.2	32.0	20.6

SOURCE: Division of Air Quality and Emissions Data, Office of Air Programs.

tegrate the various study efforts and to develop an estimate of the economic costs of the damages.

The most important category of damages from an economic point of view may well turn out to be in the area of human health. Air pollution has been linked with both respiratory and cardiovascular diseases and with excess mortality and morbidity. The potential economic dimensions are fairly obvious in nature—early death and reduced productivity—but obscure in terms of fact and "scientific" proof. This is a most difficult area to investigate because of conceptual and data problems. Nevertheless, some beginning statistical analyses have been undertaken with indications that the economic cost of mortality and morbidity due to air pollution's damage to health is probably in the neighborhood of $6 billion annually. The results of studies of health deterioration and other effects will help us to understand the longer-term environmental and ecological significance of air pollution. Obviously, any effort to gauge the magnitude of damage has to be based on a combination of documented studies of air pollution effects and considerable judgment. One attempt to distribute estimated damage costs among the major source categories is summarized in Tables 2 and 3 and presented here for illustrative purposes.

TABLE 2
ESTIMATED NATIONAL TOTAL ANNUAL COST OF POLLUTION FOR TYPES OF POLLUTANTS AND EFFECTS IN 1968
(BILLIONS OF DOLLARS)

Effects	SO_x	Particulates	Oxidant	NO_x	Total
Residential property	2.8	2.4	—	—	5.2
Materials	2.2	.7	1.1	.7	4.8
Health	3.3	2.8	—	—	6.1
Total	8.3	5.9	1.1	.7	16.1

SOURCE: Barrett and Waddell (2).

TABLE 3
NATIONAL TOTAL ANNUAL COSTS OF POLLUTION FOR TYPES OF SOURCES AND EFFECTS IN 1968
(BILLIONS OF DOLLARS)

Effects	Stationary Source Fuel Combustion	Transportation	Industrial Processes	Solid Waste and Misc.	Total
Residential property	2.8	.2	1.3	.9	5.2
Materials	1.9	1.1	.8	1.0	4.8
Health	3.3	.2	1.5	1.1	6.1
Total	8.0	1.5	3.6	3.0	16.1

SOURCE: Barrett and Waddell (2).

Gross economic damage must, obviously, be considered as a function of exposure. Presumably, damages will be reduced as exposures to pollution levels are reduced. However, because of data limitations, no proven functional relationships between pollution levels and damages have yet been established.

Obviously, the whole subject of the economic costs of pollution damage will benefit considerably from further research. As control programs and public and private expenditures grow, questions of potential benefits will come under closer and closer scrutiny.

COSTS OF CONTROL

The Federal Office of Air Programs has estimated that a billion or more dollars will be spent on air pollution control programs between 1971 and 1975 by federal, state, and local governments. Further, the full additional annualized capital and operating costs to industry of controlling particulate and sulfur oxide air pollution from fuel combustion and industrial processes in major manufacturing activities and power generation is estimated at about $2 billion.[4] The annualized cost of motor vehicle emission control could add another $2 billion a year. Thus, the additional public and private cost of air pollution control on an annualized basis could be in the $4–5 billion range by 1975 (6). These costs will be additional to whatever costs are currently being incurred.

Table 4 shows projected costs of control in stationary sources for 298 metropolitan areas containing most of the nation's population and economic activity. Investment and annual costs are indicated on the assump-

4. The concept of full additional costs is analogous for marginal costs, generally used in a static context. Full additional cost is essentially forward looking; it includes capital (fixed) and operating (variable) cost; it can be annualized to research flow of resources; and it can be discounted.

TABLE 4
ESTIMATED 1976 EMISSION LEVELS AND ASSOCIATED CONTROL COSTS FOR STATIONARY SOURCES IN 298 METROPOLITAN AREAS[a]

Source	Quantity of Emissions[b] (Thousands of Tons per Year)						Annualized Investment and Operating Costs[c] (Millions of Dollars)
	Part	SO_x	CO	F	Pb	HC	
Solid waste disposal							
Without[d]	1,500	—	5,450	—	—	2,020	
With[e]	185	—	414	—	—	293	113
Stationary fuel combustion							
Without[d]	3,867	14,447	—	—	—	—	
With[e]	930	4,697	—	—	—	—	1,006
Industrial processes							
Without[d]	6,053	6,229	10,040	73	30	1,736	
With[e]	453	1,720	539	9	10	849	1,095
Total							
Without[d]	11,420	20,676	15,490	73	30	3,756	
With[e]	1,568	6,417	953	9	10	1,142	2,214

SOURCE: "The Economics of Clean Air" (6).
a. Metropolitan areas are defined as APCO Air Quality Control Regions and are similar to Standard Metropolitan Statistical Areas.
b. Emission abbreviations are: particulates (Part), sulfur oxides (SO_x), carbon monoxide (CO), hydrocarbons (HC), fluorides (F), and lead (Pb). Blanks in the table indicate that emission levels meet applicable regulations or that emissions are negligible or do not exist.
c. Includes depreciation, operating, maintenance, and repair costs reflecting the full additional costs of owning and operating the air pollution control technology needed by 1976.
d. Estimates without implementation of the Clean Air Act.
e. Estimates with implementation of the Clean Air Act.

tion that implementation plans as called for by the legislation will materialize. Compared to the current level of annual costs of, perhaps, $0.5 billion, a projected $5.0 billion would represent a tenfold increase. It would therefore amount to about one-half of 1 percent of the present gross national product.

Air pollution control efforts and expenditures generally tend to be viewed as unproductive from the standpoint of the individual firms; therefore, a firm's financial management is not likely to respond easily to society's blandishments for cleaner air. Consequently, it would appear that society, to the extent that it wants cleaner air—and is willing to pay for it—has three basic choices with respect to the implementation of standards. One is to continue to enact new legislation and to strengthen legal enforcement procedures. A second is for government to find some way to make the private control effort show a profit by substituting some system of economic incentives. A third choice is to seek to combine the best features of both regulation and market-type incentives.

Regulation

Direct regulation of standards with enforcement fines and other penalties has generally been seen as the best way to abate and control pollution. To some extent, land-use controls and nuisance laws have been used by municipalities. The Clean Air Act, as amended, is designed to help states and designated Air Quality Control Regions develop and implement plans for the attainment of air quality standards. In the field of motor vehicle pollution control, the federal government, in accordance with provisions of the 1965 amendments to the Clean Air Act, is empowered by Congress to set emission standards for new motor vehicles. An emission control approach based on uniform national standards is based on the mobility of motor vehicles, which can and do move freely across artificial jurisdictional boundaries. Furthermore, since the majority of automobiles share a common engine and exhaust technology, they are amenable to sharing a common air pollution control technology and emission standard.

With the 1970 amendments to the Clean Air Act, the federal government—i.e., the Congress and the administration—is also adopting new and more stringent requirements. The automobile industry will be required to produce a virtually pollution-free vehicle by 1976. Naturally, this goal is meeting some opposition, and a bargaining period has been entered in which the government emphasizes pollution reduction in the interest of human health and welfare and in which industry claims technical and economic difficulties.[5]

National performance standards for emission control of stationary sources are being developed under the Clean Air Amendments of 1970.[6] These standards require the use of "best available methods" as defined by the act.[7] Emission standards of this sort are easier to apply and to enforce than air quality standards, because they define precisely the level of control an individual polluter must achieve. However, if and when capabilities improve to measure and track damages from receptor points back

5. See Davies (5) for an excellent discussion of recent regulatory developments.

6. It has been estimated that uniform application of control requirements could more than double the cost of control without adding substantially to the level of air quality. This is a complex matter which deserves more attention than can be given here.

7. ". . . the best system of emission reduction which (taking into account the cost of achieving such reduction) the Administrator determines has been adequately demonstrated" (Clean Air Act, Section III [a] [1], December 1970).

over the topography and through the atmosphere to specific emitters, specific emission control regulations tied directly to air quality requirements will become defensible.

Certainly, such a positive and well-defined ability to track from receptor point damages back to specific emitters would be desirable. It would help solve problems that arise in connection with efforts by regulatory agencies to discriminate between different emitters in terms of their effects on air quality; it would allow an escape from the economically inefficient uniform (and inflexible) control approach. The need for flexibility is recognized in the new federal air pollution control legislation, which designates Air Quality Control Regions on a priority basis in relation to their air quality and to improvement needs. If emission production, transport, effects, and demands were substantially expanded, considerations of economic efficiency would result in a variety of control requirements adopted in direct relation to each individual polluter's contribution to receptor point damages. Again, precise implementation of this approach would obviously require a capability not only to identify specific emission sources, but also to measure both quantitatively and qualitatively the nature of the pollutants and the damages they produce.

In the case of air pollution, emission measurements today are mainly the result of direct stack gas sampling in which a team of technicians physically probes a stack to extract a sample of the exit gas for analysis. In some cases, this process has presented legal difficulties, and in all cases, certain physical problems of access and construction have to be overcome. To be most effective, measurements should be continuous (or at least acceptably periodic) to assure a representative sampling over a variety of operating and meteorological conditions.

In the absence of such a complete measurement capability, most regulations have had to rely on simpler approaches involving direct visual observations by pollution control inspectors and citizens using photographic and special air samplers to supplement visual evidence. The accumulation of such evidence is generally used in the construction of *prima facie* cases against suspected polluters. The courts have shown a willingness to accept *prima facie* evidence to support fines and other penalties for offenders.

At the state level, one interesting approach to air pollution control by direct regulation has been developed in New Jersey. There, a stationary source polluter may be fined up to $2,500 per day for each day he is found to be in violation of the state emission regulation. To achieve compliance, the offender must first obtain from the state a construction permit for control equipment changes which will reduce emissions, giving evidence that his corrective actions are acceptable to state air pollution control engineering standards. Then, before resuming operations, the offender must obtain an operating permit which in effect tells the public that the offender has actually taken the corrective actions on which the construction permit was based. Further, if the corrective action has been completed within a reasonable amount of time, the offender may be forgiven up to 90 percent of his total fines. The offender must bear the initial cost of the corrective action and then proceed in normal market fashion to recover his cost as best he can, presumably through adjustments in his production costs and product prices.

Direct regulations are being applied to the control of sulfur dioxide pollution caused by combustion of fossil fuels, especially bituminous coal and residue oil. Many states now have fuel sulfur content standards and regulations to control the amount of sulfur in fuels burned within their boundaries. This approach may work well for one or two states, but as more and more try to adopt such regulations, implementation of the approach will become increasingly expensive because of the limited supplies of natural low-sulfur fuels. A possible direct advantage of a sulfur content limit is that it tends to force a substitution of lower-sulfur for higher-sulfur fuels of the same type. Later, a fuel user may switch from coal to oil or to natural gas to accommodate to the requirement. Fuel suppliers are induced to extra efforts to reduce the sulfur content of the fuel they sell. Some of the higher fuel costs required in the interest of sulfur reduction are passed along to customers as cost-of-service adjustments. As low-sulfur fuels become harder to find, the sulfur-content-limiting requirement will be abandoned in favor of alternative approaches which will place the focus where it belongs—on reducing stack emissions by any means possible, rather than concentrating on only one means of emission reduction.

To the extent that restrictions on sulfur content may work counter to the development of emission control systems,[8] this particular regulatory approach may be damaging to the long-range control effort. A simple adjustment would relate the regulation to the equivalent sulfur content of the fuel[9] and allow each plant to adopt whatever control measure or combination of measures it found to be most cost-effective for its own situation.

A principal feature of the standards-setting and regulatory approach to air pollution control is that it requires a highly complex process of

8. Restrictions on sulfur content in fuel require the use of expensive low-sulfur fuel even when emitters have installed, or could install, sulfur dioxide control systems.

9. An "equivalent sulfur content" restriction is an emission standard which would be satisfied by use of a fuel with the given sulfur content, or other control techniques which would accomplish the same emissions reduction.

research into criteria and standards plus the establishment of state and regional control agencies with inspection and enforcement procedures that rely heavily on court actions. The incentive effect of the standards approach is in direct proportion to the enforcement effort and the potential economic impact of fines and court actions. Low fines in relation to control costs will tend to be taken as a fee for pollution. High-cost fees will tend to be questioned in relation to the standards and the criteria behind them.

Economic Incentives

In economics, if there is a demand for air pollution control, the demand will be reflected in a willingness on the part of the public to pay for that control. The payment can be direct in terms of product price adjustments or indirect in terms of tax adjustments. If regulations are enforced, cost of control will be reflected in prices of products and in factor shares. Some prices will rise, some profits will fall, some factor costs will change. Some unemployment may result as polluting firms find that their markets are not strong enough to absorb added costs. If economic incentives are substituted for regulations, the impact may either remain as before or be shifted to an increased tax burden on the public. Thus, either polluting industry or the general public (or both) will incur expense in payment for improving air quality. At the same time, suppliers of pollution control technology—goods and services—will be experiencing growth. Costs of control will be seen as revenue gains and there will be increases in employment in the control supply industries. It may not really make any difference to the supplier whether the initial impetus to control comes from the enforcement of a regulation or from a new profit opportunity. The point is that resources will be reallocated and prices and profits will be involved in the reallocation process.

If, by the use of regulations, economically efficient solutions can be attained (by standard economic criteria), the only claim for consideration on the part of market-type economic incentives must be that they can attain such solutions with a smaller commitment of administrative and enforcement effort than the regulatory process. We do not know that the market type of economic incentive would be more efficient in terms of resource allocation, but we do know that it has not been tried and that it might be possible to incorporate some system of economic incentives as a supplement to regulations.

Economic incentives would include cost-plus-profit contracts, emission charges or taxes (provided that they are geared to the full additional costs of control), sale of emission rights, and full-cost subsidies or payments of any kind including tax credits that cover the full additional costs of control. The key cost calculation, of course, would subtract any offsetting by-product values such as the value of sulfur recovered from fuel or from stack gases.

Several technical considerations are important in evaluating the possible use of economic incentives. Pollution may be reduced by producers through use of substitute fuels or materials, through processing fuels and materials to clean them of pollutants prior to use, through modifications in production processes, or through proper treatment of wastes before final disposal. Because the costs of the several methods are apt to vary widely from plant to plant, it is of great importance that each polluter be free to choose that method or combination of methods which is least costly for him to apply in relation to the standards he must meet. Should an economic incentive alter the relative costs of available methods of control, it could lead to adoption of more rather than less costly methods. Furthermore, to the extent that a promising means of abatement may involve action by a supplier of fuels or raw materials, an economic incentive should be structured to encourage such actions. The desulfurization of fuels prior to use would be an example.

If new incentives are to be considered, it is important to consider them in relation to their prospective efficiencies in abatement. Furthermore, the effects of any new proposed system of incentives must be evaluated in relation to alternatives—one of which is to rely on regulation, an alternative that is favored by many experts familiar with the technical, economic, and administrative aspects of pollution control. The following are examples of economic strategies that might be used.

Cost-plus-profit contracts. Cost-plus contracts need little explanation, and they might be called disincentives. They are used extensively by governments to buy research and development, some goods, and many services. Space exploration and wars are financed almost entirely through the letting of such contracts. Presumably, if the public wanted to, it could buy pollution abatement and other environmental protection services in this way. So far, however, it seems to want the polluter to do the cleaning up—hopefully, at no additional cost.

Pollution control taxes. Essentially, a pollution control tax system would recognize the social costs of pollution damages and the need to bring about the abatement by public action. A pollution control tax system would reserve to individual polluters a considerable amount of decision making as to control method and would place the direct costs of control on the polluter himself. The polluter would find that method or combination of methods which best suited his particular situation. He would then share such costs of control as he could with customers, suppliers, and equity holders. A tax system would tend to work in the direction of efficient resource reallocation as long as the tax at least reflected the magnitude of benefits to be gained from air quality improvement.

From a governmental standpoint, the primary solution for air pollution control would require detailed knowledge of how receptor point damages relate to point source emissions over time. The optimum tax system would require a system of charges for individual point source emitters based on how much each one contributed to all individual receptor point damages. The application of such damage-related charges to polluters would induce additional control applications up to the point where: (a) additional control costs were equal to the value of incremental damages reduced, or (b) the difference between incremental damages and costs fell below some specified minimum, or (c) the total control cost exceeded a specified allocation of resources for air pollution control. Any of these three possibilities could be achieved by adjusting the level of the tax (the first possibility would occur if the pollution charges were set equal to the damages). This type of solution could also incorporate a system of payments to receptors to provide compensation for uncontrolled pollution. Ideally, the control authority would be able to vary the tax system in accordance with changing patterns of pollution production, transport, and damage considerations.

Past consideration of this solution found it to be incapable of practical application for at least four reasons: the extent of individual receptor point damages had not been established; the exact responsibility of individual emitters for the pattern of damage had not been established; there were severe administrative and legal difficulties in damage assessment; and a variable and discretionary taxing authority would have been difficult to legislate.

As with any new and untried approach, the establishment at this time of a general system of emission charges would present a number of problems. First, implementation could add, at least temporarily, to the administrative costs of government. Although relatively little is known about the administrative requirements, it would seem that the administrative costs could be minimal if the charges could be levied in rough proportion to damages and control costs and if existing governmental tax collection agencies could be relied on.

Second, it should be obvious that any system of emission charges based solely on the output of pollution would require an emission measurement or calculation capability, which either may not be available or which would be difficult to provide. Engineering calculations based on technical input-output relationships may serve well as proxies for actual emissions and could be used pending a better emission measurement capability. An example of a proxy would be an engineering calculation of the amount of SO_2 emitted from a coal-burning power plant based on established relationships among fuel inputs, processes, and the efficiencies of existing control methods.

An efficient fee schedule would have to be constructed in order to bring about the desired level of pollution reduction. Theoretically, this could be accomplished by setting tax rates at (a) levels equal to or proportional to incremental damages or (b) levels designed to produce a desirable additional investment in control. Ideally, the application of an emission control tax system would require detailed knowledge of functional relationships among damages, control costs, and the levels of control attainable as alternatives. Although much research needs to be done, there is a considerable body of knowledge regarding the technological alternatives available for some air pollution control problems and at least some understanding of the costs of applying alternative degrees of the various methods of control. Such information could be used in the structuring of a system of emission control taxes aimed at reducing pollution and gaining at least some improvement in environmental quality.

Taxes on fuel and material inputs. Because charges relating directly to pollution damages or to emissions would encounter serious measurement problems, taxes on fuel and other material inputs have been considered as alternatives. The recently proposed tax on leaded gasoline is one example. A variant of the proposal would be to levy a tax directly on the volume of tetra-ethyl and metra-ethyl lead produced. This would place the direct burden of the tax on a few companies operating a limited number of plants. Such a tax could be varied over time to produce a variety of results in terms of the use of lead in automobile fuels. It would obviously circumvent the need to measure the lead oxide emissions of some 100 million tailpipes.

Another recently proposed material input substitute for an emission tax might take the form of a unit tax per pound of equivalent uncontrolled sulfur in power plant fuels. Any sulfur recovered in the ash or collected from the stack gas would be deducted from the tax liability. This recovered sulfur would be valued at the tax rate applicable at the time. Alternatively—and depending on ease of measurement—the actual gaseous emissions of SO_2 and SO_3 could be used in calculating the tax liability. Such a tax would encourage sulfur removal through stack gas cleaning and the preprocessing of the sulfur-bearing fuel.

The tax rate would be related to the marginal costs of sulfur oxide control and set in such a way that the total tax savings available as control methods are applied would noticeably exceed the extra costs of abatement. This potential excess of available tax savings over costs of control (appropriately discounted, of course) would provide the economic incentive. The tax could be structured to include a system of credits to stimulate private research, development, and demonstration activities.

The key to the success of any tax as an emission control device is that the tax be set so that the total tax obligation is seen by the polluter as noticeably higher (or at least equal to) the full additional costs of the desired increment of control. Taxes set at less than the full additional costs of a desired incremental control would simply produce revenues rather than additional control efforts. A major potential advantage of emission control taxes (including effluent fees) is that they do not necessarily have to be set in relation to detailed standards of environmental quality. It would be sufficient to know what pollutants would be worth controlling.

As mentioned previously, the question of who would finally pay the tax would depend on the ability of firms to share costs with customers, suppliers, and equity holders. This in turn would depend on elasticities of demand and supply and on cross elasticities and substitution possibilities, as well as on the competitive cost structure of the industry. One function of a pollution control tax would be to alter consumer preferences and discourage consumption of polluting products. This is a sound economic possibility that should not be ignored by regulators seeking help from economic incentives.

Subsidies. In air pollution control, the possibilities for total direct-cost offsets to pollution control efforts diminish rapidly as control requirements and costs rise. It seems especially useful, therefore, to distinguish clearly between an economic incentive and a subsidy. If an incentive is seen as a means of providing an opportunity for maximizing profits with or without regulation, a less-than-full-cost subsidy must be seen as requiring an enforceable regulation as a precondition to expanded control efforts.

Subsidy approaches that have been tried or suggested include investment tax credits, accelerated depreciation, and performance award payments. From the standpoint of effective pollution control, there are a number of problems associated with these subsidy approaches. To the extent that they do not provide full-cost offsets, they are not apt to motivate any corrective action because they will not make air pollution control investments profitable even though the net cost may be reduced. Even if subsidies did motivate corrective action, there is no guarantee that the effect of capital-cost subsidies such as investment tax credits would not be to subsidize economic inefficiency by inducing capital-intensive solutions rather than possibly more effective and lower-cost approaches such as fuel or material changes, process modification, and better operating and maintenance practices. To the extent that the net costs and economic burdens of pollution control will be relatively low for most industries, financial aid subsidies may well prove to be more trouble than they are worth.

Pollution rights auction. If the assimilative capacity of the environment could be determined with respect to any given pollutant, the government could issue rights to pollute up to that assimilative capacity. Rights could be auctioned off to highest bidders. Bidders could include citizen groups and conservation interests, as well as polluters. Polluters' bids would bear a close relationship to their full additional costs of control discounted to present values. Citizen groups' bids would reflect aesthetic and other values that may not have been fully considered in the estimation of assimilative capacity. To the extent that a buyer's estimated need for pollution rights did not materialize, he could sell his right to another who had underestimated his need. In some regions, rights would equal disposal need; in others, the shortage of rights would bid up their price to the point where applications of control technology including shutdowns, process modifications, and relocations would adjust the volume of waste discharge to the environment's ability to absorb and neutralize it.

The information requirements associated with the effective implementation and administration of rights auctions and emission charge systems would appear to approximate those required by regulation. A strong capability to provide acceptable measurements of pollution production and control would be required to implement charges, fees, taxes, or rights. At present, there is considerable disagreement over many aspects of measurement. As long as disagreements remain, it will be difficult to implement economic incentives as well as regulatory approaches. Some institutional mechanism is needed that offers the possibility of authority compromise and agreement on the facts about the polluting behavior of the emitter system. In the financial area, businesses, stockholders, and government agencies including the Internal Revenue Service have come to rely heavily on the services provided by certified public accountants. It might be possible and it would certainly appear useful if a similar or analogous institution could be applied to the needs of environmental information. A first order of business for such an institution would be to develop acceptable practices for the measurement of pollution production, of the efficiencies of various control efforts, and perhaps of the costs involved.

The Need for Criteria

Standard-setting and regulatory approaches have been criticized by some as arbitrary and inflexible. Economic incentives and subsidies have been lumped together and proposals to tax pollutants emitted to the environment have been labeled licenses to pollute. Permits and other legislative requirements have posed difficult administrative problems.

Clearly a set of criteria is needed to help guide the development of new inducement systems. Questions of economic efficiency and equity are obviously involved. Total adherence to efficiency considerations would require adoption of those inducements that promise to maximize the present value of net benefits. But what does this mean with respect to the evaluation of specific proposals? If efficiency demands that polluters be treated with selectivity depending on whether they are large or small, old or new, in city or country locations, how will equity be served? It may be inevitable that considerations of equity and economic efficiency will always be in conflict.

The criteria selection process will reveal differences of opinion if only because those who would be disadvantaged by the application of a particular criterion will, on that basis alone, disagree if it is chosen. In the case of air pollution, differences of opinion will be augmented by uncertainty regarding the nature and meaning of air quality criteria and standards, the extent and possible resolution of the problem in the future, and the relationship of air quality to other environmental and social issues.

In view of these uncertainties, an incremental approach to selecting criteria may have advantages. The process of selecting criteria may be initiated by constructing a short list of "weeding-out" procedures. The trick is to find procedures which can be agreed upon by many groups and individuals in society in order to limit the number under consideration to a few central alternatives.

Although no approach is likely to be "best" in terms of all criteria, many will be so obviously disadvantageous in terms of one or more that for practical purposes they can be discarded.

Public understanding. Any new strategy alternative, no matter what its theoretical advantages, will be difficult to implement unless its principles and expected results are understood and accepted by those involved in the decision.

As long as a strategy is considered too complex or too abstract, there will be difficulty in understanding its implications and difficulty in convincing decision makers to adopt it. "When in doubt, don't" is a common response, and it applies strongly to public sector innovations in which a large number of individuals and organizations must be persuaded before a new idea can be developed.

Efficiency vs. equity. In order to win support over other alternatives, a program must demonstrate its long-term superiority over the others. In regard to efficiency of resource allocations, however, even highly efficient approaches will face problems, as they must be considered in terms of costs to different groups, polluters, and control agencies of the public at large. Not only must we ask what quality of air and at what price, but who will pay and how much? This question involves the difficult concept of equity or fairness: will the different individuals and groups in society concede that the costs of air pollution control are borne fairly and equitably in relation to the long-term distribution of benefits?

Compatibility. Alternatives which involve great changes from present procedures, systems, and structures are more unlikely to be successful than those which involve minimal changes. Since the federal role in air pollution is currently directed more towards research, advice, and supervision, and the state role is primarily concerned with actual implementation of policy, proposals which would radically change this situation will be more liable to failure than those which can be integrated into an existing framework.

Alternatives which are not compatible with present systems and procedures result in high transition costs. Disruption means that benefits are delayed. A decision must be made about whether a new approach is worth the disruptions. Since future benefits are uncertain while present costs are relatively certain, the chance of implementing radical changes lessens. Finally, those who find change upsetting will oppose it even if they can give no substantial reasons.

Any plan, especially where existing control technology is known to be inadequate, should make substantial provision for the stimulation of research, development, and demonstration programs. Various approaches to encourage research and development are feasible. Tax credits, for example, might be allowed for activities designed to produce new control methods and/or reduce the cost of existing methods. The financing of research, development, and demonstration projects might be facilitated to the extent that it could be made available out of a special, governmentally administered "environmental quality fund." Such a fund might be established and financed initially through revenues from taxes on polluting activities. However, it might not be wise to make research and development totally dependent on such taxes, especially where they are designed to reduce pollution and thus may be eliminated as a source of revenue.

To the extent that subsidies may qualify as incentives, there is a need for criteria to limit their application to the stimulation of pollution control. Otherwise, the general application of a subsidy could well result in considerable waste and very little additional control effort. For instance, subsidies which apply only to a portion of the "universe" of control measures—and for various reasons, most subsidies do apply only to a portion—artificially shift control practices away from unsubsidized measures and, often, away from the most cost-effective approach.

The basic and admittedly difficult test would involve the effect of a control effort cost on a firm's long-term financial position. A related test would involve determining whether or not this long-term financial position would be seriously harmed by the incurrence of control cost commitments in the short run. For example, a small, relatively profitable firm simply might not be able to marshal the financing to meet immediate capital needs. Such a firm would be a logical candidate for some assistance—perhaps most importantly for access to an available pool of funds. It might or might not make a big difference if these funds were made available at regular or low rates of interest. The danger involved in low-interest financing is simply that firms would tend to seek such financing as an alternative. An otherwise justifiable program could thus result in subsidizing economic inefficiency along with some worthwhile pollution control efforts. The pollution controller would tend to be an easy victim of the "I'll have to go out of business" argument. It must be remembered that firms go out of business every day and that it is not the job of pollution control to interfere with normal economic processes.

In short, if a firm can show a good long-term market position along with its claim of limited cash or other liquid assets, some special treatment might well be necessary to avoid undue hardship and the possible loss of a productive enterprise.

A review of the major incentive and cost-sharing alternatives seems to point away from those such as cost-plus-profit contracts and many of the subsidy approaches which would require substantial additions to government budgets. If regulations need to be supplemented, the approaches that appear most promising are those that would use a small governmental effort along with a potent economic incentive for leverage. Pollution control taxation approaches designed to utilize existing taxes such as the excise tax on motor vehicles, gasoline, and tobacco have some obvious advantages because of the enormous obstacles facing the structuring of new taxes.

Theoretically, considerations of economic efficiency may be served most effectively by allowing individual polluters to choose their own best method of control and pay the initial costs of application with a minimum amount of public subsidy. This approach recognizes that costs of control will ultimately be shared with the customers, suppliers, and equity holders. It also assumes that the evaluation of needs and alternatives is a comparatively simple process, and that extensive administrative costs are not involved. This may not necessarily be true in practice. To the extent that customers may be unwilling to bear the generally small increase in cost, they may choose other products, suppliers may find other markets, and equity holders may shift funds to other, less polluting enterprises. Not only would an economically efficient pattern of resource allocation tend to be preserved, but—even more importantly—a vital set of social values would have been introduced into the calculus.

The basic choices are now clarified. We can continue on the road of governmental standard setting with regulations and enforcement. We can introduce economic strategies as substitutes for standards and regulation. Or we may adopt what may be a more realistic and practical alternative and find a set of economic incentives that will provide effective and complementary supports to the present system of standards.

Acknowledgments. I am indebted to co-workers Alan P. Carlin, Steven Plotkin, and Dennis Tihansky for stimulation and critical comments. Edna Loehman provided valuable editorial comments. Responsibility for deficiencies is mine.

References

1. Anderson, R. J., Jr., and Crocker, T. D. "Air Pollution and Housing: Some Findings." Paper 264 read at Institute for Research in the Behavioral, Economic, and Management Sciences, December 1969, at Krannert Graduate School of Industrial Administration, Purdue University.
2. Barrett, Larry B., and Waddell, Thomas E. "The Cost of Air Pollution Damages: A Status Report." Unpublished report prepared for the National Air Pollution Control Administration, Raleigh, N.C., July 1970.
3. Battelle Memorial Institute. "A Survey and Economic Assessment of the Effects of Air Pollution on Elastomers." Contract No. CPA-22-69-146. Final report, June 1970.
4. Crocker, Thomas C. "Air Pollution and Residential Property Values in Chicago, Illinois." Contract study completed for the Air Pollution Control Office, Environmental Protection Agency, December 1970.
5. Davies, J. Clarence, III. *The Politics of Pollution*. New York: Pegasus, 1970.
6. "The Economics of Clean Air." Report of the Administrator of the Environmental Protection Agency to Congress, March 1971. Washington, D.C.: U.S. Government Printing Office.
7. Ferrando, R., and Milhad, G. "The Biological Effects of Air Pollution on Animals." *Revue d'hygiène et de Médecine Sociale* 17 (1969):295–306.
8. Gerhardt, Paul H. "An Approach to the Estimation of Economic Losses Due to Air Pollution." In *Law and Contemporary Problems*, edited by Clark C. Havighurst. Dobbs Ferry, N.Y.: Oceana Publications, 1969.
9. Gerhardt, Paul H. "An Approach to the Estimation of Economic Losses Due to Air Pollution." *Ohio's Health*, November–December 1970.
10. Havighurst, Clark C. "A Survey of Air Pollution Litigation in the Philadelphia Area." Contract No. CPA-22-69-112. Final report, December 1969.
11. Haynie, F. H. "Estimation of Cost of Air Pollution as the Result of Corrosion of

Galvanized Steel." Unpublished report, DEER, National Air Pollution Control Administration.

12. Lave, Lester B., and Seskin, Eugene. "Air Pollution and Human Mortality." Investigation conducted under a grant from Resources for the Future and published in part in *Science,* July 1970.
13. Michelson, Irving, and Tourin, Boris. "Comparative Method for Studying Costs of Air Pollution." *Public Health Reports* 81 (June 1966):505–11.
14. Midwest Research Institute. "Systems Analysis of the Effects of Air Pollution on Materials." Contract No. CPA-22-69-113. Final report, January 1970.
15. Miessner, H. "Damage to Animals Caused by Industry and Technology." *Deutsche Tieraerztliche Wochenschrift* 39 (1931):340–45.
16. Rice, Dorothy P. *Estimating the Cost of Illness.* Washington, D.C.: U.S. Department of Health, Education, and Welfare, 1966.
17. Ridker, Ronald G. "The Problem of Estimating Total Costs of Air Pollution, a Discussion and an Illustration," p. 21. Unpublished report to U.S. Public Health Service, July 1966.
18. Ridker, Ronald G. *Economic Costs of Air Pollution,* pp. 12–29. New York: Frederick A. Praeger, 1967.
19. Rubay, M. "About the Fog Observed in the Meuse Valley in December 1930 and Its Noxious Effects on Animals." *Annales de Médecine Veterinaire* 77 (March 1932):97–110.
20. Salvin, V. S. "Survey and Economic Assessment of the Effects of Air Pollution on Textile Fibers and Dyes." Contract No. PH-22-68-2. Final report, June 1970.
21. Stanford Research Institute. "Inquiry into the Economic Effects of Air Pollution on Electrical Contacts." Contract No. PH-22-68-35. Final report, April 1970.
22. Waddell, Thomas E. "The Economic Effects of Sulfur Oxide Air Pollution from Point Sources on Vegetation and Environment." National Air Pollution Control Administration, June 1970. Unpublished.

Decision-Making Problems in Water and Land Development

In chapter 5, Harry Steele describes the efforts to develop new standards for planning by government agencies for water and land resource development. He discusses the principles and standards developed by the Water Resources Council and how these principles evolved. Steele points out that in the past, not enough information was reported on alternative plans for resource development to provide information on the trade-offs between monetary and nonmonetary values. The council now recommends that several alternative plans be formulated and the differences among alternative plans illustrated in an account sheet format. A recommended plan can then be chosen on an evaluation of trade-offs. The council has recognized that evaluation requires a broader judgmental basis and more public participation.

William Lord (chapter 6) is also concerned with decision making in agencies for resource development projects. The contrast of his ideas with those in Steele's paper lies in his differing view of the decision-making process and the role of the agency in this process. Lord cites the need for the reexamination of the decision-making procedures for development projects. He contrasts "bottom up" decision making, where projects to meet local needs are generated upward, to "top down" decision making, where agency planners seek to fulfill their concept of the public interest. He suggests that there is a need to restructure decision making to incorporate the advantages of both the "top down" and "bottom up" systems. The result of his and Steele's differing views on how decisions should be made is that Lord emphasizes more strongly the need to define the distributional effects of a project on producers, consumers, and income groups, both in monetary and nonmonetary terms. Lord also disagrees with the council on the use of goals in project formulation and evaluation, and the role of a resource planner in a government agency.

The final chapter in this section, by William Johnson, deals with the problem of how to systematically obtain information for use in decision making. Although Johnson is concerned primarily with the environmental area, the process he presents for obtaining information is generally applicable. It consists of identification, description, assessment, and presentation. To illustrate this process, Johnson applies his assessment methodology to a development plan for the Morrison Creek area in Sacramento, California.

5

Multiobjective Planning of Water and Land Resources

Harry A. Steele

In recent years the Water Resources Council has been developing principles and standards for planning water and land resources. In public hearings, field tests, consultations, and reviews, the council has had a great deal of participation from federal agencies, state planning groups, universities, and the public; it has tried to develop a system that would encompass local, state, and regional viewpoints as well as the national view. The success of the council can only be judged by acceptance of the proposed principles and standards by federal, regional, state, and local planning groups.[1]

The beginning of formal evaluation procedures is often cited as the enactment of the Flood Control Act of 1936 in which Congress stated a policy relating to flood control which over the years has been broadened to other purposes. This policy was "that the Federal Government should improve or participate in the improvement of navigable waters or their

1. An earlier version of this paper was presented at a Seminar on Economics and Decision Making for Environmental Quality, sponsored by the Department of Agricultural Economics, University of Florida, Gainesville, Florida, 26 April 1971. The paper was revised in December 1971 to show a comparison of the principles and standards tentatively adopted by the Water Resources Council with the July 1970 recommendations of the Special Task Force, and the last section was added in September 1973 to indicate final changes in the principles and standards.

tributaries, including watersheds thereof, for flood-control purposes if the benefits to whomsoever they may accrue are in excess of the estimated costs, and if the lives and social security of people are otherwise adversely affected" (32).

Congress has added a great number of directives over the years, setting forth broad objectives for water and land resource planning. Analytical procedures have been developed to evaluate benefits and costs.[2] All of these efforts have recognized that *all* benefits and *all* costs must be considered, but the tendency has been to rely primarily on market or monetary considerations from a national viewpoint, with much less consideration being given to nonmonetary and intangible values or to state and regional viewpoints.[3,4,5]

The council has developed a planning system that does measure all effects, whether market or nonmarket, and considers the effects from the national viewpoint as well as from the viewpoint of states and regions.

The Water Resources Council

The Water Resources Council was established by the Water Resources Planning Act of 1965 (17), an act which initiates planning for land and water use on a coordinated basis by the federal government, states, localities, and private enterprise. The membership of the council includes the secretaries of agriculture, interior, army, health, education, and welfare, and transportation, and the chairman of the Federal Power Commission. The secretaries of commerce and housing and urban development and the administrator of the Environmental Protection Agency are associate members. The secretary of the interior is chairman.

Functions of the Water Resources Council

The functions of the council as set out in the Water Resources Planning Act are to: prepare a periodic national assessment of the adequacy of water supplies; recommend changes in water policy to the president and

2. The "Green Book" set out a systematic approach to benefit-cost analysis. It recognized the limitations of market prices in reflecting values from a public viewpoint but presented no framework for evaluating the nonmarket effect of plans (15, p. 7).

3. Maass (12, p. 219) has pointed out the inadequacy of measuring effects solely in terms of national economic efficiency.

4. Knetsch et al. (11, p. 12) argue that national income enhancement must be the primary criterion for choice among alternatives. They do argue for methods of simulating values for outputs not priced in the market.

5. Kalter et al. (10, p. 6) argue that "what is needed for a more comprehensive and politically useful analysis is an economic framework which permits evaluation from the standpoint of multiple objectives." See also Kalter (9).

the Congress; establish, with approval of the president, planning principles, standards, and procedures; coordinate comprehensive planning of water and land resources; recommend establishment of river basin commissions; review river basin plans and recommend action to the president and the Congress; assist states in water and related land resources planning through grants; and take other actions to carry out the Water Resources Planning Act and Executive Office assignments.

This paper is concerned with the function which places the responsibility on the council for establishing principles, standards, and procedures for federal participants in the preparation of river basin plans and for the formulation and evaluation of federal water and related land resources projects (reference 17, sections 102[b], 103, and 301[b]).

Special Task Force

In 1968 the council decided to review and, if desirable, to revise the evaluation practices used in planning. The council appointed a Special Task Force to conduct the review and an initial public hearing was held in Washington, D.C., on 13 January 1969, to solicit views and recommendations. A preliminary report of the Special Task Force proposing a multiobjective approach to water and land resources planning was published by the council in June 1969.[6] The council directed that the issues and proposals in the report be widely discussed and tested on existing projects.

Nine public hearings were held at which about 200 oral statements were presented and nearly 400 other statements were submitted for the record.[7] The preliminary report of the Special Task Force, of which about 5,000 copies were distributed, was the subject of discussion at numerous meetings and seminars and was extensively reviewed by several federal agencies and river basin commissions.[8]

Field Tests

The proposed procedures were given extensive field tests. Ten projects were selected for field tests, and nineteen separate tests were made. The tests were executed in two distinct steps involving the measurement of benefits and costs and the formulation of alternative plans.[9] The following

6. The preliminary report is often referred to as the "Blue Book" (23).

7. A brief summary and index to the hearing record may be consulted at the U.S. Water Resources Council Office (26).

8. The U.S. Water Resources Council (27) gives a summary of agency comments.

9. The U.S. Water Resources Council (29) gives a summary analysis of the nineteen tests. The Special Task Force was concerned about whether effects (benefits and costs) could be identified and measured under the multiobjectives. Plan formulation under the multiobjectives was thought to be even more difficult.

summary shows the ten test areas and identifies the teams making the tests on each area. Figure 1 shows the locations of the test areas and the teams.

Mountain Home Division, Southwest Idaho Water Development Project

Water Resources Council (WRC)
Corps of Engineers (CE)
University of Wisconsin (UW)

Poteau River Watershed, Arkansas and Oklahoma

Water Resources Council (WRC)
Soil Conservation Service (SCS)
Corps of Engineers (CE)
University of Oklahoma (UO)

Susquehanna River Study Area, Pennsylvania

Water Resources Council (WRC)
University of Michigan (UM)

West Fork River and Tributaries, West Virginia (Stonewall Jackson Reservoir)

Water Resources Council (WRC)
Corps of Engineers (CE)
Cornell University (CU)

Detroit River, Trenton Channel, Michigan

Corps of Engineers (CE)
Michigan State University (MSU)

Big Walnut Reservoir, Indiana

Massachusetts Institute of Technology (MIT)

Kingsport–Reedy Creek Study, Tennessee

Tennessee Valley Authority (TVA)

Lower Hiwassee, Tennessee

Tennessee Valley Authority (TVA)

Cosumnes River Division, Central Valley Project, California

Bureau of Reclamation (BR)

Columbia River and Tributaries, Washington

Cornell, Howland, Hayes, and Merryfield of Seattle, Washington (CH_2M)

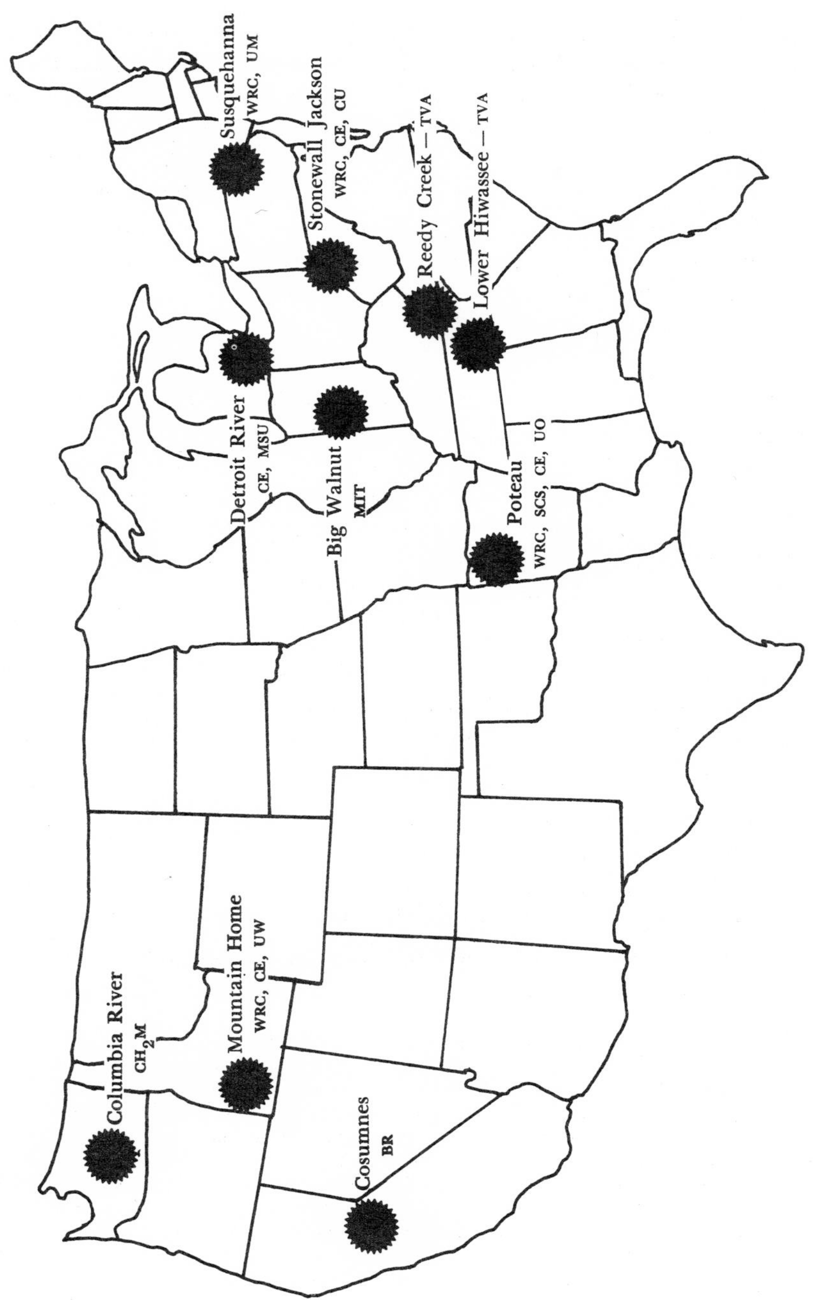

FIGURE 1. Location of field test areas.

On the basis of these tests, the Special Task Force concluded that the multiobjective approach was practical and that meaningful results and uniform application could be achieved by establishing carefully structured principles, standards, and procedures for planning.

The Special Task Force involved many people in this effort through hearings, reviews, and tests, and drew freely from the work of others. As a result, the preliminary findings made in June 1969 were greatly revised. The Special Task Force submitted its final recommendations to the Water Resources Council for consideration on 12 August 1970.[10]

Former Planning Procedures

A brief review of former procedures will help to clarify the changes that the Special Task Force recommended. Under previous procedures, plans for meeting a given problem were to be formulated under rather rigorous economic criteria; the selected plan was chosen to achieve maximum net economic benefits.[11] Adjustments could be made in this plan to take account of other considerations, such as the environment, public health, or income distribution effects, as indicated in the following steps.

FIRST PHASE: EFFICIENCY MODEL

1. Tangible benefits exceed tangible costs.
2. Benefits of separable purposes at least equal cost.
3. Scope of development provides maximum net benefits.
4. Purpose is achieved with minimum cost.

SECOND PHASE: ADJUST FOR SOCIAL OR ENVIRONMENTAL GOALS

1. Take account of intangibles.
2. Indicate the extent of departure from efficiency formulation.
3. Assess opportunity cost in terms of reduced efficiency.

This approach did not work too well. Primary weight was given to monetary values.[12] Not enough information was reported on alternative

10. "Findings and Recommendations" (24) contains a list of the Special Task Force and the many people who assisted the Special Task Force in reviews, tests, and other ways. "Principles" (25) provides the broad policy framework for planning. "Standards" (28) provides uniformity and consistency in comparing alternative plans. These three volumes of the task force report have been republished by the Senate Public Works Committee as Committee Print 92-20 (21).

11. The current planning policies, often referred to as Senate Document 97 (16), are patterned after the Green Book, but for the first time a method is provided for considering objectives other than economic efficiency. In practice there has been a requirement for a benefit-cost ratio greater than one, even though such a restraint is not required in Senate Document 97. The result has been that plans may be modified to consider other, often unspecified, objectives as long as the overall benefit-cost ratio is greater than one.

12. Maass (12) has outlined some of the problems with this approach.

plans. Decision makers did not have information made available to them on trade-offs between monetary and nonmonetary values. The system did not provide a basis for planning directly for environmental, social, or regional objectives. Adjustments in the efficiency model for social or environmental objectives were limited by the practice of requiring an overall efficiency benefit-cost ratio greater than one.

New Directions in Planning

There has been a rising tide of public concern about the environment and the quality of life. There is a growing interest in regional development. These concerns have been reflected in a series of congressional enactments and executive policies that give new directions to planning for water and land resources.[13] A consideration of these and many other factors led the Special Task Force to recommend a multiobjective system of planning. The proposed principles and standards were to be established for planning the use of the water and land resources of the United States to achieve objectives, determined cooperatively, through the coordinated actions of the federal, state, and local governments, private enterprises and organizations, and individuals.

The following section summarizes the Special Task Force recommendations made to the council in July 1970.

Special Task Force Recommendations

The task force recommended that plans for the uses of the nation's water and land resources be directed toward improved contributions to the multiobjectives of national economic development, environmental quality, social well-being, and regional development.[14] Planning for the use of water and land resources in terms of these objectives would aid in

13. "Standards" (28) gives a summary of congressional expressions for various objectives in recent legislation. After the Special Task Force report of July 1970 was available, the Congress in the Flood Control Act of 1970 (Public Law 91-611) included the following statement: "Section 209. It is the intent of Congress that the objectives of enhancing regional economic development, the quality of the total environment, including its protection and improvement, the well-being of the people of the United States, and the national economic development are the objectives to be included in federally financed water resource projects, and in the evaluation of benefits and costs attributable thereto, giving due consideration to the most feasible alternative means of accomplishing these objectives."

14. The report of the Special Task Force was published for limited circulation by the council (24, 25, 26, 27, 28, 29) and has been republished by the Senate Public Works Committee as Committee Print 92-20 (21). A bill, S. 2612, which would implement the task force report, has been introduced by Senator Jennings Randolph, chairman of the Public Works Committee (13), and Senator Henry Jackson, chairman of the Interior and Insular Affairs Committee (8).

identifying alternative courses of action and would provide the type of information needed to improve the public decision-making process.

OBJECTIVES

The task force proposed that planning for the use of water and land resources be conducted to reflect society's preferences for attainment of the following objectives:

To enhance national economic development by increasing the value of the nation's output of goods and services and improving national economic efficiency.

To enhance the quality of the environment by the management, conservation, preservation, creation, restoration, or improvement of the quality of certain natural and cultural resources and ecological systems.

To enhance social well-being by the equitable distribution of real income, employment, and population, with special concern for the incidence of the consequences of a plan on affected persons or groups; by contributing to the security of life and health; by providing educational, cultural, and recreational opportunities; and by contributing to national security.

To enhance regional development through increases in a region's income, increases in its employment, and improvements of its economic base, environment, social well-being, and other specified components of the regional objective.

Components of these multiobjectives refer to the types of outputs, environmental conditions, or regional development that are being sought as contributions to the multiobjectives. The term "component need" was used by the task force to refer to the type, quantity, and quality of the desired effect now and in the future.

BENEFITS AND COSTS

As proposed by the task force, plans for the use of water and land resources would have benefits and costs that would affect more than one of the multiobjectives.

For each alternative plan there would be a complete display or accounting of relevant benefits, costs, and effects (Table 1). Benefits of a plan are defined as positive (beneficial) contributions toward the accomplishment of the multiobjectives. Costs of a plan are defined as negative (adverse) effects on the multiobjectives.

Thus, there are national economic development benefits and costs, environmental quality benefits and costs, social well-being benefits and costs, and regional development benefits and costs. These are measured in quantitative units or qualitative terms appropriate to a particular objective. The multiobjectives are not mutually exclusive with respect to benefits and costs, and final decisions concerning the recommended plan would be made by considering the beneficial and adverse effects of alternative plans on all objectives.

National economic development objective. Benefits to the national economic development objective include all effects on national output regardless of the reason a plan may be formulated. These benefits include the value to users of increased output of goods and services, the value of output resulting from external economies, and the value of output resulting from the use of resources otherwise unemployed or underemployed. National economic development costs are resources required for a plan, losses in output resulting from external diseconomies, and losses in output from resources displaced and subsequently unemployed.

TABLE 1
System of Accounting for All Effects of an Alternative Plan

Account	Benefits	Costs	Net Benefits
National economic development (NED)	*	*	*
Environmental quality (EQ)	*	*	*
Social well-being (SWB)	*	*	*
Regional development (RD)			
Region 1	*	*	*
Region 2	*	*	*
Rest of nation	*	*	*

Environmental quality objective. The benefits and adverse effects of the proposed plan on the environmental characteristics of an area under study or elsewhere in the nation would be evaluated, with environmental effects displayed in terms of relevant physical and ecological criteria or dimensions, including the appropriate qualitative aspects. Such an evaluation would include the effects of the proposed plan on (a) open and green space, wild and scenic rivers, lakes, beaches, shores, mountains and wilderness areas, estuaries, and other areas of natural beauty; (b) archaeological, historical, biological, and geographical resources and selected ecological systems; (c) the quality of water, land, and air resources; and (d) irreversible commitments of resources to future uses.

Effects under the environmental quality objective are expressed in various quantitative units or in qualitative terms. In some instances, the effects can be expressed in terms of meeting legally established standards.

Social well-being objective. The benefits and adverse effects of a proposed plan on social well-being would be displayed, including the effects of a plan on the real income of classes or groups relevant to the evaluation of the plan; on life, health, and safety; on economic stability; on educational, cultural, and recreational opportunities; on reserve capacities and flexibilities in water resource systems; on protection against interruption of the flow of essential goods and services at times of national disaster or critical need; and on other relevant social factors.

Regional development objective. The benefits and adverse effects of a proposed plan on relevant planning regions (states, river basins, and communities) would be displayed, including income effects and effects on other components of the regional development objective, such as: (a) the number and types of jobs resulting from a plan in the region; (b) the

TABLE 2
Regional Accounting System

Effects	Region 1	Region 2	Rest of Nation	NED
Beneficial effects				
National economic development effects	+800	+200	0	+1,000
Location effects	+200	−150	−50	0
Adverse effects				
National economic development effects	+200	+50	+350	+600
Location effects	+150	−100	−50	0

effect of the plan on population distribution within the region and among regions; (c) the effect of the plan on the regional economic base and economic stability; (d) the effect of the plan on educational, cultural, and recreational opportunities in the region; and (e) the effect of the plan on environmental quality in the region under consideration.

SYSTEMS OF ACCOUNTS

A system of accounts would be established to display the benefits and costs of each alternative plan to each multiobjective (see Table 1) and to compare alternative plans (see Table 3). The display of beneficial and adverse effects would be prepared in such a manner that the different levels of achievement to each objective could be readily discerned and compared and the trade-offs among alternative plans determined.[15] The

15. The concept of a system of accounts is changing rapidly and considerable improvement is expected. The Social Science Committee of the Universities Council on Water Resources (4, 5, 32) has some promising suggestions. The Water Resources Council has asked the Office of Business Economics (Department of Commerce) and the Economic Research Service (Department of Agriculture) to develop a system of relating a regional plan to other regions of the nation (22). The Engineering Department of Stanford University (3) has developed a system of presenting economic and social effects of alternative highway plans.

system of accounts would display the benefits and costs in the region under consideration in relation to other parts of the nation.

Benefits and costs for each region would include the incidence of the national economic development effects. Thus, these effects accruing across the system of regional accounts would sum to the national total of such effects. The regional development account would also include the effects on location of related economic activities. These effects, offset by adverse location effects in other regions, would sum to zero for the nation (Table 2).

TABLE 3
DISPLAY OF TRADE-OFFS AMONG ALTERNATIVE PLANS

Objective	Alternative Plan A	Alternative Plan B	Difference (A minus B)
NED			
Beneficial effects	*	*	*
Adverse effects			
Net effects			
EQ			
Beneficial effects	*	*	*
Adverse effects			
Net effects			
SWB			
Beneficial effects			
Adverse effects	*	*	*
Net effects			
RD			
Beneficial effects			
Adverse effects	*	*	*
Net effects			

If the nation is interested in the geographical pattern of its economic growth it can influence the pattern of growth by its public investment policies. The regional development account provides a method of estimating the consequences of alternative policies for regional development.

THE PLANNING PROCESS

As recommended by the task force, plans would be directed to meeting current and projected needs and problems as identified by the desires of people, in such a manner that contributions would be made to society's preferences for national economic development, environmental quality, social well-being, and regional development. Plans for water and land resources would focus upon the specified components of the multiobjectives desired for the designated region, river basin, state, or local planning setting.

The planning process would include the following major steps: (a) specify components of the multiobjectives relevant to the planning setting; (b) evaluate resource capabilities and outline expected economic and environmental conditions without any plan; (c) formulate alternative plans to achieve varying levels of contributions to the specified components of the multiobjectives; (d) analyze the differences among the alternative plans which reflect different emphases among the specified components of the multiobjectives; (e) review and reconsider if necessary the specified components for the planning setting and formulate additional alternative plans as appropriate; and (f) select a recommended plan based upon an evaluation of the trade-offs among the alternative plans.

Essential to this process is the formulation of alternative plans to achieve varying levels of contributions to the multiobjectives and the active participation of all interests. The task force recommended that each objective be given equal consideration in the early steps of plan formulation.

The number of alternative plans to be developed for each planning effort would depend upon complementarities of conflicts among specified components of the objectives, resource capabilities, technical possibilities, and the extent to which the design of additional alternative plans could be expected to contribute significantly to the choice of a recommended plan. Emphasis would be placed on examination of those water- and land-use plans which might have appreciable effects on objectives. Appropriate methods and techniques for estimating benefits and costs would be used to provide reliable estimates of the consequences and feasibility of each alternative plan.

In cases where the trade-offs among objectives would be significant in the context of either national priorities or more localized priorities, an alternative plan would be formulated to emphasize the contributions to each such objective. One such alternative plan would be formulated in which optimum contributions would be made to the national economic development objective. These alternative plans would identify the full range of the trade-offs among significant conflicting objectives.

Four tests would be applied in the formulation of any given alternative plan: (a) the acceptability of the alternative plan to the public and compatibility with institutional constraints; (b) the effectiveness of the alternative plan in meeting component needs of the multiobjectives; (c) the efficiency of the plan in meeting component needs of the multiobjectives and a demonstration that the plan represents the least-cost means of achieving such component needs; and (d) the completeness of the plan in accounting for all investments and other required inputs or actions.

The basic steps in developing and testing alternative plans could be reiterated as necessary, with each iteration more detailed than the last. In each alternative plan screened for final consideration, the total beneficial effects to all objectives would exceed the total adverse effects to all objectives.

From its analysis of alternative plans the planning organization would select a recommended plan. The plan selected would reflect the importance attached to different objectives and the extent to which different objectives could be achieved by carrying out the plan (Table 3).

The recommended plan should be formulated so that benefits, costs, and effects toward objectives reflect, to the best of current understanding and knowledge, the priorities and preferences expressed by the public at all levels to be affected by the plan.[16]

In addition to the recommended plan with supporting analysis, other significant alternative plans embodying different priorities among the desired objectives would be presented in the planning report. Included with the presentation of alternative plans would be an analysis of the trade-offs among them. The trade-offs would be set forth in explicit terms, including the basis for choosing the recommended plan from among the alternative plans.

COST ALLOCATION AND REIMBURSEMENT

When necessary to establish reimbursement or cost-sharing policies, an allocation of national economic development costs would be made among the objectives and among components of the objectives in a manner to insure that all objectives and components are treated comparably and receive their fair share of the advantages from a multiobjective plan.

Reimbursement and cost-sharing policies would be directed generally to the end that identifiable beneficiaries bear an equitable share of costs commensurate with benefits received in full cognizance of the multiobjectives.

Since existing cost-sharing policies are not entirely consistent with the proposed multiobjective approach to planning water and land resources, it was proposed that these policies be reviewed and that needed changes be recommended.

16. Experience with multiobjective planning and related research may in time lead to methods of establishing acceptable weights earlier in the planning process. Several ongoing studies are experimenting with the multiobjective approach; the North Atlantic Framework Study and the Susquehanna Comprehensive Study are two examples. Maass (12) suggests that Congress establish weights for the guidance of planning studies. There seems to be an increasing interest in Congress in providing this type of policy guidance as evidenced by environmental and regional development legislation.

THE DISCOUNT RATE

The task force recommended that the Water Resources Council establish the discount rate to reflect the relative values that society places on benefits and costs toward the multiobjectives occurring in the future as compared with the present. It was proposed that the rate would be set for relatively long periods of time to reduce the disruption in ongoing planning activities that results from frequent change. The task force proposed a 5.5 percent rate.

NATIONAL PROGRAM DEVELOPMENT

The council would formulate a national program for federal and federally assisted water and land resource activities, including a long-range schedule of priorities among plans for projects, states, regions, and river basins.

WATER AND LAND PLANNING ACTIVITIES COVERED

The principles and standards as proposed by the Special Task Force would apply to federal participation with river basin commissions, states, and others in the preparation, formulation, evaluation, review, revision, and transmission to the Congress of plans for states, regions, and river basins; and in the planning of federal and federally assisted water and land resource programs and projects and federal licensing activities.

PUBLIC PARTICIPATION

There has been considerable criticism of the large number of interests and people that have been involved in comprehensive planning and the difficulty of effective management and decision making under the circumstances. These criticisms have resulted in reduced budget support for the comprehensive planning program. Yet, on the basis of the council's hearings and analyses, it was clear to the task force that meaningful multiobjective planning would require a broader judgmental basis and more participation of both the general public and public agencies. States and local governments are becoming much more involved. A large number of organized groups have an interest in plans for water and land resources. Conflicts of interest are being taken to the courts. In the future, more rather than fewer interests will be involved. Many questions are being raised about the institutional arrangements for planning.[17] The challenge to the Water Resources Council and other organizations charged with comprehensive planning is to organize planning activities so that

17. See Apter (1) as an example of the concern not only about the substance of the planning method but also about who does the planning.

they can be efficiently and effectively conducted while providing for meaningful and satisfying public participation in the important considerations and decisions.

THE WATER RESOURCES COUNCIL PROPOSAL

The Water Resources Council and other agencies of the Executive Office gave the task force recommendations intensive review and made extensive changes.[18] The principles and standards as tentatively adopted by the council were published in the *Federal Register*.[19]

To facilitate comparison among existing policies (Senate Document 97), the task force recommendations (July 1970), and the council's proposed principles and standards (December 1971), a summary chart has been prepared (Table 4). The table lists several items of importance in planning procedures and gives a very brief description of each of the three approaches.

This section discusses the major changes made by the council in the task force recommendations and presents some of the questions that were considered.

PLANNING OBJECTIVES

The council retained the national economic development (NED) objective and the environmental quality (EQ) objective for all planning. The regional development (RD) objective would be used only when directed. The social well-being (SWB) objective as proposed by the task force was dropped. The council redefined the NED objective to exclude benefits from the employment of otherwise unemployed resources, although these benefits would be recognized under the regional development objective as would some of the items that the task force had included under the SWB objective.

MEASUREMENT OF EFFECTS

Although the council proposal limited and redefined planning objectives, it provided for a system of accounts that would show the impact of alternative plans on NED and EQ objectives, and the RD objective when directed. In any case, the accounts would include a display of impacts on regional and social factors.

18. Discussion of some of the issues involved in these reviews may be found in the *National Journal* (6) and in several issues of the *Criteria News* (7).

19. The council's "Proposed Principles and Standards for Planning Water and Related Land Resources," along with a notice of public review and hearing and a draft environmental statement, were published in the *Federal Register*, 21 December 1971 (30).

TABLE 4

COMPARISON OF EXISTING POLICIES IN SENATE DOCUMENT 97, 87TH CONGRESS, 2D SESSION; THE SPECIAL TASK FORCE RECOMMENDATIONS OF JULY 1970; AND THE WATER RESOURCES COUNCIL'S PROPOSED PRINCIPLES AND STANDARDS IN THE FEDERAL REGISTER, 21 DECEMBER 1971

Item	SD 97	TF Recommendation	WRC Proposal
Planning objectives	National efficiency with adjustments for preservation, well-being, or regional	Multiobjectives NED, EQ, SWB, RD given equal consideration at start of planning process	Limited to NED and EQ RD only when directed
National economic	1. Output of plan valued by actual or simulated market prices 2. Redevelopment benefits	1. Output valued by willingness to pay 2. Externalities 3. Use of unemployed resources	1. Output valued by willingness to pay 2. Externalities
Environment	Preservation of open space, wild areas, and areas of unique beauty and cultural interest may be included	Enhance quality of environment by management, preservation, and restoration of natural and cultural resources	Enhance quality of environment by management, preservation, and restoration of natural and cultural resources
Social	Well-being of all the people the overruling determinant but not set out as a planning objective	Income distribution Population distribution Life, health, and safety Economic stability Educational, cultural, and recreational opportunities National security	No social objective—however, both beneficial and adverse social effects would be displayed in the system of accounts
Regional	Adjust national efficiency for regional development Include regional secondary benefits Compute separate benefit-cost ratio	Regional incidence NED Induced activities Number of jobs Regional economic stability Enhance regional environment and social well-being	Regional incidence NED Use of unemployed resources Induced activities Number of jobs Population distribution Economic stability Educational, cultural, and recreational opportunities Enhance regional EQ

Measurement of effects	Measure only monetary effects	System of accounts Measure and record all effects, quantitative and qualitative, toward 4 objectives	System of accounts Measure and record all effects on NED and EQ objectives and on RD when directed Show impact of plan on regional and social factors
Plan formulation	1. Rigorous national economic efficiency 2. Adjust for preservation, well-being, or regional	Formulate alternative plans for NED, EQ, SWB, and RD objectives Trade-offs among alternative plans	Formulate alternative plans for NED and EQ objectives and RD only when directed No formulation to emphasize SWB effects Trade-offs among alternative plans
Benefit-cost restraint	In practice, an overall $b/c > 1$ regardless of adjustments for noneconomic effects has been required	Increments for NED $b/c > 1$ No overall b/c restraint on alternative plans including multiobjectives	Increments for NED $b/c > 1$ NED and EQ combined, no overall b/c restraint When RD included by direction no overall b/c restraint
Planning interest rate	Coupon rate on long-term federal bonds to 12/24/68 Modified yield on long-term federal bonds after 12/24/68 FY 1972, planning rate at $5\frac{3}{8}$ percent	Social rate of discount Planning rate of $5\frac{1}{2}$ percent combining social time preference and opportunity cost parameters	Opportunity cost of federal investment is the real rate of return on private investment estimated at 10 percent. Planning rate of 7 percent proposed for next 5 years
Period of analysis	The lesser of physical or economic life not to exceed 100 years	The lesser of physical or economic life not to exceed 100 years, but environmental considerations may extend	The lesser of physical or economic life not to exceed 100 years, but environmental considerations may extend
Cost allocation	No provision	SCRB adapted to multiobjective plan formulation	Adapted SCRB limited to NED and EQ except when RD objective considered in plan formulation

TABLE 4—*Continued*

Item	SD 97	TF Recommendation	WRC Proposal
Cost sharing	No provision	Cost sharing to be reviewed in relation to multiobjectives Recommend 50–50 on water quality storage for EQ	Cost sharing to be reviewed in relation to multiobjectives Recommend 50–50 on water quality storage for EQ
Coverage	River basin planning Corps and Reclamation projects and Soil Conservation watersheds	Comprehensive plans All federal, federally assisted, and federally licensed water and land programs and projects	Comprehensive plans Federal water and land programs, including SCS watershed and RC&D projects
National program	No provision	Council to formulate a national program and long-range schedule of priorities for federal and federally assisted water and land activities	Council to formulate a national program and long-range schedule of priorities for federal and federally assisted water and land activities
Coordination	Provides for coordination of agency planning and for review of reports	Council to issue procedures Agency procedures to be reviewed by council for consistency Provides coordination for level A, B, and C planning	Council to issue procedures Agency procedures to be reviewed by council for consistency Provides coordination for level A, B, and C planning
Environmental impact statement	No provision	Preliminary reports of probable effects of the plan on the environmental and other objectives will be submitted to WRC and CEQ. Copies of final report to CEQ	Preliminary reports of probable effects of the plan on the environmental and other objectives will be submitted to WRC and CEQ. Copies of final reports to CEQ

PLAN FORMULATION

The council proposal provided that alternative plans be formulated to emphasize NED and EQ objectives, and when directed the RD objective. Plans would not be formulated to emphasize the SWB effects if this conflicted with the other objectives. For example, an increment of a plan could not be added for SWB effects if the addition of that increment resulted in reduction of net benefits to the NED objective.

BENEFIT-COST RESTRAINT

The council's proposal did not include an overall NED benefit-cost restraint. However, increments or segments of a plan included for the NED objective were required to have beneficial effects equal to or in excess of adverse effects on that objective. Judgments as to the desirability of a multiobjective plan would be made by comparing benefits and costs of all objectives.

PLANNING INTEREST RATE

The discount, or interest, rate to be used in planning was a major issue in the review of the task force recommendations. Consideration was given to several alternative concepts for determining the interest rate.

Social rate of time preference. This concept is based on the assumption that public investment decisions are concerned with time preferences not reflected in the private sector and that society as a whole is more concerned with provision for the future than citizens are individually. This concept also involves tests to assure that the public plan does not displace better private investment opportunities.

Opportunity cost. There are two major variations of this concept: (a) the opportunity cost of federal investment is based on average rate of return on displaced nonfederal investment and imputed time preference by considering interest rates involved in private borrowing-lending decisions for displaced consumption; or (b) the opportunity cost of federal investment is the real rate of return on nonfederal investments. Empirical estimates range from 7 to 13 percent, with the investment-consumption concept on the low side and the investment-only concept on the high side.

Cost of federal borrowing. This concept is based on the assumption that federal investment decisions are related to the cost of money to the government. Empirical estimates are usually derived by formula related to the long-term bond market being based either on the coupon rate, as in Senate Document 87–97, or the yield rate, as under the current Water Resources Council formula.

There is a large amount of literature on these concepts.[20] However, there is no agreement among economists as to which concept is most valid. Even in the Congress there are differences.[21] It is interesting that the discount rate was one issue that could not be settled by negotiation when Senate Document 97 was adopted in 1962.[22] When the change was made in 1968, the proposal for change was first announced in the president's budget message.

In its proposal published in the *Federal Register*, the council proposed using the opportunity cost of federal investment as measured by the real rate of return on private investment. This was estimated at 10 percent; the rate has been constant for several years. Recognizing both the objective of subsidizing water resource projects and the objective of an efficient combination among federal and nonfederal investment activities, the council advised that 7 percent be the planning rate for the next five years.

PERIOD OF ANALYSIS

The task force recommendation was not changed.

COST ALLOCATION

The task force had proposed an adaptation of the separable cost-remaining method of cost allocation. The council's proposal limited cost allocation to NED and EQ objectives except when the RD objective was to be considered in plan formulation.

COST SHARING

The council's proposal included the task force recommendation for 50–50 cost sharing on water quality storage for the EQ objective and for an overall review of cost-sharing policies.

ACTIVITIES COVERED

The council proposal included broad coverage for participation in comprehensive planning but restricted the coverage of federal program activities to direct federal water programs and the Department of Agriculture's small watershed and resource conservation programs.

NATIONAL PROGRAM

The council included the provision for formulation of a national program and long-range schedule of priorities for federal and federally assisted water and land activities.

20. See references 18, 19, 20, and 33.
21. See minority views (20).
22. See reference 33, p. 83.

COORDINATION

The council proposed to issue procedures for comprehensive planning and to review and coordinate agency procedures.

ENVIRONMENTAL IMPACT STATEMENT

The council proposed that, early in the planning process, preliminary reports should be made indicating the probable effects of the plan on environmental and other objectives. The proposed standards provided a means for considering environmental problems early in the decision-making process.

FINAL DEVELOPMENTS

In December 1971 the council tentatively adopted and published proposed principles and standards for widespread public review before final consideration and recommendations to the president. Many national, regional, state, and local organizations and individuals participated in this review process. Congress also expressed considerable interest. The widespread public information and participation in the preparation of the principles and standards was in marked contrast to earlier efforts such as Budget Bureau Circular A–47 and Senate Document 87–97, which were prepared and adopted without the benefit of any public discussion.

After consideration of the extensive public comments on the December 1971 draft, and consultation with concerned federal agencies, the council made its recommendations to the president. With presidential approval, revised principles and standards were published in the *Federal Register* on September 10, 1973, and became effective on October 25, 1973. Major changes occurred in the planning objectives and choice of the discount rate.

According to the final changes, planning is to be guided by the objectives of national economic development and environmental quality. Each objective will be given equal consideration in the conservation, development, and use of the nation's water and land resources. Beneficial and adverse effects on these two objectives will be measured and displayed for each alternative plan. Plans will be formulated considering the trade-offs between the two objectives.

In addition, an accounting of beneficial and adverse effects on regional development and social well-being will be displayed, where appropriate, for each alternative plan. However, in contrast to the task force recommendations, these two accounts will not be considered in formulating alternative plans; they will be a source of information in choosing among alternative plans.

In the discount-rate concept adopted by the council, the government's investment decisions are related to the cost of money to the government. The rate has been established at 6⅞ percent for the balance of fiscal year 1974 and will be changed annually by not more or less than ½ of 1 percent as determined by estimates provided by the Treasury Department. This is a major departure from the opportunity-cost concept proposed in the December 1971 draft; the formula may well produce higher rates over the next five years than the 7 percent rate proposed in 1971 for a five-year period.

Many other changes were made, some of which may later prove to be of major significance. The important problem now is how to implement them. The council has left to each agency head the troublesome question of the application of the new "Principles and Standards" (31) to the large backlog of plans which have been authorized by the Congress.

References

1. Apter, Robert L. *An Analysis of the Water Resources Council Principles and Standards for Evaluation of Water and Land Resource Projects.* Denver, Col.: Rocky Mountain Center on Environment, n.d.
2. "Atomic Energy," title 10, ch. 1, pt. 50. Implementation of National Environmental Policy Act of 1969. *Federal Register* 36, no. 175 (9 September 1971).
3. Bishop, A. Bruce; Oglesby, C. H.; and Willeke, Gene E. *Socio-Economic and Community Factors in Planning Urban Freeways.* Project on Engineering-Economic Planning, Stanford University, in cooperation with State of California Transportation Agency, Department of Public Works, Division of Highways, and U.S. Department of Transportation, Federal Highway Administration, September 1970.
4. Butcher, Walter R.; Rettig, Bruce; and Brown, Gardner M. *Proposed New Procedures for Evaluating Water and Land Resources: Some Comments from an Academic Viewpoint.* University of Washington and Washington State University. Pullman: State of Washington Water Research Center, June 1971.
5. Committee of University Social Scientists, under auspices of the Universities Council on Water Resources. "Proposed New Procedures for Evaluating Water and Land Resources: Some Comments from an Academic Viewpoint." Preface, draft of 22 March 1971.
6. Corrigan, Richard, and Clark, Timothy B. "Resources Report/Budget Office Agencies Struggle Over Standards for New Water Projects." *National Journal,* 6 February 1971.
7. *Criteria News,* issue 40 and subsequent issues. Washington, D.C.: National Waterways Conference, Inc.
8. Jackson, Henry M. Statement in support of S. 2612, *Congressional Record,* 5 October 1971.
9. Kalter, Robert J. "Multiple Objective Planning: Reflections on the Current Scene." Agricultural economics staff paper, no. 28. Ithaca, N.Y.: Cornell University, March 1971.
10. Kalter, Robert J.; Lord, William B.; Allee, David J.; Castle, Emery N.; Kelso,

Maurice M.; Bromley, Daniel W.; Smith, Stephen C.; Ciriacy-Wantrup, S. V.; and Weisbrod, Burton A. *Criteria for Federal Evaluation of Resource Investments.* Ithaca, N.Y.: Water Resources and Marine Sciences Center, Cornell University, August 1969.

11. Knetsch, Jack L.; Haveman, Robert H.; Howe, Charles W.; Krutilla, John V.; and Brewer, Michael F. *Federal Natural Resources Development: Basic Issues in Benefit and Cost Measurement.* Washington, D.C.: Natural Resources Policy Center, George Washington University, May 1969.
12. Maass, Arthur. "Public Investment Planning in the United States: Analysis and Critique." Reprinted from *Public Policy* 18, no. 2 (Winter 1970).
13. Randolph, Jennings. Statement introducing S. 2612, National Water and Related Land Resources Policy Act, *Congressional Record,* 29 September 1971.
14. U.S. Code Title 33, section 701a, Flood Control Act of 1936.
15. U.S. Congress. *Proposed Practices for Economic Analysis of River Basin Projects.* Report to the Inter-Agency Committee on Water Resources, prepared by the Subcommittee on Evaluation Standards. Issued May 1950, rev. May 1958. Washington, D.C.: Government Printing Office.
16. U.S. Congress. Senate. *Policies, Standards, and Procedures in the Formation, Evaluation, and Review of Plans for Use and Development of Water and Related Land Resources.* Prepared under the direction of the President's Water Resources Council. Senate Document 97, 87th Cong., 2d sess., May 1962. Washington, D.C.: Government Printing Office, 1962.
17. U.S. Congress. Public Law 89–90, 89th Cong., 1965.
18. U.S. Congress. *The Planning-Programming-Budgeting System: Progress and Potentials.* Hearings before the Subcommittee on Economy in Government of the Joint Economic Committee. 90th Cong., 2d sess., 14, 19, 20, and 21 September 1967. Washington, D.C.: Government Printing Office, 1967.
19. U.S. Congress. *Economic Analysis of Public Investment Decisions: Interest Rate Policy and Discounting Analysis.* Hearings before the Subcommittee on Economy in Government of the Joint Economic Committee. 90th Cong., 2d sess., 30–31 July and 1 August 1968. Washington, D.C.: Government Printing Office, 1968.
20. U.S. Congress. *Economic Analysis of Public Investment Decisions: Interest Rate Policy and Discounting Analysis.* Report of the Subcommittee on Economy in Government of the Joint Economic Committee. Joint Committee Print, 90th Cong., 2d sess. Washington, D.C.: Government Printing Office, 1968.
21. U.S. Congress. Senate. *Procedures for Evaluation of Water and Related Land Resource Projects.* Findings and recommendations of the Special Task Force of the U.S. Water Resources Council, with a foreword by Senator Jennings Randolph. Committee Print, serial no. 92–20, 92d Cong., 1st sess. Washington, D.C.: Government Printing Office, September 1971.
22. U.S. Department of Commerce. "Toward Development of a National-Regional Impact Evaluation System and the Upper Licking Area Pilot Study." Staff paper in economics and statistics, no. 18, March 1971.
23. U.S. Water Resources Council. "Procedures for Evaluation of Water and Related Land Resource Projects." Report by the Special Task Force. Washington, D.C., June 1969.
24. U.S. Water Resources Council. "Findings and Recommendations." Report by the Special Task Force. Washington, D.C., July 1970.
25. U.S. Water Resources Council. "Principles for Planning Water and Land Resources." Report by the Special Task Force. Washington, D.C., July 1970.
26. U.S. Water Resources Council. "Procedures for Evaluation of Water and Related Land Resource Projects." Summary and index of public response to the Special Task Force report. Washington, D.C., July 1970.
27. U.S. Water Resources Council. "Procedures for Evaluation of Water and Related Land Resource Projects." Summary of federal agency technical comments on the Special Task Force report. Washington, D.C., July 1970.

28. U.S. Water Resources Council. "Standards for Planning Water and Land Resources." Report by the Special Task Force. Washington, D.C., July 1970.
29. U.S. Water Resources Council. "A Summary Analysis of Nineteen Tests of Proposed Evaluation Procedures on Selected Water and Land Resource Projects." Washington, D.C., July 1970.
30. U.S. Water Resources Council. "Proposed Principles and Standards for Planning Water and Related Land Resources." *Federal Register* 36, no. 245, pt. 2 (21 December 1971), Washington, D.C.
31. U.S. Water Resources Council. "Principles and Standards for Planning Water and Related Land Resources." *Federal Register* 38, no. 174, pt. 3 (10 September 1973), Washington, D.C.
32. Universities Council on Water Resources. "Evaluation Processes in Water Resources Management and Development." Report of the Task Force on Water Resources Evaluation, sponsored by the Office of Water Resources Research, U.S. Department of the Interior, 1971.
33. Western Agricultural Economics Research Council, Committee on the Economics of Water Resources Development. "The Discount Rate in Public Investment Evaluation," pts. 1, 2. In *Water Resources and Economic Development of the West*. Conference proceedings, report no. 17. Denver, Colorado, 17–18 December 1968.

6
Information Requirements for Environmental Decision Making

William B. Lord

Americans these days are much concerned with where we are headed as a society. Our image of ourselves as a nation leading the world in the search for the good life has been shaken. The self-assurance which we developed over two centuries as we settled a virgin continent, attained an unprecedented level of material prosperity, and became the most powerful nation in the world has been shaken by racial strife, continued poverty, and environmental deterioration at home, and by our inability to export our values to other nations abroad. We are alarmed, confused, and sometimes resentful because so many of our young have rejected the goals which we have struggled so hard to attain.

Coupled with this new mood of self-examination is a growing awareness that our technology and our institutions have given us great power to affect the development of our society, a power which historically has been largely undirected but which need not be so. In particular, we now realize that the fifth of our productive capacity which is controlled directly by government can and does influence profoundly the ways we live. This realization has led to a quickening of interest in how our collective options can be revealed so that our future may be more a deliberate and rational choice than unanticipated circumstance.

There are many ramifications of this growing interest in the process of public choice. Perhaps the most obvious is the wholesale adoption, if not use, of program budgeting by the federal agencies. States and other units of government are rapidly following the federal lead. On a more limited scale, the U.S. Water Resources Council's attempt to develop a multiple objective planning approach in place of the traditional benefit-cost analysis represents a pioneering effort in the field of public expenditure evaluation.

In this paper I will discuss some of the problems which arise in attempting to illuminate the alternatives for public choice, with particular reference to the relationship between the processes by which such choices are made and the kinds of information which economists and other technical specialists might provide if better decisions are to be taken. I am indebted to my colleagues Daniel W. Bromley, Irving K. Fox, Robert J. Kalter, A. Allan Schmid, John R. Gordon, and Stephen C. Smith for many of the ideas herein, as well as for the stimulus behind the development of those which are properly mine.

The Decision Process

J. Willard Hurst has remarked, in his insightful book *Law and the Conditions of Freedom in the Nineteenth-Century United States,* that Americans are a pragmatic people, not much inclined to the development of general theory. Our policies are largely the result of the making of very practical decisions in very concrete contexts. We are suspicious of those who proclaim high-sounding abstract goals and then attempt to apply them in the solution of specific problems. Our national goals have been more expressions of the trend of decisions already made than the proclamation of new directions yet to be pursued.

As an example of our traditional process of "bottom up" decision making (the term was suggested by Stephen Smith), consider the way in which federal water resource projects originate. Normally, such projects begin at the local level. There are exceptions, of course, and frequently spectacular ones. The Bureau of Reclamation's Marble and Bridge Canyon dams grew out of a long-standing regional problem—financing the major system of engineering structures which were thought necessary to resolve conflicts over the use of the waters of the Colorado River. Nonetheless, the vast majority of federal water projects grow out of the interaction of a local water-related problem and a local office of one of the federal water agencies. The problem to be addressed is usually seen in a quite limited geographical context; for example, a specific community experiences a destructive flood, a particular taxing district feels that its tax base is too limited and seeks industrial development, a harbor is too small or too shallow to accommodate commercial vessels, or an irrigation district finds that its financial capabilities are inadequate to provide desired water supplies. At the same time, a federal water agency is seeking opportunities to "maintain the work load" or to expand its program. The federal water planners then attempt to design a project which will be responsive to the local need and which will be consistent with their agency's mission.

Projects which originate in this way produce ecological and socio-economic changes which are usually primarily local in their direct impacts. Broader interests may be affected, particularly as the indirect or nth round effects induced by the project are felt. But such effects are often quite diffuse in their incidence and of low intensity as far as most affected interests are concerned. Consequently, the project is seen as a matter of primarily local concern, and there is much truth in that view.

Once planned at the local level, and politically accepted there, the project proceeds upward through agency channels to the Washington level. In the process it must clear a series of hurdles as it undergoes technical, economic, political, and, most recently, environmental reviews. In some cases, opposition may form and be expressed politically as broader project impacts become apparent. If so, differences must be resolved, possibly through reformulation of the project plan. Often, however, no major opposition appears and the project finds its way into the agency's backlog of projects awaiting authorization and funding. How soon, if ever, it will be constructed depends on such matters as congressional committee work loads, federal budget constraints, local ability to meet cost-sharing requirements, and, most important, upon the political utility of the project in the complicated game of congressional, presidential, and interest-group bargaining and accommodation. But much of this utility derives from the basic ability of the project to solve the problem for which it was originally designed—that is, from its favorable local impacts, at least as seen by some locally powerful groups.

There is, of course, a measure of broad national interest in all such projects. This is partly due to the fact that almost all federal water projects rely heavily upon federal financing, no matter how circumscribed may be the incidence of their benefits; it is clearly a matter of national concern to ensure that taxpayers' funds are wisely spent (this is the rationale for the B/C ratio constraints). And, this national interest arises partly from the value such projects may have as currency in bargaining for major federal legislation. But the existence of this national interest in all federal water projects, and the even greater national interest in some projects—such as the Central and Southern Florida Flood Control Project, which alters a major national asset (Everglades National Park)—should not be allowed to obscure the fundamental role of such projects in meeting local needs and solving local problems.

"Bottom up" decision making, our heritage from English common law, has many virtues. It is well suited to the society which favors evolutionary over revolutionary change. It also has its vices. It is slow to respond, and narrow and myopic in its vision. By way of illustration, I return to the example of federal water resource development programs.

At the national level, the sum total of many small decisions which our society makes may produce results which carry great significance for the quality of our lives. Often such "system effects" go unrecognized, or at least are little considered in our decentralized and incremental group pluralist decision process. For example, continued reservoir development for hydropower production, flood control, navigation, water supply, and slack water recreation may seem quite justifiable when examined on a piecemeal project-by-project basis. The end result of such development, however, may be a profound change in our river systems which threatens the existence of some plant and animal species (indeed, entire ecological communities), forecloses opportunities for scientific and recreational use of wild rivers and wilderness areas, substantially halts the creation of fertile farmland through silt deposition, and destroys the possibility of recreational boating on white water or even fast-flowing streams.

Beyond this, the overall effect of a number of public works and other federal spending programs, incurred largely to satisfy local, special interest, and congressional desires, may well encumber a substantial portion of discretionary federal government spending capability, leaving inadequate funds for meeting truly national objectives. Taxpayers may revolt against higher taxes while state and local officials complain that the federal government has preempted the most productive taxing possibilities. Such viewpoints may be true, so far as they go, but they fail to recognize that much federal spending is incurred to meet local or regional desires—desires which may be of comparatively low priority if considered in the context of a full range of local objectives.

Water resource planners should provide information necessary to examine proposed water projects and programs in relation to other objects of both local public expenditures and federal expenditures. National trade-offs are no less important than local trade-offs, and adequate evaluation procedures should facilitate both. On the national level, it is crucial that water resource evaluation procedures provide information in terms of generally applicable national objectives which are appropriate to a wide range of federal programs. In short, the planning and evaluation procedures adopted should be fully consistent with, and indeed an integral part of, the government's planning-programming-budgeting system.

Government agencies at every level survive and grow because they are able to serve the needs of particular interest groups. These groups, in turn, provide the political support which an agency must have in order to obtain the legislation and funding upon which it depends. Our federal water agencies are primarily developmental in orientation and have formed close alliances with interest groups whose objectives are also developmental. Other agencies, with other orientations, are drawn into the federal water planning process through the review procedure. The prospect of a hostile review must always be considered by the planning agency. It deals with this possibility by coordinating with the reviewing agency at the local level and by making (usually) minor modifications in the project to meet the more serious objections of the reviewing agency and/or by including in the project some feature desirable to that agency (a new wildlife refuge or fish hatchery, for example).

"Top down" decision making finds great support in academic circles. Indeed, most of the normative literature on decision making would lead one to believe that it is the method most generally employed. Roughly speaking, this literature suggests that the process begins with the establishment of the broad goals of public policy, proceeds to the derivation of operationally defined objectives from the stated goals, turns next to the search for alternative means for attaining the objectives, and concludes with the evaluation of those means in terms of their cost-effectiveness for objective attainment. It is not always clear how the goals, with which the process begins, are established. Presumably they are to be found in the statements of legislative bodies or other elected officials. Once they are established, however, the rest of the process becomes a matter of technical analysis.

"Top down" decision making is an attractive process in many ways. It is attractive to the technical specialist because it defines a role for him which he understands well and which permits him to contribute importantly to the decision process without becoming enmeshed in all the complexity and ambiguity of the political job of making choices. It is attractive because it promises to produce policies which are comprehensive and internally consistent. It is attractive because it seems to offer hope for making federal programs more responsive to truly national goals and less dominated by the desires of local areas and special interests. Most of all, it is attractive because it offers a framework within which the powerful tools of systems analysis and the available reservoir of scientific knowledge can be brought to bear on problems of public policy.

Against these virtues of "top down" decision making must be set one great disadvantage—its potential for major errors in direction. All decisions are shaped by goals and objectives which have been previously established. Yet, it is these goals and objectives which are the most slender reeds of all. Neither the American electorate nor its elected representatives think in terms as general and abstract as these goals and objectives must be. Broad agreement can be found on such goals as individual freedom and security, for example, but only because such terms are not translated into specific rules about who may and may not act in particular ways. When so translated, consensus evaporates and the real work of the political process in hammering out livable compromises begins. To suggest that political decisions be confined to achieving agreement on goals and objectives so that technical specialists may then define and select alternative means is to misconceive the genius of the American political process. What matter how skilled the helmsman if the compass doesn't work?

How can we achieve some modification of our traditional "bottom up" decision process which will improve its vision without sacrificing its responsiveness? Approaching it another way, how can we employ the analytical techniques and approach of "top down" decision making in the context of a group pluralist political system instead of the hierarchical context with which it is more often identified? It would be presumptuous for an economist to attempt to answer such a question. But it may not be too presumptuous to explore the kinds of information which economists could supply to serve such a decision process well and even to suggest that the availability of such information may also help to hasten the evolution of the process itself.

The implications of this discussion for planning and evaluation are at least twofold. First, the planning process must address the local problems which give rise to it and must provide politically acceptable resolutions of those problems. Second, the planning process must also reveal the broader implications of alternatives in order that the various local and national consequences of federal programs may be revealed. Only if this is accomplished can the group processes of political bargaining and accommodation function effectively in discovering the public interest.

To return again to my earlier example, the bargaining context within which federal water resource decisions are made is presently inadequate in at least two respects. First, the range of interests participating at the local level is too limited and the distribution of bargaining power is weighted inordinately in favor of the development-oriented groups which comprise the traditional clientele of the water agencies. Second, the political system within which decisions are made, and especially the cost-sharing rules in force, militate against a local realization that all federally financed projects and programs are mutually competitive in the budgetary sense. Difficult choices must be faced among such dissimilar alternatives as dams, highways, and hospitals if local decision making is to be retained, as it probably should be, as the principal basis for projects and programs whose impacts are mostly local. To raise such decisions to the national level requires the involvement in each case of a vast majority of congressmen who have no essential interest in the outcome, hence encouraging the logrolling behavior which has been so widely criticized.

This is not to say that matters of national interest are not at stake in federal water resource programs and that no decision making should occur at the national level. I have already alluded to aspects of the national interest inherent in these programs. But the key in most cases is the program, not the individual project. Decision makers at the federal level should concern themselves far more with broad water resource programs and far less with specific water resource projects.

The information display which should emerge from the water resource planning process should achieve three results which are not now achieved. First, it should reveal fully both the positive and the negative impacts of proposed projects upon the full range of local interests likely to be affected substantially if the project is implemented. Second, it should reveal any important positive and/or negative impacts upon other localities. Third, it should facilitate a national consideration and comparison of entire programs, in terms which are meaningful in the light of truly national objectives.

An information display which adequately performs these functions will serve well an improved institutional context for water resources decision making. Also, and of greatest importance, is that it will help bring such an improved institutional context into being. If groups whose interests are not now adequately considered in the decision-making process are fully informed as to how they will be affected by these programs and projects, they will take steps to achieve a more effective voice in such decisions. Broader participation in decision making, if supported by a comprehensive information-gathering system, is likely to be more effective than technical constraints, such as the familiar benefit-cost ratio, imposed at the national level. But, concern at the national level also should be shifted to programs, so that the broad implications of entire systems of projects may be revealed and weighed at that level, the only place where they can be fruitfully considered.

A System of Accounts

Considerations such as the foregoing seem to my colleagues and me to argue persuasively for a system of accounts as the basic information display in evaluating alternatives for public choice. Neglecting for the moment the very important matter of how alternatives are formulated in the first place, it seems crucial that each alternative can be described in terms of its effects on the various groups and interests in our society. This notion is by no means new to students of public choice, although I wish to emphasize the display of effects in terms of the welfare of identifiable interest groups to a greater extent than has been done in the literature on, say, social indicators or regional accounting.

Difficult conceptual and empirical problems arise in determining which of the multitude of interest groups in our society should be selected for explicit information display. For any given alternative, the subset of such groups obviously must be a very small part of the set of all possible groups. This is a problem for political scientists and sociologists, but economists can contribute in some ways. Industry-oriented groups are often important, and the ready availability of national income and product data and other information, provided by the Standard Industrial Classification system, is a great empirical asset. Our interest in income redistribution, and particularly in the alleviation of poverty, suggests the possibility of displaying effects by personal income classes. Then, too, a very important aspect of many federal programs is their effect upon the location of economic activity. Surely project and program effects should be displayed by region or other locational classification. The relatively recent Office of Business Economics delineation of economic regions should be an invaluable contribution in this regard, although one might argue for river basins, congressional districts, or an alternative taxonomy on some grounds.

One crucial classification of project or program effects relates not to the incidence of effects, as just discussed, but to the type of effect. A basically tripartite classification seems appropriate in this respect, showing separately those effects which are measurable in commensurate units (usually dollars), those which are measurable but not in commensurate units, and those which cannot be quantified in any meaningful way and so must be described qualitatively. Daniel Bromley has suggested a further subdivision of the first of these categories into those effects which are directly market-valued and those which are assigned dollar values through shadow pricing, opportunity cost techniques, or administrative fiat when no market values are in fact available.

At this point, it may be helpful to provide an illustration of how an information display might look. Figures 1a, b, and c illustrate the necessary components of an information display in terms of impacts on industry groups, consumer groups, and income classes. Such an analysis would be made for the project region, the contiguous region, and the rest of the nation. I draw upon a recent study of the Water Resources

Industry group / Type of impact	Project farmers	Nonproject farmers	Agricultural suppliers	Agricultural processors	Recreation services	Business and industry	Consumers
Monetary, market-valued							
Monetary, nonmarket-valued							
Nonmonetary (a)							
Nonmonetary (b)							
Nonmonetary (c)							

FIGURE 1a. Project impacts by industry group.

Consumer group / Type of impact	Warm-water fishermen	Cold-water fishermen	Bird hunters	Big game hunters	Power boat users	White-water boaters	Hikers
Monetary, market-valued							
Monetary, nonmarket-valued							
Nonmonetary (a)							
Nonmonetary (b)							
Nonmonetary (c)							

FIGURE 1b. Project impacts by consumer group.

Type of impact \ Income class	0–$3,000	$3,000–$4,500	$4,500–$6,000	$6,000–$9,000	$9,000–$12,000	$12,000–$15,000	$15,000+
Monetary, market-valued							
Monetary, nonmarket-valued							
Nonmonetary (a)							
Nonmonetary (b)							
Nonmonetary (c)							

FIGURE 1c. Project impacts by income class.

Council's proposed evaluation procedures for this illustration, with the caveat that the specific categories of type and incidence of effects leaves room for much improvement.

For at least some kinds of effects, it may be useful to introduce a general zero-sum constraint, unless the planner can demonstrate convincingly that the game is non-zero-sum. Thus, we might require, as a general rule, that net dollar benefits to those regions and groups which are shown to gain if a particular alternative is adopted be offset by explicitly shown equivalent (in the aggregate) losses to other regions and groups, except for the net national gains to be expected. More concretely, regional development benefits could not exceed losses to other regions by more than the net national benefits in familiar benefit-cost terms.

A system-of-accounts approach to the evaluation of public choice, while posing many difficult conceptual and empirical problems, promises to be much more useful in the kind of decision-making system which exists in the real world than conventional benefit-cost analysis. One great sin of benefit-cost analysis (and of its theoretical basis, welfare economics) has been its propensity to destroy highly important information on the incidence of effects through excessive aggregation. In essence, the political problem has been assumed away, rather than addressed constructively.

I shall not deal with the many difficult and interesting scientific problems of determining what entries to place in the system of accounts. These are the problems of predicting the behavior of natural and social systems subject to the perturbations introduced by collective action. Most of us, along with our colleagues in many other disciplines, build our careers on developing such predictive models. It would be foolish to pretend that we have solved all of these problems, or that we are even close to solutions for many. But, further work along the system-of-accounts line may serve to reveal priorities for future efforts and thus make our work even more productive.

Plan Formulation

The system-of-accounts approach is well suited to the task of facilitating the evaluation of alternatives from many points of view. It is less well suited to the task of designing alternatives for such evaluation. The planner who has followed my argument thus far is likely to be highly skeptical of a proposal which increases both the information which he must collect and the potential for controversy over his recommended alternatives, while at the same time providing few guidelines to aid him in developing those recommendations. I cannot deny the increased burden which the information requirements of the system-of-accounts approach places upon the planning process, although I would point out, first, that the development of national predictive models such as that used by the Economic Research Service, U.S. Department of Agriculture, to predict shifts in agricultural production promises much in the way of more efficient analysis and better standardization; and second, that it may be quite rational to spend somewhat more money than we now do on planning before embarking upon such costly, irreversible, and debatable projects as we are now building in the field of water resources. I will return later to the issue of controversy in the decision process. At this point, I turn to the very real and legitimate need for more direction for the planner in his task of formulating alternatives. Such consideration raises once again the issue of goals and objectives and their role in the planning process.

I will begin with an examination of the basic distinction between ends and means and then consider the basic notion of a goal or objective as a tool in the problem-solving process. I will then examine specific goals and objectives relevant to federal water resource programs and attempt to place the recommendations of the Water Resources Council in perspective. Finally, I will offer suggestions for what I believe to be a more fruitful approach.

The Ends-Means Hierarchy

Much of the literature in decision making makes a sharp distinction between ends and means. In the planning-programming-budgeting literature, for example, the distinction is posed as one between ends, which are output-oriented, and means, which are input-oriented. Thus, the reduction of flood damages may be the end, or objective, of a particular water resource program, and the means to achieve that objective may be the construction of dams, levees, and channel improvements, and such nonstructural measures as flood warning, floodplain zoning, flood-proofing, and risk-related flood insurance. While this distinction between ends and means in this particular water resource program seems clear at first glance, second thoughts come quickly. On the one hand, it is clear that the reduction of flood damages is certainly not an ultimate end for government activity. It is hardly conceivable that we should wish to eliminate flood damages altogether, for to do so would doubtless involve a cost far greater than the benefits provided. It is also possible that we should want to provide flood protection to areas now sustaining no flood damages, if by so doing we could provide attractive sites for new industrial development in an area of low incomes and high unemployment, where lack of suitable development sites may appear to be a constraint upon such development. In other words, flood damage reduction is not desired for its own sake, but serves some higher end or ends. From this point of view, then, flood damage reduction is not an end, but a means toward human well-being, regional development, or other higher ends. Similarly, there are a variety of tasks to be performed in order to build a flood-control structure. One of these tasks is to acquire the land upon which the structure will be built. Acquiring that land is then a means toward achieving the end of completing the flood-control structure.

One of the implications of blurring the ends-means distinction is that ends can no longer be regarded as given and means as totally open to choice. What is an end in one particular context is merely one of the many alternative means in some broader context.

It should be possible, then, to postulate a whole hierarchy of ends-means relationships. At or near one end of such a hierarchy would be very broad and general statements of social ends, which we shall call *goals.* These broad national goals may be defined as general statements of the aims of public policy. They are widely accepted because they express fundamental and long-standing cultural values. Because of their generality, national goals are equally relevant to a wide range of public and private activities. They are the ultimate standards against which public policies and programs in water resources, as in all other areas, must be evaluated.

The breadth and generality of national goals renders them inadequate for the formulation of policies, programs, and projects. This task requires far more specific guidelines. Goals indicate the general direction in which public programs should move. They do not reveal what or how much to do.

In the long run, even national goals must be regarded as instrumental and subject to change. They are evolving manifestations of a particular culture. As that culture changes and adapts in response to changing conditions, its expressed goals must change as well, for these goals are basically only a means by which a society orders the behavior of its members and its institutions to insure its survival. Changing conditions will change the survival value of different behavior patterns and, in turn, the stated goals of economic growth and environmental quality in our society. Our affluence has made further rapid economic growth seem less crucial, particularly if it must come at the expense of environmental deterioration.

Objectives for formulating federal policies and programs may be defined as specific statements of what those policies and programs are meant to accomplish. They are limited in scope and, because of their specificity, are much less likely to command general agreement than are national goals. Objectives are instrumental in nature, which is to say that they are intellectual tools for use in the problem-solving process and are subject to frequent reevaluation in terms of their ability to serve higher ends. Objectives often appear to be, and often are, competitive with each other and somewhat controversial.

Objectives are established for particular policies or programs. They are expressed in terms of the direct outputs or proximate results of the operation of each policy or program, not in terms of ultimate effects. Whenever possible, objectives should be quantitatively stated, thus permitting an estimate of how much a specific action alternative will contribute toward attainment of each objective.

The results of a program or project may be defined as the direct effects of that program or project. As such, they are a subset of the larger set of total effects. Total effects, in turn, are all the differences which implementation of the program or project will make in the real world. Even as the results are only a part of total program or project effects, so objectives express only some of the results. Objectives arise because certain results are perceived to flow from certain actions (programs or projects) and these results are desirable in the eyes of at least some persons or groups. An objective thus expresses an intention to implement a particular program or project at a certain level in order to produce a specified level of some output or result.

When a program is so implemented, some of its other results may seem desirable to some interests, and new objectives may arise as a consequence. An example is reservoir recreation, which was originally an unintended side benefit resulting from flood control and irrigation programs. It has now become a full-fledged objective in its own right.

Objectives, then, are directly derived from program results or outputs, although they never express the full range of outputs actually produced, to say nothing of the even broader range of program effects. These effects must be studied and identified insofar as is practical, however; it is only by knowing these effects (such as that of water quality on industrial location decisions) that water programs and their objectives can be related to national goals.

Goals, objectives, and action alternatives lie on a continuum from generality to specificity—from end to mean. Dividing lines are largely arbitrary. All are tools for problem solving and are appropriately viewed as means in the context of a more general problem.

More concretely, a policy or a program is devised in an effort to resolve a particular perceived problem. One or more objectives are established on the basis of an analysis and definition of the problem. A variety of alternative means for the attainment of these objectives are then explored and those means which appear to be most effective are chosen and implemented. Finally, as the objectives approach or reach attainment, it can be seen whether the problem has been successfully resolved. If not, the process starts over, with a reanalysis of the problem and the establishment of new objectives (the old ones having been proved inappropriate). If the problem has been resolved, however, the objectives are validated and the entire experience becomes history. This history is then available as a source of analytical ideas and plausible objectives for use when another, more or less similar, problem arises.

The problem-solving approach outlined above is basically scientific in nature. It is somewhat more formalized and structured than much of the problem solving which actually occurs in our political system. Explicit objectives are not always established for federal policies and programs or, more commonly, the stated objectives of a policy or program are not the real objectives which guide it. And the real objectives of any policy or program are to a greater or lesser extent inconsistent with national goals, although this is difficult to determine because national goals themselves are so poorly articulated.

Water Resources Goals and Objectives

The Water Resources Council Task Force has suggested that four objectives should guide federal water planning and evaluation. These four objectives are national economic development, regional economic development, environmental quality, and the well-being of people. Each is quite obviously very general in nature and very broad in application. Each can apply to almost every activity of government, not merely to water resources. None would suggest that these broad general statements, which I would call goals, are irrelevant to the evaluation of public alternatives. On the contrary, they are extremely important, for everything which government does must be examined for its implications in each area. However, such an examination cannot be conducted solely by water resource planning agencies because such agencies are unable to consider the full range of alternatives available to the public in achieving these goals. This is not to say that water resource plans should not reveal the efficiency, regional development, and environmental quality implications of proposed projects and programs—it is essential that they do so; but it is to say that water resource plans cannot hope to justify recommended water resource developments on the basis of these very broad and general goals. The essence of planning to achieve a particular end is to examine all relevant means to the attainment of that end and select the most effective one. This cannot be done in water resource planning when the ends employed are so broad and general that alternatives for achieving them comprise only a tiny portion of the full range of relevant alternatives.

On this view, the four "objectives" for water resources planning advanced by the Water Resources Council are of very little use for water resource project formulation. They are useful for evaluating water resource projects and programs, but at a *much higher level* than that of the water resource agencies of the federal government. What is needed for effective planning is a set of objectives expressing the proximate results, or outputs, of water resource projects and programs, which will be useful in guiding planners in their search for what is better to build. In this respect, the traditional purposes of water resource project development seem more useful and more germane than do the new objectives.

In particular, it does not seem necessary or even possible for a water resource agency to formulate an environmental quality plan, or a plan for achieving regional development, or a plan for maximizing personal well-being, or even a plan for achieving national economic development. Given the limited range of constituencies, the professional specialization, and the narrowly defined missions of such agencies, it is scarcely possible that they could do so. It seems only realistic to suggest that agencies prepare plans to solve the kinds of problems which they are politically, legislatively, and technically equipped to solve and that the evaluation process reveal the additional effects which such plans might be expected to produce in other areas of concern. Organizations responsible for economic development, environmental resource management, and other types of planning can then use such information to determine how consistent the proposed water resource developments are with the plans which they prepare. Inconsistencies can be identified and remedied through adjustments in the plans of the several organizations.

This position carries with it the corollary that program and project objectives of a more specific, operational, and limited nature must be carefully defined early in the planning process. It is impossible to provide a complete list of such objectives because they will in part be unique to each problem situation and project. Among the examples which can be offered, however, are a stated number of acres to be brought under irrigation in a particular locality, improving a waterway to accommodate a stated type and volume of commerce, and reducing flood damages by a stated amount. If such objectives are clearly set forth, debate can center at one level on the most desirable way of attaining them and at another level on the desirability of pursuing them at all (although these questions are obviously interrelated).

Conflict Resolution

By now it should be clear that my view of the planning process is built upon the notion of group pluralism. The public interest, including statements of goals and objectives which express it, is discovered through the presentation of alternatives for action to the many divergent interests with a stake in the outcome. The planner's role is to formulate alternatives to solve a concrete problem as he sees it and to investigate and report upon the wider ramifications of those alternatives. A system-of-accounts approach is a useful format for such reporting. As the various interest groups react to the alternatives initially presented, the disagreements between them will emerge clearly. The most creative part of the planner's job is to take note of those disagreements and formulate new alternatives with the purpose of discovering one which will be acceptable to most of the contenders, as they work out their necessary compromises. Overt conflicts are brought into the open early in planning, and are resolved for the most part before the planning agency makes its final recommendations for action.

I believe that this process is an improvement upon present procedures, wherein planners are responsive only to a subset of affected interests and therefore make recommendations which turn out to be controversial as they are subsequently studied and reviewed. Too often the outcome may be inaction, or a project rammed through over major opposition, or a replay of the entire planning process. In either of the first two cases, the action or inaction which results is likely to fall well short of a public interest solution. In the latter case, the eventual outcome may be more satisfactory, but planning becomes inordinately expensive, time-consuming, and frustrating to the planners themselves. Surely it is time to experiment with alternatives to this system.

7
Assessing Environmental Impacts of Resource Development

William K. Johnson

Decisions involving development of our limited and valuable land and water resources are made on the basis of different types of information: economic, engineering, political, legal, institutional, environmental, and social. Because our country has, during the past 100 years or so, experienced an era of tremendous development, certain types of information are founded upon more trustworthy data and time-tested analytical techniques than others. Economic and engineering information is usually of this nature. Literally thousands of development projects of all kinds make up the data base and serve as cases for testing and refining various techniques. Likewise political, legal, and institutional information has a long history as a result of development. Congressional acts, judiciary decisions, and agency policies have been established which have a significant influence on development decisions. Environmental and social information, on the other hand, has not been available or used in the decision-making process to the extent these other types have. The data base is limited, and analytical techniques are in their infancy. Where data and techniques are available, they are often based on laboratory experiments and the step into the real world is often a giant one.

Increased public concern in recent years for greater consideration of environmental and social factors has caused the decision maker to become much more sensitive to this type of information. One of the most notable influences to date has been the passage of the National Environmental Policy Act of 1969 (NEPA). This act applies to every "major Federal action significantly affecting the quality of the human environment." Those "actions" affecting the environment require a detailed five-point statement by the responsible official (decision maker) covering the environmental impact of the proposed development. Preparation of such a statement requires development of considerable environmental information (here and in subsequent sections, "environment" is intended to mean the human environment which includes some social features), and the adequacy of this information to comply with the law is being challenged in the courts (4, 5). This challenge stems both from our increased awareness and concern and from our general lack of data and evaluation techniques. For the decision maker to have reliable environmental information, new methods, techniques, and tools must be developed.

Considerable work has been under way in recent years to improve our development and handling of environmental and social information. The U.S. Water Resources Council has proposed four general accounts to display information for decision makers on national economic development, environmental quality, regional development, and social well-being (23). The applicability of these accounts to real-world planning has been tested in several cases with mixed success (24). Others have suggested a matrix-type display for use in evaluation (9, 15, 22). These accounts, or matrices, offer a general framework for organizing and displaying information, but an assessment, either quantitative or qualitative, is necessary in order to develop the information to be displayed.

This paper discusses a method for systematically developing environmental information.[1] Termed an assessment methodology, it seeks to make an input into the decision-making process relevant to environmental information. Information may be presented through a system of accounts, matrices, or written summaries. When all types of information (economic, environmental, etc.) have been displayed, trade-offs and value judgments are made by the decision maker during evaluation. To illustrate the application of this methodology, a preliminary planning study has been selected which involves proposed development of both land and water resources.

An Assessment Methodology

In a previous paper (11), I have suggested a general methodology for assessment. Figure 1 shows the basic steps: identification, description,

1. All thoughts and opinions expressed in this paper are those of the author and do not necessarily reflect those of the U.S. Army Corps of Engineers.

assessment, presentation. Identification is essentially an inventory of developmental and environmental features associated with the proposed development. Developmental features would include dams, levees, channels, power plants, and transmission lines. Environmental features would include people, fish, wildlife, vegetation, land, and many others. Various ways have been suggested to identify these features systematically (7, 14, 15), but regardless of the method used, the objective of the identification step is to inventory those features which might have an impact on the environment and those features affected. This inventory would be prepared for all alternative plans, including the no-development alternative.

Following identification, the next step is to describe the two types of features in terms of their physical, chemical, biological, and other characteristics. What channel work would be done? What reservoir outlet works would be specified? What is the nature of land use? What fish and wildlife species might be affected? Many of these kinds of questions can be answered with available quantitative data—if not exactly, at least within a

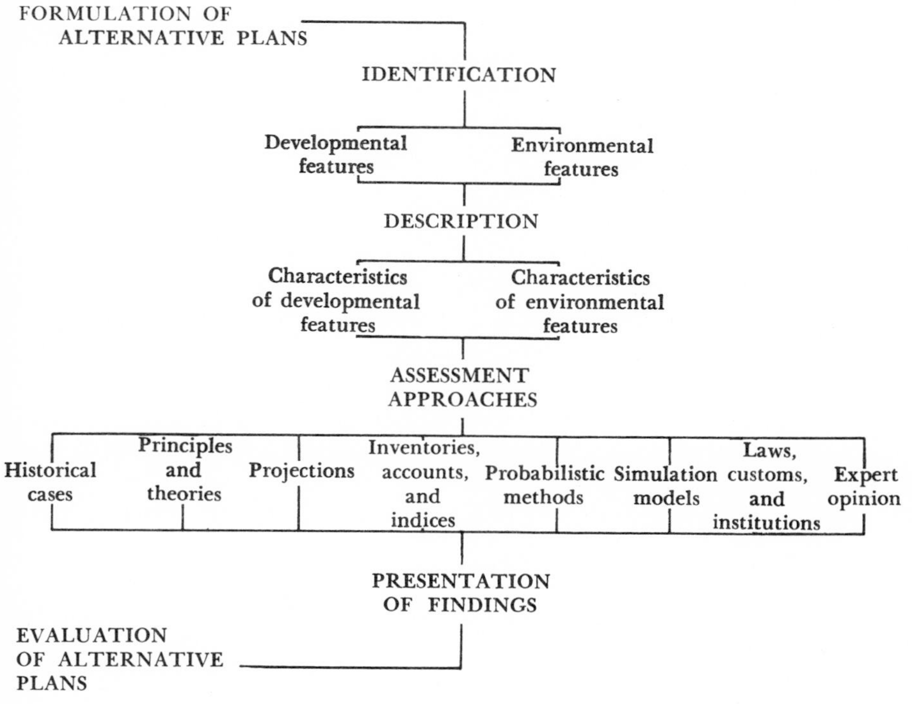

FIGURE 1. Assessment methodology.

range. For others, where quantitative data are not available, estimates must be made. In either case, the objective is to describe these features in as much detail as possible. This provides the foundation for the next step—the actual assessment.

Several approaches to assessment are shown in Figure 1. They illustrate a general classification of techniques useful in assessing impacts after the important features have been identified and their characteristics described. For an assessment of any particular feature, it is likely that several approaches would be utilized, depending on the nature of the development and environment, the range of feasible alternatives, and the availability of data, funding, manpower, and time. Collectively they form a basis for predicting different kinds of impacts.

Historical cases, whether they deal with the effect of water temperatures on specific species of fish in a particular stream or, more generally, with the social and environmental impact of water development in a river basin (10), provide a basis for predicting impacts where similar conditions exist. Generally, the greater the similarity between the historical case and the potential development, the greater the reliability of the assessment.

Principles and theories formulated in the natural and social sciences are also useful in assessment. Ecological theory, for example, can be helpful in defining interrelations and responses between elements of different types of ecosystems (3).

Projections are a widely used prediction technique today. Using data collected from available sources, projection models are constructed to make many different kinds of predictions. Often these models are quite specific and their range of applicability is limited. Others are more general and find application in a variety of problems (16).

Inventories, accounts, and indices of physiographic, biological, and anthropological features provide a systematic approach to analyzing and subsequently assessing environmental impacts. Examples of the kinds of environmental features that might be considered and various analysis methods are discussed by Steinitz (16). These methods utilize tabular, graphical, and computer techniques.

Probabilistic methods are those methods of analysis which assign quantitative values to the probability of an event occurring or not occurring. For example, the computation of the number of times a flood would exceed a certain magnitude would be considered a probabilistic method. Mathematical models which utilize probabilities of various elements are another example. Given the probability of several independent events, probability theory allows us to compute the combined probabilities. Unfortunately, in resource development the events are often interdependent, making the application of this approach difficult. Research currently under way in the areas of decision theory, probabilistic models, and operations research is directed toward making these methods more readily applicable to real-world problems.

Simulation models are especially useful in assessment, because they seek to answer the "what if" question. They may be mathematical, analog, physical, pictorial, or a combination of these. Hydrologic simulation (17) provides data relevant to the water balance in a system and the effects that various types of resource development have on this balance. These data are then useful in predicting impacts on fish, wildlife, vegetation, and land. Other models are available to simulate such things as water quality, outdoor recreation supply and demand, and future urbanization.

Laws, customs, and institutions are important and useful tools in assessment because they form boundaries and paths for resource development. In some cases, the definitive nature of existing laws provides a basis for predicting probable future conditions. In other cases, legal, social, and institutional criteria are undergoing such rapid change that it becomes difficult to anticipate how these new conditions might affect the development's impact. As environmental law develops and matures, it could become a major tool for defining the boundaries of assessment. Likewise, congressional action directed toward reorganization of federal agencies and definition of their responsibilities helps to define environmental impact.

Expert opinion provides an integrative means for utilizing many approaches and a variety of data. Through the expertise of individuals or the collective knowledge of a panel, assessments can be made which represent the familiar "best judgment."

Application to the Morrison Creek Stream Group

To illustrate the application of this assessment methodology to an actual resource development plan, the Morrison Creek Stream Group near Sacramento, California, was selected. Preliminary planning studies for the area have been made by Sacramento County, a local engineering firm, and the U.S. Army Corps of Engineers. The Corps' study began in 1964 and was directed toward determining the advisability of providing improvements for flood control and other related purposes. It is not the purpose of this paper to discuss or evaluate these studies, but rather to simply use the natural features of the basin and a proposed development plan to illustrate the assessment application. Three major aspects—the natural features, a development plan, and the assessment methodology—comprise the illustration.

NATURAL FEATURES—MORRISON CREEK BASIN

The natural features of the Morrison Creek Basin are described in the Corps of Engineers' environmental statement (18) as follows:

> Morrison Creek Stream Group Basin lies in the inland Central Valley of California, in Sacramento County [Figure 2] and encompasses the southern part of the city of Sacramento, two military establishments, several small towns, and extensive subdivision and commercial development in the county area outside the city limits. The basin covers 192 square miles and is drained by a network of poorly defined small streams of low gradient. Elevations range from 300 feet above mean sea level in the eastern part of the basin, in the foothills of the Sierra Nevada, to below sea level in the downstream part of the basin. The basin has a semi-arid, two-season climate with dry, hot summers and heavy rainfall in the cool winter months. All winter drainage from the basin flows through the Beach-Stone Lakes area and connecting channels, which discharge into downstream tidal delta channels and are subject to tidal influence, thus having a dependable year-round source of fresh water.
>
> Lands in the basin are generally of marginal quality, and agricultural use is primarily limited to irrigated and nonirrigated pasture. The Sacramento metropolitan area is one of the most rapidly growing urban areas in the nation, and the basin is in rapid transition from agricultural to urban use.
>
> The quality of the natural landscape of the upper basin cannot be considered to be of outstanding merit. In the lower basin (Beach-Stone Lakes area), however, the permanent fresh-water lakes and connecting channels have luxuriant riparian vegetation and represent a scenic and environmental resource of great importance to the people of the area. Much of the area floods annually and, therefore, has remained in agricultural use. It contains remnants of diversified and interrelated water, marsh, and grassland wildlife habitat which was once typical of the California Central Valley, but which has become increasingly meager as the valley has been intensively developed for agricultural and urban uses.
>
> The pattern of annual flooding in the Beach-Stone Lakes area has prevented incursion of adjacent urban development into the area, and the variety of wildlife is unusually large considering the proximity of the highly developed metropolitan area. North Stone Lake and South Stone Lake each have a permanent surface area of approximately 500 acres during dry summer months, and both lakes support a good warm-water population of catfish, black bass, and other species. Upstream channels cannot support a significant permanent fishery because of their intermittent nature.

A DEVELOPMENT PLAN

Plans for development of Morrison Creek Basin are directed toward controlling flooding in the basin, improving outdoor recreational opportunities, and preserving the wildlife habitat. Alternative plans, both structural and nonstructural (floodplain zoning), were an essential part of

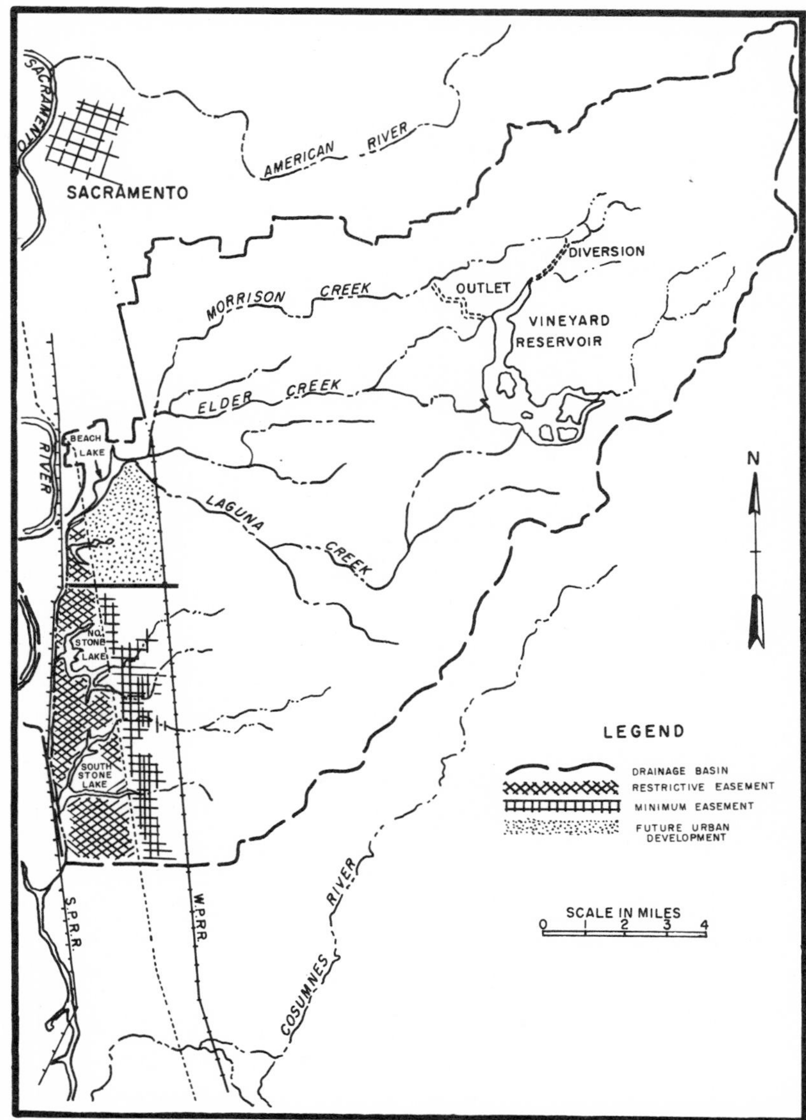

FIGURE 2. Morrison Creek Stream Group.

preliminary planning for the area, but for purposes of this analysis only a proposed plan is discussed to illustrate the application of the assessment methodology.

In the upper basin (east of the Western Pacific Railroad), three structural features are proposed: Vineyard Reservoir for storage of flood flows from the upstream drainage areas of tributary streams; a diversion structure and appurtenances for diverting Morrison Creek flows to Vineyard Reservoir; and levee and channel improvement on the streams downstream of the reservoir.

In the lower basin three structural features are proposed: a leveed floodway to the Beach Lake area to convey flows from the upper basin to the lower basin; a pumping plant to pump drainage into the floodway from the local area east of Beach Lake; and a 7,800-acre flood retardation basin in the Beach-Stone Lakes area for temporary detention of flood flows, preservation of wildlife habitat and environmental aesthetics, and public recreation.

In addition to major structural features, recreational facilities in the form of picnic sites, trails, boat ramps, and swimming beaches would be provided in both the Vineyard Reservoir and the Beach-Stone Lakes areas.

IDENTIFICATION

Developmental features are readily identified from the plan description above. Environmental features affected by the proposed plan are not so easily identified, but they may be compiled from a checklist of environmental features, knowledge of the basin, and experience in water resource development. Environmental features are summarized in the following section.

DESCRIPTION

Pertinent characteristics of the development features are described in Table 1. These are only a small part of the total data available on the dam, spillways, channels, levees, pumping station, etc.

Information describing physiographic, biological, and anthropological features is presented below. Most of this information was obtained from the review report (19), which not only contains data collected by the planning agency but also includes information furnished by other federal and state agencies. Several important considerations, such as development effects on features outside the basin and effects of future urbanization on surface water quantity and quality, were included in the report but are not discussed here.

Physiographic features. (a) Land use. The basin includes the southern part of the city of Sacramento and adjacent suburban development.

TABLE 1
Description of Development Features

Vineyard Reservoir

	Elder Creek Pool		Laguna Creek Pool
Storage (acre-feet)		11,000	
Maximum pool		11,000	
Minimum pool	1,000		1,000
Average recreation pool on June 1[a]	3,600		1,200
Surface area (acres)			
Maximum pool		1,600	
Minimum pool	180		280
Average recreation pool on June 1[a]	500		360
Depth (feet)			
Maximum	16		10
Minimum	a		a
Average on June 1[a]	13		6
Outflow capacity (cfs)			
Morrison Creek		500	
Elder Creek		300	
Laguna Creek		1,000	

Levee and Channel Improvements

	New levees (miles)	Channel improvement (miles)	Project design flow	
			cfs	Location
Morrison Creek	3.7	13.2	6,700	WPRR
Morrison Creek Diversion Channel	0	1.6	3,150	Diversion
Morrison Creek Outlet Channel	0	2.1	500	Dam
Elder Creek	2.1	7.9	2,300	Jct. Morrison Cr.
Florin Creek	2.3	2.2	780	Jct. Elder Cr.
Gerber Creek	0	3.6	730	Jct. Elder Cr.
Unionhouse Creek	4.0	6.6	1,690	WPRR
Strawberry Creek	0	3.0	750	Jct. Unionhouse Cr.
Laguna Creek	7.0	13.1	4,250	Mouth
South Laguna Creek	0	5.3	920	Jct. Laguna Cr.
Laguna Tributary No. 1	0	4.2	980	Jct. Laguna Cr.
Beach Lake Floodway	6.7	3.5	12,700	Jct. Morrison and Laguna Creeks

Beach-Stone Lakes Flood Retardation Basin

Basin	
Area purchased in fee	7,800 acres
Area of minimum easements	3,200 acres
Gross storage (elevation 13.0)	
Confined between WPRR and Interstate Highway 5	59,000 acre-feet
With backwater east of Interstate Highway 5 south of Elliott Ranch Road	66,000 acre-feet
Drainage pumping plant capacity	650 cfs

Continued

TABLE 1—*Continued*

Recreational Facilities	
Vineyard Reservoir	
Initial project	
Picnic sites	85
Boat launching ramps	1,000 square yards
Swimming beach	200′ x 120′
Trails	5 miles
Future additions	
Picnic sites	40
Boat launching ramps	400 square yards
Swimming beach	200′ x 50′
Steam channels	16.1
Beach-Stone Lakes Flood Retardation Basin	
Initial project	
Picnic/group sites	50
Trails	10 miles
Future additions	
Trails	10 miles

a. Evaporation is estimated to lower pools about 2 feet between June and September.

Lands in the basin are primarily irrigated and nonirrigated pasture, although the basin is in rapid transition from agricultural to urban use. Land in the basin is generally of marginal agricultural quality, while land in the lower basin has freshwater lakes and riparian vegetation of considerable resource value. Frequent flooding of the lower basin has kept this land in agricultural use. A sanitary landfill exists adjacent to the proposed Vineyard Reservoir. Information on land ownership, acreage under different uses, flood-prone areas, and lake areas is available.

(b) Surface water quantity and quality. Hydrologic data such as air and water temperature, precipitation, flood records, flood frequencies, soil infiltration rates, standard project floods, channel capacities, flow velocities, overbank areas, etc., are available to describe the hydrology of the basin. Stream water quality is expected to be similar to that of two nearby rivers, the American and the Cosumnes (19). Water quality data available include pH, turbidity, dissolved oxygen, total dissolved solids, and various chemical constituents. Agricultural land is expected to be a plentiful source of nutrients entering the streams from surface runoff.

(c) Groundwater quantity and quality. Wells for both domestic and industrial use have been drilled in the area as sources of water. There has been a report of poor taste and odor, and the sanitary landfill is suspect. Soils in the area are relatively impervious and percolation is slow.

Biological features. (a) Aquatic life. A good warm-water fishery exists in the Beach-Stone Lakes area and Snodgrass Slough (southeast of South Stone Lake). This fishery includes largemouth bass, bluegills, warmouth, white catfish, brown bullheads, and striped bass. Some information describing food sources, nutrient requirements, and temperature effects is available for these species. A warm-water fish hatchery is located adjacent to Laguna Creek near Elk Grove. Tributary streams are naturally intermittent, and fisheries in these streams are negligible. It is expected that the proposed Vineyard Reservoir will support several species of warm-water fish.

(b) Wildlife. Upland game animals in the area include California quail, ringnecked pheasants, mourning doves, cottontails, and black-tailed jackrabbits. Fur animals present in limited numbers include muskrats, weasels, minks, raccoons, skunks, beavers, gray foxes, and coyotes. Large numbers of migratory waterfowl winter in the Beach-Stone Lakes and Snodgrass Slough areas. Major species of waterfowl using the area are snow, Canada, and white-fronted geese and mallard, teal, American widgeon, wood, and pintail ducks. Snodgrass Slough has two unique features: it contains one of the largest populations of river otters in Sacramento Valley and provides some of the last remaining tule marsh habitat once typical of the Sacramento-San Joaquin Delta. Riparian vegetation provides habitat for over 150 wildlife species. Some information is available on food-source requirements of the game and waterfowl in the area.

(c) Plant life. In the upper basin above Beach Lake, vegetation is largely grasses on the generally flat terrain, and riparian plant species near the small streams and farm ponds. In the lower basin, the interrelated water and marsh resources provide a higher-quality landscape which supports the rich diversity of wildlife and fisheries. Limited data are available on factors influencing the nutritional value of vegetation.

Anthropological features. (a) Land use. In the vicinity of Vineyard Reservoir, the development plan will change land use from rural-agricultural to recreational- and water-oriented use. About 400 acres would be acquired for recreation in the vicinity of Elder and Laguna creeks. Land in the reservoir vicinity is privately owned and therefore could be developed in many different ways. Reducing flood danger by levee and channel work between Vineyard Reservoir and Beach Lake will allow a better-planned and higher-grade area and to some extent more rapid development, especially around Beach Lake. Below the Beach Lake Floodway 7,800 acres of agricultural land would be acquired in fee for a flood retardation basin, and a minimum-type flowage easement would be acquired for 3,200 acres of adjacent land to be inundated under standard project flood conditions. This minimum easement would not prohibit future private reclamation of these lands. While the acquisition in fee and minimum easement would not immediately change the natural state of the land, use by man would do so, and thus the anthropological nature of the change. Two quite different uses emerge: open space and urbanization—open space near the reservoir and in the flood retardation basin, and urbanization that will follow reductions in frequency of flooding, between the retardation basin and Vineyard Reservoir.

(b) Recreational and visual quality. The Beach-Stone Lakes area is highly regarded for its recreational and visual quality. Even so, its use is limited to a few nature study groups and sportsmen because of restricted access to private property. Most public use is either along public roads and railroads bordering the area or by trespass. Also, the area is undeveloped for recreational use. The remaining area in the basin is agricultural land which supports a limited hunting interest.

(c) Historical and archaeological features. Historic and archaeological sites are present in the study area. Several main routes to the gold fields in the mother lode and a number of known archaeological sites are among the potentially significant features.

ASSESSMENT

Land use—physiographic impact. Inundation of 1,600 acres at Vineyard Reservoir and changes in land use brought about by flood reduction and fee and easement purchases are three significant physiographic impacts. Assessment of the land inundated is rather obvious, as are all other direct changes in the natural landscape caused by the structural development features. Land-use changes are more difficult to project and assess. Urbanization will take place whether the development is built or not. Rational design and population estimates by urban planners provide the techniques to project the extent and nature of urbanization. To assess the impact of flood reduction, the same rational design techniques together with historical cases are necessary. By looking at cases where flooding has been reduced in other areas, we can compare, analyze, and assess the urbanization pattern in the Morrison Creek Basin. Similarly, historical cases near Vineyard Reservoir enable the planner to study how land use changes when a reservoir is constructed near an urban area. This type of reservoir is a familiar feature near urban areas in California.

In the vicinity of the Beach-Stone Lakes area, legal and institutional policy is particularly applicable, since some 7,800 acres are proposed to be taken in fee and another 3,200 acres as minimum easement. Using the projected urbanization for the area as a base, this base could be modified—first, to account for recreational potential and second, to consider the legal and institutional effects of the fee and easement acreages. Legal and institutional considerations would include constraints on the ownership, development, maintenance, and use of the land.

Surface water quantity and quality. Vineyard Reservoir and the

Morrison Creek Diversion would alter the hydrology of the area by storing, diverting, and evaporating runoff. Of particular interest are the capacity of Vineyard Reservoir to control floods in the wet season and provide for recreation in the dry season, the quantity of water released to the downstream channels, and the quantity of water available to the Beach-Stone Lakes area. Models are available to simulate the operation of the reservoir and downstream stream system (17). Input data include the natural, or preproject, hydrology and the physical characteristics of the development features. The output indicates the hydrologic modifications that will result from the development features. Urbanization can be considered by modifying runoff data. The average values shown in Table 1 were computed by a rough simulation procedure using hand computation.

Simulation models are also available for representing water quality parameters, e.g., sediment, biological oxygen demand (BOD), dissolved oxygen, thermal energy, and chloride concentration, in reservoir and stream systems (20, 21).

To assess reservoir water quality, basic principles of limnology are useful. While many factors contribute to lake eutrophication, research indicates that three of the most important are water temperature, nutrient content, and mean depth (2). Water temperature has a controlling influence over life in water. Warmer water temperatures stimulate greater biological activity. Nutrients, particularly nitrogen and phosphorus, contribute to aquatic growth. Finally, shallow reservoir depths increase the opportunity for algal concentrations.

At Vineyard Reservoir, the available description indicates that water temperatures will be high during the summer, nutrient levels at the reservoir site appear to be more than sufficient for eutrophication, and average reservoir depth is expected to be about thirteen feet in Elder Creek Pool and six feet in Laguna Creek Pool on June 1, with an estimated two-foot loss due to evaporation between June and September. In addition, there will be no outflow or inflow during the summer season. Each of these conditions is conducive to eutrophication.

A second approach to assessing the potential for aquatic growth is to review case histories of similar reservoirs. One such development is fifteen miles west of Vineyard Reservoir, the Putah Creek recreational area, which has been plagued with algal bloom for several years. Although the water surface area is much smaller, other conditions are about the same: a warm climate and water temperature, a rich nutrient supply from agricultural land and range animals, and shallow depth (about four feet). The problems encountered at Putah Creek have been studied extensively at the University of California in Davis, and the information resulting from these studies is available for assessment.

The potential leaching from the sanitary landfill near the reservoir must also be considered. This is a special problem which does not lend itself clearly to either case histories or principles and theories, although they would be involved. Expert opinion (soils specialist, water quality specialist) is possibly the most feasible approach for determining any impact the landfill might have and what structural or nonstructural measures might be used to minimize this impact.

Groundwater quantity and quality. Any effects on groundwater from the planned development are likely to be associated with Vineyard Reservoir. One potential problem is leaching from the sanitary landfill, which appears already to be causing poor groundwater quality. With additional geologic information on the size, location, and depth of the aquifer, expert opinion (groundwater geologist) could probably assess the potential impact.

Aquatic life. Water conditions at Vineyard Reservoir are such that it could support a good warm-water fishery. An assessment of specific numbers and rate of growth would require expert opinion (aquatic biologist) based on information derived from similar warm-water reservoirs. It could also support populations of mosquitoes and other aquatic insects whose impact could best be assessed by expert opinion.

In the Beach-Stone Lakes area the aquatic life already present could be affected by changes in water supply and water quality. More specifically, such parameters as food source, water quantity, water temperature, sediment load, dissolved oxygen, and toxic load could affect the fishery and other aquatic life. Due to the specialized nature of the problem, expert opinion (aquatic biologist, aquatic ecologist) would be required.

Wildlife. An assessment of the impact on wildlife is tied directly to the impact on land use. One reason wildlife is plentiful in the Beach-Stone Lakes area today, even though it is near an urban area, is that frequent flooding has prevented urbanization. Development to prevent flooding would allow more rapid urbanization, which would in turn reduce or possibly eliminate wildlife.

A more immediate impact would result from inundation of 1,600 acres at Vineyard Reservoir and preservation of 7,800 acres in the Beach-Stone Lakes area. Wildlife within the proposed Vineyard Reservoir area is presently minimal, and with proper control and vegetative plantings, an equal population could be established with the reservoir. In Beach-Stone Lakes the acreage taken in fee would protect the present wildlife population unless the area were extensively developed for recreation.

An assessment of specific numbers of species affected could best be made through an inventory and expert opinion (zoologist).

Plant life. Plant life, like wildlife, would be most directly affected by land use; and the two are, of course, tied together because plant life is necessary to support wildlife. Vegetation in the upper basin is not considered of particularly high quality, so it is likely that plantings associated with project development could maintain or even improve present conditions. The lower basin has luxuriant riparian vegetation characteristic of the habitat that once covered much of the California Central Valley, and it has almost completely disappeared in the face of intensive agricultural and urban development. The Beach-Stone Lakes area is the only large remaining area in California exemplifying this ecosystem, and 7,800 acres for the retardation basin would maintain this flora and fauna. As in the case of wildlife, an inventory of specific species together with expert opinion (botanist) could best assess the specific impact.

Land use—anthropological impact. Important here are such factors as the ratio of urban space to open space, availability of recreational land, and the nature of the urbanization, i.e., residential, industrial, commercial. To assess the nature of urbanization—knowing generally the lands which may be expected to be urbanized—requires a look at the history of development in the area and in other areas and at laws, institutions, and customs, i.e., the County General Plan, zoning ordinances, ability to change zoning ordinances, and lastly, land-use simulation models (6, 8, 12).

Recreational and visual quality. The primary recreation features are Vineyard Reservoir and the 7,800 acres purchased in fee for the Beach-Stone Lakes Flood Retardation Basin. Where recreational features similar to these have been provided near other urban areas, it would be useful to know the extent to which such features are used and the nature of the recreational experience. Projections of recreational use are available from various state and federal studies. Inventories (16) could be an effective way to determine both the quantity and quality of recreational opportunity. They could then be compared with an inventory of existing recreational features.

Expert opinion (recreation planner) would be particularly useful for an assessment at Vineyard Reservoir because an assessment of water quality would indicate whether eutrophication is possible. The question is: how would this affect the recreational experience? This is difficult to answer because of the many variables that enter into the evaluation of reservoir recreation (25). Water quality may affect some uses, but not others; or it may affect all uses. While historical information and projections form a general information base, this base should be modified to consider the specifics of Vineyard Reservoir, primarily the water quality.

Finally, the recreational assessment should consider legal and institutional factors. At both Vineyard Reservoir and the retardation basin, the recreational experience would be enhanced by development of picnic sites, boat ramps, beach, trails, etc. However, the question of who will provide these facilities, and when, becomes important. Sacramento County, the state of California, and the Corps of Engineers all have an interest, but are limited in the extent of their participation by financial and institutional constraints. For example, the Federal Water Project Recreation Act (PL 89–72) and the chief of engineers' policy (ER 1165–2–4) discuss this type of recreation development and the extent of federal and local contributions.

An assessment of visual quality in the Morrison Creek Basin should include all development features: reservoir, channels, pumping station, floodway, and retardation basin. This impact may be assessed in several ways. Probably the most systematic and objective approach is the use of indices similar to those discussed by Steinitz et al. (16).

Historical and archaeological features. Identifying and describing historical and archaeological features may be the most difficult steps in assessments of this type. Once they are identified, steps can be taken to preserve their value. Only where a proposed development would destroy them would there be an apparent conflict. Thus, the impact is likely to be quite obvious.

Conclusion

The proposed Morrison Creek Stream Group development illustrates both the applicability of an assessment methodology for developing environmental information and the associated difficulties. Predicting the future is always difficult, and it is even more so when dealing with impacts of complex resource development features. Yet, environmental information is an important and necessary input in the decision-making process, and every attempt should be made to develop reliable information for this purpose. The methodology presented here is a process by which the planner can generate this information. There is no assurance that better information will always be developed using this methodology, as opposed to a less systematic and more informal approach; but it is believed that through this methodology the planner is more likely to develop more complete and relevant information for use in decision making.

References

1. Baldwin, Malcolm F. "The Environmental Impact Statement of the National Environmental Policy Act: Criticisms of Agency Performance and Recommendations for Reform." Speech given at the Stanford University School of Law for the Law Forum and the Environmental Law Society, Stanford, Calif., 9 December 1970.
2. California Water Quality Control Board. "Eutrophication—A Review." Publication No. 34, 1967.
3. Cooper, Charles F., and Jolly, William C. "Ecological Effects of Weather Modification: A Problem Analysis." School of Natural Resources, University of Michigan, Ann Arbor, May 1969.
4. Environmental Defense Fund, Inc., et al. v. Corps of Engineers, et al. (Gillham Dam Project). U.S. District Court, Eastern District of Arkansas, filed 19 February 1971.
5. Environmental Defense Fund, Inc., et al. v. Corps of Engineers, et al. (Tennessee-Tombigbee Waterway). U.S. District Court, District of Columbia, filed 21 September 1971.
6. Goldberg, Victor. "Land Use Conflict and Public Policy." Working Paper Series No. 5, Department of Economics, University of California, Davis, October 1970.
7. Hagan, Robert M. "Ecological Impacts of Water Projects in California." ASCE Irrigation and Drainage Specialty Conference, Miami, Fla., 4–6 November 1970. Draft copy.
8. Highway Research Board. "Urban Development Models." Special Report 97, Washington, D.C., 1968.
9. Hill, Morris. "A Goals Achievement Matrix for Evaluating Alternative Plans." *Journal of the American Institute of Planners*, January 1968.
10. Hogg, Thomas C., and Smith, Courtland L. "Socio-Cultural Impacts of Water Resources Development in the Santiam River Basin." Water Resources Research Institute, Oregon State University, Corvallis, October 1970.
11. Johnson, William K. "Assessing Social Consequences of Water Deficiencies." ASCE Irrigation and Drainage Specialty Conference, Miami, Fla., 4–6 November 1970.
12. Kaiser, Edward J., et al. "Predicting the Behavior of Predevelopment Landowners on the Urban Fringe." *American Institute of Planners Journal*, September 1968.
13. Luce, Charles F. "The Need for Alternatives in Water Resource Planning." ASCE Water Resources Conference, Phoenix, Ariz., 11 January 1971.
14. McHarg, Ian. *Design with Nature*. New York: Natural History Press (Doubleday and Company), 1969.
15. National Water Commission. Annual Report for 1969 of the Panel on Ecology and the Environment, p. 62.
16. Steinitz, Carl, et al. "A Comparative Study of Resource Analysis Methods." Department of Landscape Architecture Research Office, Harvard University, Cambridge, Mass., August 1969.
17. U.S. Army Engineer District, Sacramento. "Analysis of Recreational Use of Selected Reservoirs in California." Contract Report 1, July 1969.
18. U.S. Army Engineer District, Sacramento. "Environmental Statement—Morrison Creek Stream Group." September 1970.
19. U.S. Army Engineer District, Sacramento. "Review Report for Flood Control on Morrison Creek Stream Group, California." Vols. 1–3. April 1970, rev. August 1970.
20. U.S. Army Engineers. Sediment Transport Computer Program (preliminary). Hydrologic Engineering Center, January 1971.
21. U.S. Army Engineers. Computer Program HEC 3, Reservoir System Analysis. Hydrologic Engineering Center, February 1971.

22. U.S. Geological Survey. "A Procedure for Evaluating Environmental Impacts." Circular 645, Washington, D.C., 1971.
23. U.S. Water Resources Council. "Standards for Planning Water and Land Resources." Washington, D.C., July 1970.
24. U.S. Water Resources Council. "A Summary Analysis of Nineteen Tests of Proposed Evaluation Procedures on Selected Water and Land Resource Projects." Washington, D.C., July 1970.
25. Water Resource Engineers, Inc. "Prediction of Thermal Energy Distribution in Streams and Reservoirs." Prepared for the Department of Fish and Game, State of California, 30 August 1968.

Law as a Choice Mechanism for Environmental Quality

In the first paper in this section, Donald Levi and Dale Colyer outline some of the current legal remedies available for use against polluters, and review some of the newer but untested theories suggested to aid the concerned citizen. Current legal remedies are based on common law and statutory law. Newer approaches are based on broader definitions of public rights. All approaches will have economic consequences which are discussed by the authors.

Joseph Little's paper shows that law is a dynamic process in dealing with social problems. Using as an example a dredge-and-fill case known as the Zabel-Russell, he illustrates how the concept of public versus private right has altered over the twenty-year period during which Zabel and Russell sought to obtain legal permission to dredge and fill 11.5 acres of submerged land in Boca Ciega Bay near St. Petersburg, Florida. Before the case was over, local, state, and federal bodies were involved in the legal process. Paralleling the progress of the Zabel-Russell, a new emphasis on the importance of public interests over private rights has culminated in the National Environmental Policy Act.

The paper by John Timmons brings the background of a land economist to bear on problems of identifying and achieving environmental quality levels. Though his paper is not primarily about law, it is included in this section because he makes certain proposals for the achievement of environmental quality which have to do with changes in the legal rights and institutional structures. Timmons proposes two criteria to be used to set environmental quality standards. These are the "next use" criterion and the "irreversibility" criterion. The "next use" criterion defines when quality standards are required and on what basis standards are set when one use of a resource conflicts with another. The "irreversibility" criterion forms a basis for formulating universal resource quality standards. Timmons also proposes that a doctrine of public trust be incorporated in private rights of resource use. New institutions would be needed to regulate the rights of trusteeship, and Timmons suggests the creation of environmental control districts for this purpose.

8

Legal Remedies for Attacking Environmental Problems

Donald R. Levi and Dale Colyer

A leading legislator has commented that our concept of environmental law is as "outdated as the Ptolemaic theory of the universe" (20, p. 666). Yet, during the last few years it has become generally accepted that the supply of natural resources is not infinite, that serious environmental and pollution problems exist, that we are faced with an ecological crisis, and that the situation must be improved substantially. The crisis is a direct result of the rapid increases in population, technology, and material well-being and results in a dilemma between the desire for improvements in the level of living and the necessity for protecting the environment. Resolving this dilemma is a highly complex issue due to both the magnitude of the problem and the existence of widely varying values and vested interests of the people and organizations involved. However, most serious students in this field probably agree that action is essential to preserve not only the quality of life but even its potential.

Any individual wishing to help in solving the problems of the environment will tend to feel relatively helpless in view of the complexity of the problem and the advanced level at which rational solutions must be implemented. However, there are several contributions the individual can make. These include simple physical acts such as using nonphosphate detergents, lead-free gasoline, returnable bottles, birth control methods, etc., as well as political activities such as supporting and voting for environmentally oriented candidates, writing letters to legislators, and joining environmental protection groups.

Another approach is to institute lawsuits, either as an individual or as a member of a group, against polluters, potential polluters, or those unwilling to carry out their public responsibilities to protect the environment. Although the legal process may be long and costly, it does provide a means by which the individual can have a significant impact on specific, generally localized situations. The purposes of this chapter are to outline some of the legal remedies available for use against polluters, analyze their substantial procedural deficiencies, review some of the newer, unusual theories suggested to aid the concerned citizen, and discuss some economic implications of the various types of remedies.

While the legal definition of pollution varies with the different remedies and jurisdictions, there is a fairly widely accepted economic definition. For the purposes of this chapter, the Ayres and Kneese concept (5, p. 282) is used. Thus, pollution is viewed as an externality—something which affects one person or group but is under the control of another—which is associated with the disposal of the residuals of production and consumption. In this disposal process "free" resources, water and air, are used to dispose of the wastes. Such resources, however, are scarce and valuable in a modern, affluent, densely populated, mass consumption economy. An economic approach to pollution is to internalize—make the user pay—the full cost of using such valuable resources. Mishan (17) has adequately reviewed the literature on externalities and related welfare concepts, and therefore the emphasis here will be on specific legal remedies and their implications.[1]

Common Law Remedies

A frequent basis for legal actions against individuals has been provided by common law—that body of law which originated in England and has been constructed through the years from judicial decisions based on custom and precedent. Where the requirements of specific common law remedies are met, these may be available to use against polluters and, in some cases, potential polluters. These remedies are primarily concerned with private property rights and hence cannot be expected to be readily adaptable to protecting the public interest. Those which have been or might be useful in the environmental arena include nuisance, trespass, and water rights laws.

1. This chapter is based, in part, on a paper presented at the annual meeting of the American Agricultural Economics Association, Carbondale, Ill., 17 August 1971.

NUISANCE

A nuisance exists whenever there is interference, by another party, with the basic right that everyone has to the enjoyment and use of his property. Air, water, solid wastes, and recently noise pollution have been considered nuisances. Whether a specific instance of pollution is such an interference is usually considered as a matter of fact which a jury must decide based on the evidence presented.

Generally, to maintain a nuisance action, the plaintiff must show some financial or irreparable physical damage. Thus, a nuisance suit might consist, on one side, of a nearby resident or group of residents complaining of the effects of air, water, solid waste, or noise pollution from some existing facility; it may be an industry, municipality, or perhaps a rancher or farmer operating an intensive feeding facility. Any of these may involve a substantial investment in plant and equipment and furthermore may be a financial boon to the area by providing jobs and services for other local residents, i.e., substantial benefits may be accruing from the offending plant.

The nuisance lawsuit may request damages for the harm done and/or an injunction to halt the operation and prevent future damages (pollution). This latter type of award may be necessary to really halt the pollution. However, many legal jurisdictions use a "balancing-of-interests test" in deciding whether to grant the injunction (24, p. 674). That is, the relative interests of all parties are considered and if the polluter and others have substantial interests which require maintaining the operation, the injunction may not be granted. A common result is to award damages for past harm but to deny the injunction. A developing trend is to require modification of the facility to reduce or eliminate the effects of pollution, while permitting continued operation.

The unfortunately common result of denying relief other than damages can permit an undesirable industry to move in, build a plant, and then cause a significant lowering, through the effects of pollution, of the sales values of the surrounding property, or in some cases actual physical damage. While the industry is liable for the damages, the reduction of the property values—frequently to very low levels—amounts to "inverse condemnation" (24, p. 680).[2] It is the application of the balancing-of-interests doctrine which permits, essentially, private property to be taken for private use without the consent of the owner.

Another basis for denying the injunction, in some states, is the ex-

2. Inverse condemnation in its simplest form refers to the situation in which a landowner complains of public use of his land (or interference with his use), and *he initiates* the condemnation proceeding, i.e., he must sue to receive compensation for the loss which has already occurred.

istence of a zoning ordinance. Where an area is zoned for a particular use and is so being used, the user may be insulated from injunctive action. However, there appears to be no logical basis for this, since the existence of zoning does not determine if there is unreasonable interference with another's enjoyment or use of his property.[3] Several courts have accepted this argument and it seems that the trend is away from such insulation.

Where an interference is considered a public instead of a private nuisance, there is a somewhat greater likelihood that the injunction will be granted.[4] A public nuisance affects the rights of the general public, and the public's interest is more likely to outweigh the polluter's than is that of another individual or smaller group. Therefore, it may be significant that the statutes of several states classify air, water, and solid waste pollution as public nuisances.

The remedy of nuisance has been less useful to environmentalists than it could be, because of the reluctance of courts to grant injunctions. While damage awards may internalize some of the costs of pollution, they do little to reduce the harmful effects except insofar as the continual threat of suits could cause offenders to reduce pollution to avoid litigation. A strong possibility of an injunction, however, should be more effective since it would reduce the use value of the facility to zero. Money awards alone are inadequate where irreparable damage is allowed to continue. However, given the difficulty of quantifying an aesthetically pleasing environment, it appears that nuisance-based injunctions are not likely to become common unless directed by specific statutory law.

TRESPASS

The remedy of trespass provides a second common law basis for lawsuits against certain types of polluters. Trespass involves an intentional and unprivileged entry onto land, whereas with nuisance an unreasonable interference must occur. Since trespass need not affect enjoyment, it would appear to require less proof from a plaintiff to use this remedy. A requirement of direct physical entry by a person or object, however, circumscribes the use of the concept. For instance, the entry of air pollutants such as smoke, dust, or gas fumes has been held to be too insubstantial to be considered trespass (25). Courts have also held that direct entry has not occurred if an intervening force such as wind or water brings the pollutants onto the property of the affected party (3, p. 488).

3. To illustrate simply, county zoning in no way affects the odors from a 20,000-head feedlot or the death of fish from stream pollution

4. Unfortunately, agencies charged with abatement and control have seldom sought enjoinment on this theory. This may be due to being understaffed and underpaid, physical impossibility, or the political "atmosphere." Occasionally, vague laws and overlapping responsibilities may inhibit enforcement.

In Oregon, however, a relatively recent case in which pollutants were transported by air was decided in the plaintiff's favor (16). A group of Oregon farmers sued for damages and an injunction because fluoride gas from an aluminum plant drifted onto their properties and damaged their crops. While the case must be considered as favorable from the standpoint of environmentalists, a discouraging aspect was the denial of the injunction. The court used the balancing-of-interests doctrine as justification for the denial. Since the economic usefulness of the surrounding property is reduced by continued pollution, the value of the land is reduced and, in effect, the property is taken without consent for private use—an example of inverse condemnation as cited in the preceding section.[5]

WATER RIGHTS

Water rights of individuals owning property along streams and bodies of water were developed by common law procedures. While these cannot aid in fighting other types of pollution, they may provide a basis for legal action in some specific instances concerning water. Most states in the eastern part of the United States follow the riparian rights system while those in the more arid West subscribe to the prior appropriation doctrine. A few follow the "California Doctrine," which combines the two systems.[6]

Approaches to using water rights to fight pollution focus on quality factors, i.e., the right to unpolluted water of a certain quality. Under the riparian doctrine each eligible landowner is entitled to make a reasonable use of water in a riparian source.[7] Reasonableness depends to some extent on the other uses being made of the water, both with respect to quantity and quality. Under some circumstances this may include using water for waste disposal.[8] An opposing, minority view of the riparian doctrine holds that a riparian landowner has the right for riparian water to flow by in its natural condition, undiminished in either quantity or quality (7, pp. 493, 614). This natural flow theory would permit inter-

5. If the pollution were not allowed to continue, the operators of the aluminum plant could "clean up," halt operations, "bribe" surrounding owners to allow the pollution through negotiated settlements, or buy the land area affected. For an example of results where the clean-up or buy-out alternative was faced, see Crocker (8). It is interesting here that the polluter purchased the surrounding property and later found it advantageous to clean up the emissions to preserve the value of the new land. This resulted because all costs were then internalized for the polluting firm, including damage to their land and crops.

6. Since it generally reflects both of the other two systems, the California Doctrine will not be discussed here.

7. In its simplest definitional form, a "riparian source" is a natural lake or stream.

8. Of course this cannot be such as to constitute pollution under state water pollution control agency water quality standards.

pretation which would be very useful in combating water pollution, but unfortunately it has not been widely adopted because—at least partly—of its potential for limiting economic development.[9] At the time water doctrines were being determined, growth was viewed as very desirable while environmental protection was not generally viewed as a problem, since the supply of natural resources was thought to be effectively unlimited.

In some states with the prior appropriation system, precedents have been established that declare an individual to have a vested right to the quality of water which existed at the time the appropriation began. Washington is an example of a state where this principle is used (18). However, in general, neither the prior appropriation nor the riparian rights system provides a strong basis for antipollution suits due to a large body of contrary precedent. It has, for example, been held that "a riparian owner has no proprietary right in a beautiful scene presented by a river anymore than any other owner of land could claim a right to a beautiful landscape" (15, p. 892).

SOME IMPLICATIONS CONCERNING COMMON LAW REMEDIES

Obtaining a money award for damages from the effects of polluting acts tends, from an economic standpoint, to internalize for the polluter some of the former externalities, thus increasing his total costs. To the extent that such an approach is effective, the usual consequences of internalization would result: higher product prices, lower production, and related reallocations. But unless all interests are fully compensated, the offender may be allowed to continue to operate at a greater than optimal rate of pollution—if indeed such a thing as an optimal rate exists. Furthermore, it may be cheaper for a firm to pollute and pay the damages than to clean up. By means of this procedure surrounding owners have their property rights taken without their consent, even though they may be compensated. Furthermore, they must initiate the actions, hire lawyers, and devote time to the lawsuit to obtain even that limited result. Such procedures also involve substantial transaction costs—the lawyers' fees and court costs—as well as the opportunity cost of the time involved.[10] Furthermore, substantial differences may exist in the economic strength of the contending parties, with many polluters having an advantage in assets and income as well as a legal staff. Although suits which award substantial damages, or the threat of such suits, may cause firms to take preventive action, they

9. Water law systems are relatively modern, and a product of the society in which they were developed. Early in our history, the natural flow theory was felt undesirable because growth was a conscious social goal. Today the theory may find more backers as we recognize that growth has some undesirable aspects.

10. For a discussion of transfer costs see, for example, Randall (21).

cannot be considered adequate to fully protect the environment. Something more is needed than just punishing past pollution, especially where the use of the natural resources reaches such a point that the effects become nearly irreversible or are reversible only at very high costs. The loss of property value by the victim may be the least of the undesirable results in the long run. Therefore, it is necessary to seek legal remedies other than those provided by the common law, remedies which might be used as preventive measures as well as means to correct past wrongs.

Some Statutory Remedies

Statutory law—both specific, environmentally related acts and more general provisions—provides bases for legal actions of various types. Many such laws exist in each state and at the federal level, and therefore only those more general and more appropriate for environmental protection will be reviewed. In general they will be those more suited to preventive actions, although some are means of suing for damages resulting from acts of pollution.

CLASS ACTIONS

A class action may be brought by a few members of a general class, with the same rights or complaints, on behalf of the whole class. In general the claims of each member would be relatively small. In a pollution case this might be a means of insuring that a more complete bill for damages is presented, i.e., that more of the externalities will be internalized. There has been at least one such action in the area of water pollution (30). In 1939 a suit was brought by fifty-six plaintiffs against a slaughterhouse; while possible at that time, such a suit appears less likely at the federal level now because of a recent decision which requires that each class member meet the federal diversity case jurisdictional requirement (29).[11] Thus, no clear precedent currently exists for class actions in the environmental area.

DECLARATORY JUDGMENT ACTIONS

Governmental administrative agencies may act, fail to act, or permit acts which may be harmful to the environment. In such cases citizens may seek a review of such actions or attempt to enjoin them by use of a declaratory judgment action. The Federal Declaratory Judgment Act,

11. This refers to class actions filed in federal courts. Generally such an action must involve a federal question or be a situation where the case can be diverted from a state court because the plaintiff could not get a fair hearing, usually a situation of a nonresident suing a resident. If in a class action at least one member of the class is a resident, then the diversity requirement is not met, since it is assumed that a resident could get a fair trial.

which can be used if a federal agency is involved, provides that "in a case of actual controversy within its jurisdiction, . . . any court of the United States . . ., upon the filing of appropriate pleading, may declare the rights and other legal remedies in such declaration . . ." (10). A similar provision applies to state agencies in the thirty-five states which have adopted the Uniform Declaratory Judgment Act. At both levels a suit can be initiated to seek a decision on the validity of some specific agency action or to determine whether environmental factors are being adequately considered by the agency in relation to some specific problem.[12] Under some circumstances, the individual(s) may go directly against the polluter, too.

MANDAMUS

Although no longer called by that name, the remedy of *mandamus* is still available under the Federal Rules of Civil Procedure.[13] A "writ of *mandamus*" is a court order requiring a particular public officer to perform his duty in the manner required by law. Thus, when the duty of a public official is to carry out actions involving environmental factors (as, for example, under the National Environmental Policy Act), a private individual may seek a writ of *mandamus* to require that the duty be performed.

REFUSE ACT OF 1899 AND QUI TAM

Among the potentially useful federal laws directed specifically at pollution is the Rivers and Harbors Act of 1899, commonly referred to as the Refuse Act of 1899, which prohibits individuals, corporations, and municipalities from discharging "refuse" into navigable waters or their tributaries (22).[14] Conviction can result in fines of $500 to $2,500 for each day of violation, and an informer who gives information leading to the conviction shares in the fine, receiving one-half of the sum (22, p. 411). In general the effectiveness of antipollution laws depends upon adequate enforcement, and if vigorous action is not forthcoming such laws are not adequate remedies.

The Refuse Act, however, may allow circumvention of poor enforcement by the initiation of a *qui tam* action. A private individual can initiate an essentially criminal action and share in the penalty under

12. This latter facet is particularly relevant since the passing of the National Environmental Policy Act of 1969, as will be discussed later.

13. Though abolished in name at the federal level, "the remedy . . . [formerly] . . . known as mandamus, is still available . . . and is governed by the same principles as formerly governed its [*mandamus'*] principles" (13, p. 25).

14. "Refuse" has been broadly interpreted to include all foreign substances and pollutants (34, p. 230).

qui tam. In general, when a statute permits the sharing of the penalty and does not prohibit them (as in the Refuse Act of 1899), *qui tam* actions are allowable.[15] A congressional committee report has concluded that this does apply to the Refuse Act of 1899 (33). If so, and if individuals or groups are willing to initiate such actions when federal authorities will not act, it could provide a very strong weapon in the legal antipollution arsenal. Of course, it can be effective only against water pollution.

Furthermore, as in other cases such actions are not riskless. The individual or group must, as in all other actions, be willing to take on the transaction costs of legal fees, court costs, evidence accumulation, etc., without assurance of conviction and recompensation. Since, again, economic strength may vary, there is no assurance that an individual acting alone can carry out the lengthy litigation process which is apt to follow initiation of *qui tam* or other legal actions. A more equal contest would be assured if the appropriate federal officials would act on the evidence provided by the individual(s).

NATIONAL ENVIRONMENTAL POLICY ACT OF 1969

Among the more recent laws designed to provide more adequate consideration of environmental aspects of societal activities is the National Environmental Policy Act of 1969 (19). The stated purpose of this act is to "declare a national policy which will encourage productive and enjoyable harmony between man and his environment; to promote efforts which will prevent or eliminate damage to the environment and biosphere and stimulate the health and welfare of man; to enrich the understanding of the ecological systems and natural resources important to the nation; and to establish a council of environmental quality" (19, § 4321).

The act requires all federal agencies to take into account the environmental effects of any proposed activity by meeting several specific conditions. One of the more important is the requirement for a report on the environmental effects of proposed laws or actions (19, § 4332). These reports are to include a detailed statement on the environmental impact of the proposal, any adverse effects which cannot be averted, alternatives to the proposed action, short- and long-run relationships, and any irreversible or irretrievable consequences.

Although this appears to be a significant improvement, Representative Richard Ottinger has stated that the "widely publicized new legisla-

15. While not specifically authorized by the Refuse Act of 1899, *qui tam* actions have been permitted in other areas where the enabling legislation neither authorized nor forbade this type of action (35). See also the Natural Resources Subcommittee discussion of *qui tam* (33).

tion gives the appearance of action without substance. It lulls the public into a false confidence that something is being done" (20, p. 671). There is no penalty to assure that the stated policies will be carried out, although the requirements do provide a basis for legal action against noncomplying agencies.

An early test of the act was provided by the *Environmental Defense Fund* v. *Hardin* case, which challenged the USDA fire ant control program (9). The act was interpreted as requiring the agency to consider the environmental effects and to make conclusions therefrom in "good faith." The court refused to substitute its or the environmentalists' judgment for that of the agency and thus refused to grant a preliminary injunction.[16] However, in a later case against the Atomic Energy Commission, the U.S. Court of Appeals for the District of Columbia severely criticized the AEC for its failure to adequately consider environmental factors in licensing atomic power plants (13). Although not enjoining construction of the particular plant involved, the court did say that the AEC should consider halting construction pending a new environmental review. As a result the AEC changed its procedures for environmental evaluation to include factors other than radiation and to allow outsiders to raise such issues. The particular case involved the Calvert Cliffs reactor on Chesapeake Bay and was concerned with thermal pollution. As a result, cooling towers and other changes are sometimes necessary for power plants licensed after January 1970, when the National Environmental Policy Act became effective.

Other Approaches

The existing statutory and common law remedies do not seem to have the necessary breadth and generality needed to protect the environment. Therefore, constitutionally related and other approaches to suing for environmental protection have been proposed but are still in the theoreti-

16. More specifically, the interpretation required agencies (a) to complete a "diligent research effort, undertaken in good faith, which utilizes effective methods and reflects the current state of the art of relevant scientific discipline," (b) "to prepare and distribute an environmental impact statement concerning proposed programs," and (c) "to 'initiate and utilize ecological information in the planning and development of resource-oriented projects' " (9). "Thus, in reviewing the . . . program under consideration here, the Court will not substitute its judgment for that of the Secretary on the merits of the proposed program but will require that the Secretary comply with the procedural requirements of the National Environmental Policy Act as outlined above." Consequently, the conclusion was that "Congress did not intend by the Act to relocate or diminish the decision making responsibility currently existing . . . , but it did intend to make such decision making more responsive and more responsible." All quotes are from the order of 14 April 1971, denying the request for a preliminary injunction sought in the case.

cal stage, i.e., they have not been tested. These remedies would be used to force governmental authorities to protect the environment and to maintain natural resources for public use.

GUARANTEE OF A CLEAN ENVIRONMENT

One theory maintains that a fundamental but unenumerated right to a clean environment is guaranteed under the ninth amendment to the U.S. Constitution. The amendment concludes with a statement that enumeration of certain rights in the Constitution "shall not be construed to deny or disparage others retained by the people" (34). Although not yet applied to the environmental area, such an interpretation has been made concerning other rights.[17] This line of reasoning also holds that under the due process clause of the fifth amendment the federal government is prohibited from interfering with those unenumerated rights. Similarly, the fourteenth amendment prohibits the states from such interference.

Others do not believe this approach has much chance of being implemented and have proposed that the U.S. Constitution be amended to expressly guarantee a pollution-free environment (20). Similar attempts have been made or proposed for some state constitutions (24, p. 686).

PUBLIC TRUST DOCTRINE

A noted legal authority, Joseph L. Sax, has held that "of all concepts known to American law, only the public trust doctrine seems to have the breadth and substantial content which might make it useful as a tool of general application for citizens seeking to develop a comprehensive legal approach to resource management problems" (26, p. 474).[18] To fulfill this role the public trust concept must (a) contain some concept of a legal right in the general public, (b) be enforceable against the government, and (c) be capable of an interpretation consistent with the objective of improved environmental quality.

The public trust approach holds that rivers, lakes, seashores, parks, and other public property are held in trust for public benefit. To prevent conversion of this to private benefit, Sax advances the basic public trust doctrine that "when a state holds a resource which is available for the free use of the general public, the court will look with considerable skepticism upon any governmental conduct which is calculated either to reallocate that resource to more restricted uses or to subject public uses to the self-interest of private parties" (26, p. 490). He further argues that

17. E.g., see *Griswold* v. *Connecticut* (12), where an unenumerated right of privacy was used to strike down a Connecticut statute declaring it a crime to teach birth control techniques to anyone (a case involving a licensed physician and a married couple).

18. Only the basic skeleton of the public trust doctrine is outlined here. For a more detailed treatment see Sax (26), used extensively in the following discussion.

the public interests which concern environmentalists are substantially different from constitutionally protected rights, which he concludes are "the rights of permanent minorities" (26, p. 560). Both approaches remain in the conjectural stage, but they may provide a broader-based approach for action by a private individual than is possible under the other remedies discussed.

Standing to Sue

A procedural constraint in the form of the requirement for "standing" has frequently made it difficult for the environmentalist to obtain legal remedies against either the polluter or the lax public official. Standing to sue has traditionally required one to have a "personal stake in the outcome of the controversy" (11, p. 10). This requirement is in no way related to the merit of the action but reflects the concept that one must be personally affected before being permitted recourse to the courts. From the standpoint of prohibiting unnecessary lawsuits for the purpose of harassing officials and others or because of the existence of overcrowded dockets, a logical basis for the requirement can be advanced. On the other hand, it can be argued that everyone is affected by pollution since the quality, even the possibility, of everyone's life is ultimately modified by each and every act of pollution. Historically, however, merely an interest in the environment did not provide one with standing.

Significant modifications in holdings with respect to standing have been made in recent years, especially in the environmental area. In a 1965 case (27), *Scenic Hudson Preservation Committee* v. *Federal Power Commission* (FPC), the FPC had licensed Consolidated Edison to construct a hydroelectric project at a site considered uniquely beautiful as well as of historical significance. Local groups combined and sought a reversal of the licensing. The court held that the FPC should have a concern for preservation of historical and scenic sites and, importantly, that the plaintiffs had standing.

In both the 1965 and a similarly decided 1967 case (23), the plaintiffs were local citizens, municipalities, or citizen groups residing in or near the area. Thus, a 1969 case (6) involving the Sierra Club, a national conservation organization, is especially significant. They were held to have standing in a case involving the secretaries of the army and transportation, as well as the Corps of Engineers, who had issued permits for construction projects, also along the Hudson River. Because the plaintiff had no personal stake, due either to residing nearby or to financial reasons, this case appears to have expanded the concept of standing sufficiently to allow groups with an interest in the environment to bring suit against those agencies they feel are not adequately considering environmental factors.

Thus, likelihood of judicial review has been made more probable. Traditionally, agencies formulated policies within broad legislative guidelines and could be challenged only if their actions were "arbitrary, capricious, an abuse of discretion, or otherwise not in accordance with law" (2). Now such a challenge should be denied only when the legislative intent is clearly contrary, and furthermore, in this respect the Federal Administrative Procedure Act should be given a "hospitable" interpretation (1, p. 141).

A more recent case, however, has cast doubt on the validity of the preceding conclusions (27). In another circuit the Sierra Club was held not to have standing when it attempted to prevent the commercial development in Yosemite National Park. This issue probably will eventually be settled by a discussion of the Supreme Court, which granted *certiorari* on 22 February 1971, but in the meantime the issue will remain clouded and open to divergent rulings.

Some improvement toward expanded standing at the state level exists as evidenced by a recent act in Michigan. This 1970 law states that "the Attorney General, any political subdivision of the state, . . . any person, partnership, corporation . . . may maintain an action in the circuit court having jurisdiction where the alleged violation occurred or is likely to occur" (32). The stated purpose of the act included the provision of "declaratory and equitable relief" in order to protect the air, water, and other natural resources. Other states are considering or have proposed similar acts. In Ohio, for example, the governor recently proposed such an extension as part of an environmental protection package.

The initiation and carrying out of lawsuits by persons not directly affected by an act of pollution or environmental damage, except insofar as everyone is affected by such acts, can be especially important in environmental protection. There is an increased probability of such suits resulting from a broadening of standing since the number of people willing and able to undertake such actions is relatively small. Many more agencies and potential polluters will examine the environmental effects of proposed activities if they are apt to be held accountable. However, since so many activities may have deleterious results and early action is essential for full protection and to prevent the building of the economic interests so frequently advanced for allowing continued pollution under the balancing-of-interests doctrine, even the full broadening of standing may not be sufficient. Such is especially probable in areas where the citizenry is apathetic or even sympathetic to the polluter because of economic interests in the form of jobs, trade, or other benefits being or expected to be received. Although not the ultimate solution, lawsuits filed by environmentally concerned persons can be an aid in reducing the level of ecologically harmful activities.

Some Economic Implications

Every act of pollution prevention, clean-up, and any other measures designed to improve the environmental condition as well as every act of pollution and environmental damage has economic consequences. Different persons and groups are affected differently by various approaches to pollution control or failure. Although the economist has a particular way of viewing pollution (see Solow [30]), the purpose here is to examine the implications of specific classes of legal remedies which individuals may use for attempting to gain the objective of a better or at least less deteriorating environment. Two aspects are of interest: preventing unacceptable pollution from new sources and eliminating or reducing old sources. In both situations, containing pollution will be likely to make production more costly, reduce levels of production, increase prices, and cause substantial reallocation of income and wealth.

When a new facility is being planned, the economics is relatively simple in concept. If the discounted expected net returns are not sufficient at least to cover the investment outlay, the facility should not be built.[19] Thus, imposition of environmental quality control standards, which impose at the beginning the need for internalization of the costs, may reduce the flow of net returns via higher operating costs and/or raise the investment costs sufficiently to make the investment unprofitable. Under such circumstances the environmentalist needs remedies to insure that all costs are adequately internalized, i.e., that all environmental cost factors are adequately considered. Thus, bases are required for moving against licensing agencies or directly against a potential polluter to either prohibit the incomplete plan or impose modifications to insure that all costs are adequately considered and internalized. Of course, in cases where irreparable damage to irreplacable resources is likely to occur, prohibition via enjoinment or other techniques is required, because in these circumstances there is no way to internalize all the costs.

However, attempting to do something about a particular existing situation is more complex, involving as it does complicated economic interrelations and the vested interests of the various parties. On one side are the producers and consumers of products and services (including governmental agencies) while on the other are the parties (including the

19. Government projects evaluated by the benefit-cost procedure use this method of discounting as well as capital budgeting procedures used by many industrial firms.

general public) being harmed by the pollution. These are not mutually exclusive groups, but fairly distinguishable in their separate roles. With imposition of new controls, or internalization of costs through, say, damage awards, the economic value of the facility is affected, i.e., its use value is reduced if no way is found to offset the increased costs. If the economic use value is reduced, someone's assets are affected and it cannot be expected that those individuals would not try to protect their interests, especially where perhaps their livelihood and a substantial portion of their economic wealth are closely associated with the affected facility. While it can be argued that such a "penalty" is just and necessary for environmental protection, some polluters may be made to suffer for shortcomings imposed by the failure of society to plan adequately for environmental quality. Some may have been persuaded to invest in the polluting facility as a public service to provide jobs, income, or other benefits. Thus, solutions ideally should be implemented in such a way as to consider the equity of all parties. Lawsuits for damages and injunctive relief, for instance, may not adequately consider legitimate interests of the offending party. Therefore, the balancing-of-interests approach, while inadequate from the environmentalists' viewpoint, was developed to consider the real interests of both sides.

Conclusions

Complexity characterizes the entire area of pollution abatement, control, and prevention, although an ever-present concern must be environmental protection—a concern for the quality and existence of life. Ad hoc actions and piecemeal approaches cannot be expected to result in adequate solutions. Rational policies developed from analyses of complete systems and including primary, secondary, tertiary, and other effects are essential. While much effort has been devoted to the subject in recent years, some new laws passed, and a greater concern expressed from many quarters, implementation of such a comprehensive approach still appears to lie far in the future. Given the existing situation, those persons vitally concerned must use the means which are available. The legal approaches discussed in this chapter are one set of tools that can be used. It may be that effective use of such remedies can help to induce the necessary reforms and hasten the movement toward a more rational, systematic approach to the problem.

References

1. Abbott Laboratories v. Gardner, 387 U.S. 136 (1967).
2. Administrative Procedure Act § 10, 5 U.S.C. §§ 701, 706 Supp. 4 (1969).
3. Arvidson v. Reynolds Metal Co., 125 F. Supp. 481 (W.D. Wash. 1954).
4. Association of Data Processing Service Organizations, Inc., v. Camp, 397 U.S. 150 (1970).
5. Ayres, R. U., and Kneese, A. V. "Production, Consumption, and Externalities." *American Economic Review* 59 (1969):282–97.
6. Citizens Committee for the Hudson Valley v. Volpe, 302 F. Supp. 1083 (1969).
7. City of Richmond v. Test, 18 Ind. App. 482, 48 N.E. 610 (1897).
8. Crocker, T. D. "Externalities, Property Rights and Transaction Costs: An Empirical Study." Working Paper No. 2, Program in Environmental Economics, University of California, Riverside, 1971.
9. Environmental Defense Fund v. Hardin, Civil Action No. 2319–70 (D.C. Dist of Columbia).
10. Federal Declaratory Judgment Act 62 Stat. 964 (1948), amended 63 Stat. 946 (1949), 28 U.S.C. § 2201 (1948).
11. Flast v. Cohen, 392 U.S. 83 (1968).
12. Griswold v. Connecticut, 381 U.S. 479 (1965).
13. Hammond v. Hull, 133 F. 2d 23 (1942).
14. Holden, Constance. "Court Decision Jolts AEC." *Science* 173 (1971):799.
15. International Shoe Co. v. Heatwole, 30 S.E. 2d 537 (W. Va. 1944).
16. Lampert v. Reynolds Metal Co., 372 F. 2d 245 (1967).
17. Mishan, E. J. "The Post War Literature on Externalities: An Interpretive Essay." *Journal of Economic Literature* 9 (1971):1–28.
18. Naches v. Cowiche Ditch Co., 87 Wash. 224, 151 Pac. 494 (1915).
19. National Environmental Policy Act of 1969, 42 U.S.C.A. §§ 4321–47 (Supp. 1970).
20. Ottinger, Richard L., *Legislation and the Environment: Individual Rights and Government Accountability*, 55 Cornell L. Rev. 666 (1970).
21. Randall, Alan. "Market Solutions to Externality Problems: Theory and Practice." *American Journal of Agricultural Economics* 54, no. 2 (May 1972):175–83.
22. Rivers and Harbors (Refuse) Act of 1899, 33 U.S.C. 407 (1899).
23. Road Review League, Town of Bedford v. Boyd, 270 F. Supp. 650 (S.D.N.Y. 1967).
24. Roberts, E. F., *The Right to a Decent Environment; E = MC²: Environment Equals Man Times Courts Redoubling Their Efforts*, 55 Cornell L. Rev. 674 (1970).
25. Ryan v. City of Emmetsburg, 232 Iowa 699, 4 N.W. 2d 435 (1942).
26. Sax, Joseph L., *The Public Trust Doctrine in Natural Resource Law: Effective Judicial Intervention*, 68 Mich. L. Rev. 473 (1970).
27. Scenic Hudson Preservation Committee v. Federal Power Commission, 354 F. 2d 608 (2d Cir. 1965).
28. Sierra Club v. Hickel, 433 Fed. Rep. 2d 24 (9th Cir. Ct., 1970).
29. Snyder v. Harris, 394 U.S. 332 (1969).
30. Solow, Robert M. "The Economist's Approach to Pollution and Its Control." *Science* 173 (1971):498–503.
31. Storley v. Armour and Co., 107 F. 2d 499 (8th Cir. Ct., 1939).
32. Thomas J. Anderson, Gordon Rockwell Environmental Protection Act of 1970, M.C.L.A. §§ 691.1201–.1207 (1970).
33. U.S. Congress. *Qui Tam Actions and the 1899 Refuse Act.* Committee on Government Operations, Conservation and Natural Resources Subcommittee, House Print. Washington, D.C.: Government Printing Office, September 1970.
34. U.S. Constitution, Amend. 9.
35. U.S. *ex rel.* Marcus v. Hess, 317 U.S. 537 (1942).
36. U.S. v. Standard Oil Co., 384 U.S. 224 (1966).

9
Legal Strategies for Achieving Environmental Goals: A Florida Case Study

Joseph W. Little

Legal strategies for achieving environmental goals have undergone great change over the past few years and will continue to do so until generally acceptable and effective goals are formulated. Hence, one's legal strategies must be strongly time- and circumstance-oriented. The law, being merely society's compelling tool for regulating human behavior, can in the main do no more than truncate undesirable modes of behavior at whatever extreme the majority lays down as the tolerable limit. Although creative legislation and litigation can do much to define goals and limits of acceptable behavior, experience has shown over and again that successful legal regulations reinforce public mores and do not create them. In the context of environmental control, this means that those people looking to the law as the savior of the environment must use it creatively, never edging too far ahead of the public's contemplation of the need for regulating the particular environmentally abusive behavior under attack and ever pulling the limits of tolerable behavior toward a more protective curtilage by whatever means are at hand. Therefore, in mapping out a strategy for achieving any given environmental goal one needs to test carefully the prevailing public sentiment and the current posture of the law vis-à-vis the unwanted behavior. One may then find that his task is conceptually easy in that existing legal controls can adequately bring the offensive behavior into line. Or, more frequently at present, one may find that either public sentiment or existing laws or both thwart the immediate achievement of one's goals.

In studying the legal strategies for protecting the environment, it is inherently more interesting to turn to the process of creating changes in modes of acceptable legal control than it is to map out an application of existing law. Accordingly, this paper will deal with the process of change. Fortunately, Florida has produced several fascinating models to examine.

As in most states, Florida's entire legal structure for regulating pollution has come of age rapidly in the past few years, growing at least to adolescence from a former infantile stage. More than in most states, however, Florida has seen important changes in its ability to control behavior which is exploitative of its natural environment. This is fitting, of course, since, being more abundantly blessed with natural treasures than most states, Florida has more to protect and more to lose. Because of my personal preference for thinking about nature rather than about pollution and because of the fascinating subjects Florida's recent past offers for study, I have chosen to examine an illustrative process of how legal control is attained over what was formerly legally acceptable but extremely abusive behavior.

Three important situations have been of recent interest. One is the now defunct Dade County jetport battle that saw the Everglades hanging in the balance. The second is the Cross-Florida Barge Canal controversy that pits the remains of the Oklawaha River ecosystem against the vested interests of Florida and the minions of the U.S. Army Corps of Engineers. The third is the practice of dredging and filling estuarine areas that not only threatens to destroy a vital link in the chain of life for most of Florida's fish and marine creatures, but is also an irreplaceable element of the natural charm of the state. I have accepted the third situation to discuss here. The choice is easily explained. Despite the fact that the battle for gaining control over indiscriminate dredging and filling has been going on longer than the other two controversies (if one disregards the "ancient" pre-1962 history of the canal), it is probably the least well known and deserves to be better known both for its significant advancement for environmental protection and also to acknowledge a debt of gratitude to the people who achieved an important environmental goal. Furthermore, in terms of creating definite, substantial changes in the law, both legislative and judicial, it has been by far the most productive of the three situations to date. To a very important extent, this situation is the first one of major consequence in which the public interest, being protected by an aroused group of ordinary citizens, prevailed over the vested economic interests of rich Florida developers. After decades of submergence, the public interest has surfaced in what portends to be a massive assertion of dominance over private exploitation.

Today in Florida, powerful legal controls exist for regulating dredge-and-fill operations on the basis of environmental factors alone, whereas only a few years ago no controls existed. The remainder of this paper will first lay down the background of the dredge-and-fill controversy, then trace the process that led to change, and finally attempt to assess the importance of what has occurred. Whether a strategy really existed and what it was, if there was one, seems inextricably entwined in the historical evolution of the struggle.

Dredging and Filling

Dredging and filling is the process of making dry land out of submerged and tidal wet lands by scooping earth from one portion of the water's bottom and piling it on another. Usually, but not always, people dredge and fill to make money. Waterfront sites for homes, commercial ventures, and now condominiums bring in a return to developers many times greater than the total cost of the finished landfill. The venture is extremely lucrative for the few individuals fortunate enough to control the tidal and land bottoms being filled.

On the other hand, dredging and filling is an extremely costly process to a great many people who cannot claim any direct personal ownership of the lands involved. Dredge-and-fill projects occur on the margin of the sea. Those who fill and build on seafront sites claim for themselves the sole right to view the sea from one part of the world, and often they erase the adjoining beaches, robbing the rest of the population of its right to enjoy nature's bounty. Thus, indiscriminate dredging and filling levies a very heavy price against the public's aesthetic and recreational treasury.

But more than temporal pleasures are involved. Most destructive dredge-and-fill operations occur in estuarine areas, which include "tidal rivers, marshes, bays and river mouths, the inshore edge of the ocean, and the land areas which interact with [them]" (3). It is this rich area at the "edge of the sea and its estuarine waters . . . upon which most marine life depends. Here is where to find mussels and clams, shrimps, lobsters and crabs, sea ducks and shore birds, plus almost all of the fish we catch from the sea" (4).

These natural facts translate into several conclusions of vital concern to the public interest of Florida. One is that the joy of fishing, dear to countless Floridians, is jeopardized by continued destruction of life-spawning estuaries. The second is that the lure and charm of the state as a retreat for visitors who are attracted by plentiful fish will be sharply diminished if the good fishing fails. Finally, Florida's commercial fishermen will find themselves deprived of their chosen livelihood if dredging and filling continue unabated.

Attempts have been made to cast dredge-and-fill losses in monetary terms. Taking Boca Ciega Bay as their example, two scientists concluded that the destruction of marine life caused by fills embracing 20 percent of the bay (3,500 acres) resulted each year in a loss of $1.4 million (33). This estimate was predicted upon an annual loss of $300 per filled acre for eliminated fishery production and of $100 per filled acre for ruined recreational value. Capitalized at 5 percent, the estimated annual losses stemming from the filled bottomlands of Boca Ciega Bay represent a public investment of $28 million. Although I do not know what income was received by the state in exchange for the filled acreage, I am confident that it was much less than that sum. Other estimates of the potential economic damage caused by dredge and fill have been made. Taking a different analytical approach, an economist in 1965 "conservatively" estimated the annual value of "good fishing" to Florida to be not less than $1.75 billion (19). Florida's economic future is therefore clearly tied to the preservation of estuarine and other fish-breeding areas.

Exactly how much of Florida's estuarine areas could be filled before intolerable economic losses would be exacted is hard to say. To a large extent, however, cold economics is beside the point to the people trying to protect the environment. They know that each spoiled acre subtracts one from the diminishing limited supply that remains, and that man can destroy in mere days what nature toiled for thousands of years to create. In essence, estuaries are essentially nonregenerative resources. When we have destroyed them, they and the life they support will no longer exist. Therefore, man must be regulated, if not stopped, in his pillage of this important part of nature, whatever the economic consequences to the privileged few may be.

Before discussing achievement of control over that form of exploitative behavior, we should bring out another economic factor. Bottomlands frequently contain rich lodes of oil and other minerals (such as limestone in the bottom of Lake Okeechobee). The question of who controls their exploitation is extremely important both in determining who takes the profits and in deciding what consideration is to be given to environmental protection while they are being extracted. In the course of the situation to be explored here these factors receive little attention. As shall be seen, however, they are strongly affected by the outcome.

Background of an Epic Legal Saga

Dating back to origins in the common law of England, lands lying under navigable waters along with those lying in the margin between the line of mean low tide and that of mean high tide were known as sovereignty lands, meaning that their ownership resided in the sovereign or state. Although sovereignty lands could in some circumstances be put to private uses, they were impressed with an inalienable servitude in favor of public uses such as navigation, fishing, and bathing. In protection of the inalienable public servitude, a "public trust" doctrine was devised by American courts, stemming mainly from a U.S. Supreme Court opinion holding that the state of Illinois' conveyance of the submerged lands fronting the city of Chicago to a private developer was invalid because violative of the inalienable trust. Unfortunately, Florida developed an emasculated form of public trust doctrine that not only let sovereignty lands fall into private hands but also relinquished the state's right to control uses made of them, including dredging and filling.

As a result of this peculiar legal posture and its confluence with Florida's post–World War II development boom, dredging and filling began in earnest in the late 1940s. Boca Ciega Bay was a favorite target. As one fill after another struck beauty and life from the bay, conservationists became alarmed. Before their eyes the natural bounty that they had assumed to be unassailable by man was being gobbled up. How, they asked, can this exploitative behavior be brought under control? Taking 1950 as a watershed date, one can say confidently that it could not be. As early as 1856, the Florida legislature conveyed certain sovereignty lands to riparian owners in order to encourage the building of docks and wharves for commerce (25). In 1917 the Florida legislature conveyed most of the sovereignty lands of the state to the Trustees of the Internal Improvement Fund (TIIF)—now composed of the Florida cabinet—to be held and disposed of "as they see fit" (8). Then in 1921 the legislature purported to convey additional large chunks of sovereignty lands to riparian owners, allowing for dredging and filling as did the earlier grants, so long as commerce was not obstructed (26).

As a result of these grants and of TIIF's power to sell sovereignty lands, much of the bottom of Boca Ciega Bay, as well as huge tracts of sovereignty lands throughout the state, fell into the hands of speculators (29).

Inevitably, as use was made of the bottomlands, the question was raised as to whether the state could legally destroy the public's interest by conveying away lands impressed with the public trust. In a 1924 opinion,[1] since reconfirmed (12), the Florida Supreme Court held that the public trust could be abrogated by statute. In short, these cases seemed to state this proposition: the sovereign creates the trust; the sovereign can eliminate it. Pushing the abrogative rule to the extreme, the public trust doctrine was further limited in 1946 when the Supreme Court stated: "[I]f the grant of sovereignty land to private parties is of such nature and extent as not to substantially impair the interest of the public in the remaining lands and waters, it will not violate the inalienable trust doctrine" (17).

Under that rationale, presumably the whole east coast of the state could have been sold, dredged, and filled because the public interest in remaining areas, meaning the west coast, would not have been impaired.

With the coming of the financial crisis of the late 1920s and the 1930s also came fractionation of the ownership of the land. In 1950 many private owners were readying to "improve" their lands by dredging and filling. The law seemed to be on their side: the inalienable public trust had been supplanted by the inalienable private right to dredge and fill.

In terms of environmental integrity (not to mention governmental integrity), this state of the law was intolerable. What follows is an account of the quest for change that has in large measure returned public interest to its rightful place in making decisions involving the use of sovereignty lands.

In the middle 1950s two men named Zabel and Russell purchased about fifteen acres of Boca Ciega Bay bottomland with the intention of extending their fifteen-acre upland trailer court out onto a landfill in the bay. The price they paid is a matter of controversy; opponents of the fill say about $100, whereas the landowners' lawyers say maybe $6,000. Either price would be a bargain. The land was originally sold by TIIF in 1925 under the authority of the 1917 law. Accordingly, the title carried with it the right to dredge and fill to the channel.

In 1955, after conservationists (in losing a number of dredge-and-fill battles) had aroused public opinion sufficiently, the Florida legislature created the Pinellas County Water and Navigation Control Authority (PCA) and gave it authority to regulate dredging and filling of submerged lands within Pinellas county (9). Among eight factors to be considered in issuing permits were the effects on natural beauty and recreation and

1. *State ex rel. Buford* v. *City of Tampa*, 88 Fla. 196 (1924). A dissenting judge disagreed, saying, "Tide lands and lands covered by all the navigable waters in a State are called sovereignty land as distinguished from ordinary public lands, the latter being subject to sale and private ownership in fee simple absolute, while the former have the limitations of tenure and uses for public purposes"; id., p. 214.

"conservation of wildlife, marine life and other natural resources." This was a first step in attempting to bring dredge-and-fill projects under control.

The next significant step was taken in 1957. In that year the Florida legislature enacted the Bulkhead Act (10), which allowed for setting a line seaward of which filling would not be permitted. The purpose was to restrict the former practice of filling to the channel by setting bulkhead lines shoreward of the channel. The Bulkhead Act also removed from TIIF the authority to dispose of sovereignty lands as they saw fit, and replaced it with new authority to sell only in situations that would not be contrary to the public interest. Thus, the noose of regulation on exploitation was beginning to form.

As required by the 1955 legislation, Zabel and Russell applied to PCA to establish a bulkhead line across their submerged lands and to issue a permit to dredge and fill 15 acres; the application was subsequently amended to reduce the proposed fill to 11.5 acres. As we shall see, almost thirteen years were to elapse while that and related applications were being processed. Out of the multitude of legal skirmishes came a clarification of the state law regarding dredge-and-fill operations, and much protective legislation was influenced. Most importantly came the federal court ruling that a federal agency (the U.S. Army Corps of Engineers) must consider conservation factors in issuing permits to dredge and fill private lands in navigable water and may refuse to issue a permit on environmental considerations alone.

That element of control was not available in 1950. Its importance must not be discounted, however, because of the meager 11.5 acres involved in its determination. The ruling has potential nationwide applicability, extending to not less than 27,000 square miles of submerged and tidal coastal lands (34) and to uncounted thousands of square miles of bottoms under fresh navigable waters.

When the case began, two small landowners were claiming the right to dredge and fill. Before it was terminated by the U.S. Supreme Court's refusal to review a decision contrary to their position, the small-timers had been reinforced by large land developing and mining interests from across the country. They all fell together.

The Struggle

LOCAL AND STATE PROCEEDINGS

Zabel and Russell filed their application with the PCA sometime before fall 1958, making two requests: that a bulkhead line be established across their submerged lands and that a permit be issued to dredge and fill a designated area. The first of several anecdotal events occurred at this time. The council of the town of South Pasadena, the municipality in which the property lay, voted by a 4 to 1 margin to support the application. This was the council's prerogative under the statute establishing PCA which gave municipalities "the right to be heard." The interesting point is that the membership of the council at that time included a certain Mr. Zabel.

However, the municipality's recommendation was not binding on PCA. Following prescribed procedures, the latter body appointed a hearing examiner to investigate the proposed project and make a recommendation as to the disposition of the application. During the ensuing months three public hearings were held. Applicants were represented in these hearings by a local lawyer well versed in dredge-and-fill matters. His tactic was to show that neither the environment nor the navigability of the surrounding area would be harmed by the project. Evidence was adduced in support of both these contentions. The position advanced on damage to the environment is of particular relevance to what was to follow in later years: at this point in the controversy the applicants presented expert testimony alleging that the area had been made sterile by previous dredge-and-fill projects; that the area was a biological desert; and that it could not be harmed further by additional filling. This position was taken in 1958 and 1959.

More than 200 objections to the project were registered with PCA and fifteen witnesses testified against it at the hearings. Most of them were local residents who spoke mainly in terms of comparisons, reciting how a formerly beautiful, clean, productive, enticing bay had been spoiled by earlier fills. (See Figure 1, indicating the extent to which Boca Ciega Bay had been changed by fills. Figure 2 is an enlargement of a small area of the bay, showing where the proposed Zabel-Russell fill would have been made.)

Leading the objectors at this time were two individuals. One was a local lawyer whose property interests in a nearby tract of land were threatened by the project. In short, his interest was economic; the Zabel-Russell fill would be harmful to any fills he might later plan for his property and could diminish its value as well. The other principal objector, a dedicated conservationist and the central protagonist throughout the dispute, was a local resident who represented Boca Ciega Bay. Judging from the recollections of a number of people closely involved in the struggle—some praising, some condemning—her work and persistence were of great importance in reaching the final goal.

On 23 July 1959, the PCA hearing examiner issued his findings with a recommendation that the application be denied, saying in part, "Appli-

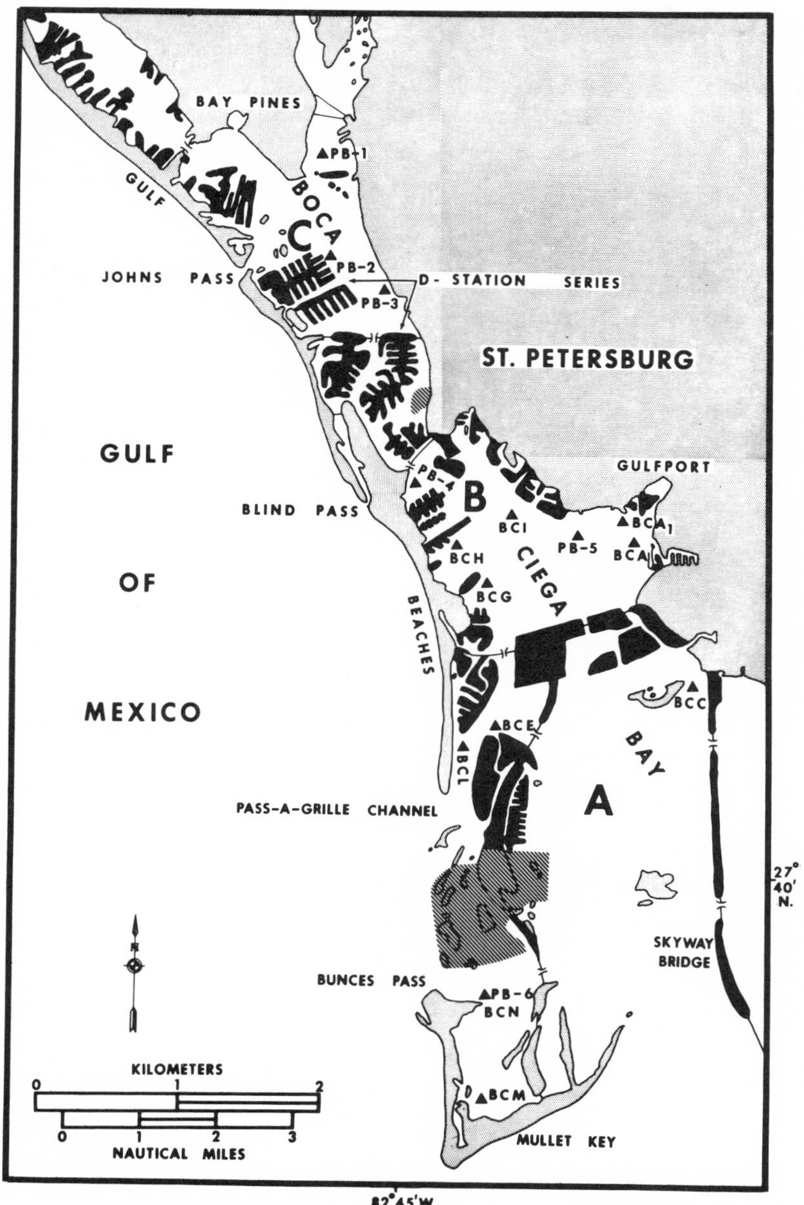

FIGURE 1. Boca Ciega Bay showing station locations (BC and PB series, and biomass stations A, B, and C), bayfill areas (black), and proposed bayfill areas (shaded). Source: *Fishery Bulletin* 67, no. 2 (October 1968).

cants have failed to establish that the proposed plan of development will have no adverse effect on the use of the waters of Pinellas County for transportation, recreational or other public purposes, flow of water or tidal currents and erosion and shoaling of channels in the area necessarily affected by the proposed development. . . ." On 12 November 1959, PCA "confirmed" the hearing examiner's report without extended debate and denied the application.

In a practical sense, here was a break from the past. A permit was denied in protection of the public interest. Had proceedings stopped here,

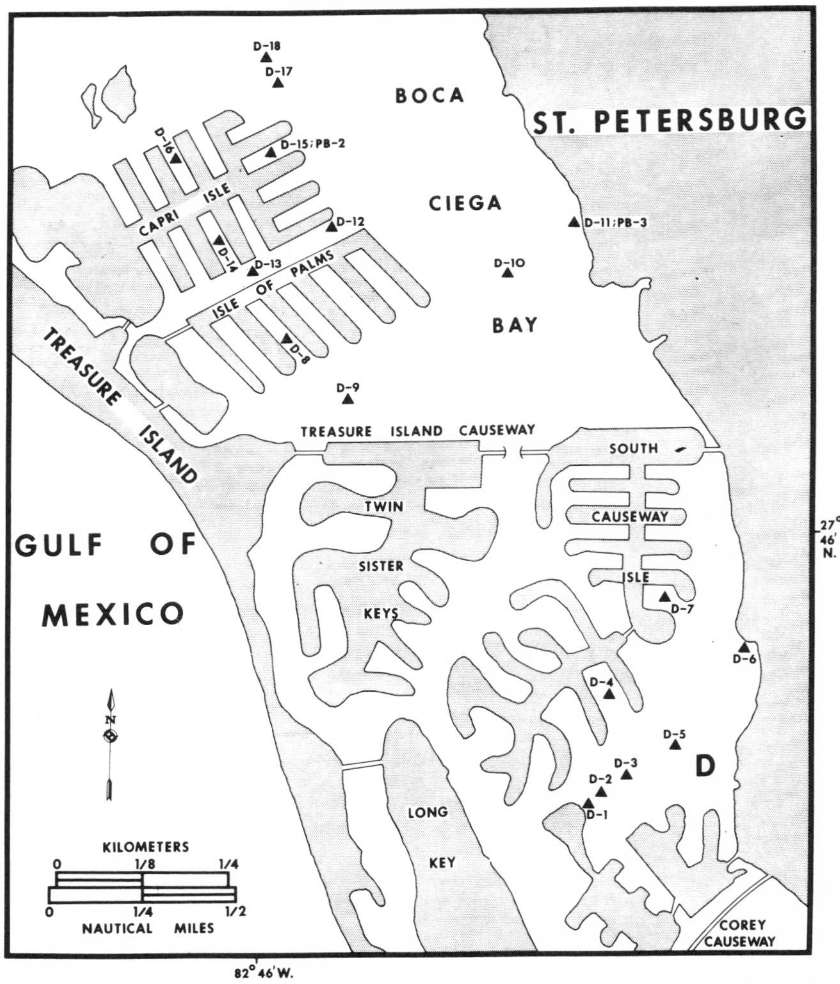

FIGURE 2. Boca Ciega Bay north of Corey Causeway showing station locations (D–1 through D–18, and biomass station D). Source: *Fishery Bulletin* 67, no. 2 (October 1968).

however, later and better-supported permits would have continued to come in, putting great pressure on the local approval agency; it would have approved at least some of those that would have damaged the bay. With a somewhat ironic consequence, the dogged determination of the applicants assured that the matter would not drop so easily. They pressed through every avenue of legal recourse available to them in pursuing a permit to dredge and fill their land.

Their first step into court was to appeal the permit denial to the circuit court of the Sixth Judicial Circuit of Florida. The appeal alleged that the permit had been erroneously denied on the merits and that, in any event, the denial was an unconstitutional action. The constitutional argument went as follows: The land in question had been part of a large bloc sold by TIIF in 1925 under the authority of the 1917 law. In practice, conveyance under that statute carried with it an absolute right to dredge and fill. To deny that right, under the authority of the Bulkhead Act of 1957 or otherwise, could have the effect of denying the property owner the only possible use of his lands. A denial under that circumstance would constitute an unconstitutional taking of private property without compensation. Such a taking is forbidden by the Florida Constitution.

On 7 November 1961, the circuit court held against Zabel and Russell on the merits, finding that the hearing examiner's conclusions were supported by the record of the hearings (20). As for the constitutional argument, the court said that applicants were "estopped" to raise them because of having previously relied upon the validity of the statute in saying that the denial was erroneous on the merits.

Appealing to the Florida First District Court of Appeal, the applicants continued to voice both their contentions: that the denial was erroneous on the merits and that it was an unconstitutional act. In May 1963 the district court of appeal issued its opinion, again denying the permit (41). On the merits the circuit court's holding was affirmed, but the constitutional argument was handled differently. In the interim between the rendering of the circuit court's opinion and the issuance of the district court's opinion, the Florida Supreme Court had ruled that the Bulkhead Act of 1957 was constitutional in its application to a case before that court (16). In the *Gies* case, as it was called, certain other landowners argued that the Bulkhead Act of 1957 could not be applied to restrict their right to fill to the channel lands purchased long before the Bulkhead Act was enacted. On the particular facts of the *Gies* case, the state supreme court held the act to be constitutional. Therefore, relying upon *Gies* as authority, the district court of appeal ruled that the denial of the Zabel-Russell application was not unconstitutional.

At this point two interesting changes occurred. One was that the lawyer who had originally led the objectors dropped out of the case. He sold his interest in the nearby lands and professed no continuing interest in the environmental question. The second was that obtaining the Zabel-Russell fill permit became a pure contest of principle with no lingering economic goals. According to the Zabel-Russell lawyer, his clients at this time had determined that the proposal was no longer economically feasible because of advancing costs. According to Russell's lawyer, "Mr. Russell was a firm believer in our system of free enterprise and believed that the genius of our country was the right to ownership of property. He also believed that the state could not sell this land and then take [it] away without paying compensation. It is for these reasons that Mr. Russell financed the deal after he determined that economically and feasibly [the dredge-and-fill project was not viable]." The lawyer himself was determined to get the permit if only "to hang it on the bathroom wall."

Pressing their constitutional arguments upon the Florida Supreme Court, Zabel and Russell finally hit upon a successful formula. In a split decision (42) with three justices dissenting, the high court agreed that to deny the permit would be an unconstitutional taking of private property without compensation under the facts of the Zabel-Russell application. Distinguishing the factual situation of the *Gies* case, the court pointed out that the PCA hearing examiner's finding was that *applicants* had not shown that the public interest would *not* be damaged by the project. Since the original sale of the land bottoms in question was made under the 1917 legislation, it carried with it the absolute right to dredge and fill in the absence of proper exercise of either the police power of the state or the retained sovereignty servitude in the lands. In order to exercise properly either power, according to the court, the *state* must bear the burden of proving that a "material adverse effect" to the public interest would otherwise occur. Therefore, every decision on the application up to that point had been wrong because all had depended upon the examiner's original finding that placed the burden of persuasion upon the applicants. Hence, on 20 January 1965, it appeared that Mr. Russell's lawyer would get his bathroom ornament. The lawyer says that he was surprised with the results; he had expected to lose in the Florida courts on the basis of the *Gies* case and to win eventually in the federal courts. Ironically, just the reverse was to occur.

The Florida Supreme Court quashed the lower appellate court's opinion and remanded the case for "disposition consistent herewith." An earlier line penned into the opinion created some confusion as to just what such a disposition might be and added a melodramatic twist to the case. In that regard, it should be recalled that almost seven years had elapsed since Zabel and Russell had first proposed the project. In the meantime an original principal objector had sunk out of sight and the landowners themselves purportedly had abandoned their project, if not their quest for vindication. Laying the basis for more dispute, the supreme court said, "The examiner did not find, nor could he have on the record, that any material adverse effect on the public interest had been demonstrated."

Upon receiving the case on remand from above, the district court of appeal vacated[2] its earlier opinion and ordered the circuit court to comply with the supreme court's ruling. On 9 April 1965 the circuit court in turn ordered PCA to issue the permits sought. At that point opposing conservationists strenuously argued that the supreme court's opinion had been misread; that it left open the holding of further hearings in which the public could prove material adverse effect. Challenged on that ground, the circuit court's ruling bounced up to the district court of appeal for review. Foreclosing any prospect of further proceedings on the merits, the appellate court upheld the circuit court's order, saying that it "complies with our mandate and is consistent with the opinion of the supreme court" (22). According to the district court, the supreme court's allusion to the examiner's findings when it said "nor could he have [found any material adverse effect]" ruled out further hearings.

On an uncertain date following that final try to the district court of appeal, PCA issued a permit "subject to approval of the project by the Trustees of the Internal Improvement Fund." This condition was gratuitously added by PCA as it continued to look for a way to halt the project. Although TIIF arguably had a right to review the action, the statute creating PCA did not set it up as a mere fact-finding and advisory body of TIIF.

By this time, however, PCA was as thoroughly and resolutely committed to its position as the applicants were to theirs. Determined not to overlook any opportunity to oppose, they sent off a delegation (it is reported) to urge TIIF to disapprove the conditional permit. At this point judicial tempers were raised. Hauling the PCA members before the bench, the circuit court judge threatened them with contempt of court for refusing to issue an unqualified permit as they had been ordered to do. Not without argument, the commissioners wilted under the ire of the court and issued therewith a clear permit on 4 May 1966. Nine days after the process had begun, Zabel and Russell had obtained state clearance for their project.

Aside from the massive public interest that had been created, dredge-and-fill opponents found themselves no better off in 1966, in some respects, than they had been in 1957. Although the Bulkhead Act of 1957

2. 5 May 1965 (unreported opinion).

provided some protection for lands sold after the date of its passage, the supreme court's *Zabel* left it holding severely diminished control, which seemed to have been established in the *Gies* case over lands sold prior to that date. Florida law under *Zabel* continues to be that the public must show "material adverse effect" on its interests in order to apply the Bulkhead Act's restrictions to deny fills in lands sold under the early laws. One later qualification can be noted. In 1970 the powers of TIIF were enlarged to allow for acquisition of submerged lands through condemnation "in the public interest and for a public purpose" (13). Although the way in which this power will be exercised remains to be seen, arguably it allows a means for returning lands, such as the Zabel-Russell tract, to the public domain.

FEDERAL PROCEEDINGS

Exercising its congressional power (37) to regulate commerce, Congress in 1899 enacted the Rivers and Harbors Act (27), which forbids erecting obstructions to navigable capacity of "any waters of the United States," except as affirmatively authorized by Congress under permit issued by the Department of the Army. Through the years this statute has operated mainly as a navigational servitude. Impact upon navigation was the sole criterion to be satisfied in permit issuance.[3] By the late 1950s, however, public reaction to environmentally exploitative projects that were not a hindrance to navigation (and indeed often enhanced it) created congressional pressures for widening the scope of considerations given under the "regulation of commerce" rubric. Rather than invest a separate agency with an environmental permit power, Congress enacted the Fish and Wildlife Coordination Act of 1958 (23) to impose that additional duty upon the army. The Coordination Act requires that the approving agency consult with the Department of the Interior and the head of the pertinent state agency "with a view to the conservation of wildlife resources by preventing loss of and damage to such resources as well as providing for the development and improvement thereof in connection with such water resource development" prior to modifying "the waters of any stream or other body of water."

A stated purpose of the act was to give consideration to "wildlife conservation" *equal* to that given other factors, such as expanding the national economy. This bit of resource philosophy was determined to be of profound importance in ensuing decisions—although at the time Con-

3. This is true with very few exceptions. The two cases most alluded to in the *Zabel* proceedings were *United States ex rel. Greathouse* v. *Dern*, 289 U.S. 352 (1933), and *Miami Beach Jockey Club, Inc.*, v. *Dern*, 86 F. 2d 135.

gress adopted it there was apparently little discussion of possible future consequences. In an attempt to give proper attention to wildlife conservation, agencies were enjoined to give "full consideration" to the reports and recommendations made by the various conservation-oriented agencies.

Although a Memorandum of Understanding had been executed by the secretaries of the army and department of the interior concerning the implementation of the statute, the full scope of its mandates had not been filled out when the Zabel-Russell application came to the Army Corps of Engineers, which is the permitting agency for the army. It is conservative to speculate that navigational servitude was still the principal factor in most permit applications.[4] As we shall see, however, that practice changed with the processing of the application to fill 11.5 acres of the remaining bottom of Boca Ciega Bay.

The Zabel-Russell application to the Army Corps of Engineers (CE) was accompanied by a flood of protest mail. More than 700 objectors countrywide registered their complaints. Of course, this deluge stemmed at least in part from the organized activities of "big conservation," which had now joined the fray. It must also have been about this time that big vested economic interests began coming in on the side of the landowners.

Owing to the storm of controversy, Colonel Tabb, then CE district engineer, called for a public hearing in St. Petersburg, near the proposed project. This near-situs hearing, as opposed to a district headquarters hearing, is itself extraordinary, owing, no doubt, to the intense public interest.

It is pertinent here to describe CE's method of processing permit applications. The secretary of the army is charged by the Rivers and Harbors Act with authorizing projects upon the recommendation of the chief of engineers (27). For efficiency in administration the secretary has delegated approval of projects "which are entirely routine and which involve no difference of opinion on the part of engineer authorities, nor doubt as to the law, facts or regulations, nor any opposition or other considerations which should be decided by higher authority" to the chief of engineers, who in turn has redelegated approval authority to division and district engineers (see footnote 4). The Zabel-Russell application turned out to be one that found its way to the top, largely because of the furor of public controversy. Two other factors were important: (a) CE would not usually issue a permit when state or local authorities declined to consent, and (b)

4. The following statement appears in an Army Corps of Engineers document entitled "Permits for Work in Navigable Waters," Corps of Engineers, Department of the Army, 1962, general policies on issuing permits: "The decision as to whether a permit will be issued must rest primarily upon the effect of the proposed work on navigation." Application of the Fish and Wildlife Coordination Act is later described.

in controversial cases CE would hold hearings in which an applicant had a right to present relevant evidence, but no right to cross-examine opposing witnesses—this was the nature of the hearing called in St. Petersburg.

Following its policy of contacting local agencies, CE called for comments on the Zabel-Russell application after it was filed. PCA replied, "No protest," as did TIIF, Central and South Florida Flood Control District (who in fact had no jurisdiction), and the Board of Pilot Commissioners for the Port of St. Petersburg (BPC). According to the leader of the conservationists, TIIF held a hearing before filing the no-protest position, but without giving any public notice that it was to occur. Making the situation even more difficult for the environmentalists, TIIF had three false starts toward a hearing before it was finally held.

The emergence of BPC supplies another episodic sidelight to this story. Apparently that body, which was chartered by statute to undertake certain responsibilities concerning pilotage, had never claimed any interest in dredge-and-fill applications prior to this juncture in the Zabel-Russell proceedings. At the time, however, one of the landowners' lawyers served as secretary of BPC. He resigned that position. Thereafter, BPC claimed an interest in the controversy, filing both a "no protest" statement and, later, a report of a BPC-commissioned study of the possible effects of the proposed project upon navigation in the vicinity. According to the BPC study, navigation would be "greatly aided" by the project (40).

Filing protest against the application were the Florida Board of Conservation on behalf of the state, the County Health Board of Pinellas County, and, somewhat courageously, the Board of County Commissioners of Pinellas County. It took courage for the county commissioners to submit their protest because they as individuals were the *very same persons* who constituted the PCA. Officially they were schizophrenic, compelled by court order and threat of contempt to approve as members of PCA but equally compelled by their convictions to protest as members of the Board of County Commissioners; but as individuals they were one-minded. Nevertheless, in issuing the protest some of them must have wondered whether the court's order controlled them as individuals as well as PCA members.

More than 200 objectors appeared at the St. Petersburg hearing in November 1966. Many of them were the same citizens who had testified eight years earlier in the PCA hearings. But this time their intuitive objections were buffered by professional criticisms. For example, the Bureau of Sports Fisheries and Wildlife of the U.S. Fish and Wildlife Service, in a letter of 3 August 1966, opposed the petition "because of the value of the area encompassed by this permit as a nursery area for marine fishes and the damage . . . which would result." Indeed, instead of being a "biological desert," as claimed by the landowners' biologist in 1958, the area was now seen as one replete in life-supporting flora and invertebrates, making it "one of the last remaining undestroyed nursery areas in central Boca Ciega Bay."

The environmental testimony had changed drastically between 1958 and 1966. According to Zabel's lawyer, no legitimate biologist would support their earlier position of no harm to the environment: "For every biologist we could turn up, they could produce twenty-five." Moreover, under the CE hearing rules no cross-examination of witnesses was allowable. It became necessary, therefore, for Zabel-Russell to change their legal stance at the CE hearing. This they did, adopting a singular position that was to couple with another equally singular one later taken by CE to give the case its ultimate vital importance. First, the landowners in effect stipulated that biological damage would ensue from the project. Next, relying upon the implications of the Florida Supreme Court's opinion in the state proceedings, the landowners claimed absolute ownership in the fee simple absolute of the bottomlands in question, giving them the right to "sterilize the bottom," if they so chose. Thus, Zabel and Russell bluntly admitted that environmental damage would occur and denied the existence of any federal authority to stop it.

Although some small amount of testimony was given concerning harmful effects on navigation, the bulk of the evidence on the point supported the general contention that no effects of that sort would occur. Consequently, when on 30 November 1966 Colonel Tabb recommended that the permit be denied on the grounds that the project would be contrary to public interest (despite the fact that it "would have no material effect on navigation"), the second crucial legal position began to crystallize.

On 11 January 1967, the division engineer concurred with Colonel Tabb's recommendation, stating "widespread opposition" as his reason. Receiving the case up the line, the chief of engineers supported the decisions of his underlings. Finally, on 28 February 1967, Secretary of the Army Resor denied the application, giving as his reasons that the project: (a) would result in a distinctly harmful effect on the fish and wildlife resources in Boca Ciega Bay; (b) would be inconsistent with the purposes of the Fish and Wildlife Coordination Act of 1958, as amended (16 U.S.C. 662); (c) was opposed by the Florida Board of Conservation on behalf of the state of Florida, and by the County Health Board of Pinellas County and the Board of County Commissioners of Pinellas County; and (d) would be contrary to the public interest.

The absence of any exercise of the navigation servitude was striking. Of equal prominence was the presence of environmental rationale in denying a federal permit under the Rivers and Harbors Act authority.

From the point of view of many vested interests, this action represented a damaging break from past practices. Approval at the state level as a carte blanche to use up the lands of the state freely, so long as navigation was not hurt, now began to pale in importance. Moreover, the possible ramifications of the new CE position began to be felt more widely.

Among the wider concerns was the question of exploiting mineral rights under submerged lands. One directly related example was the store of valuable limestone deposits in the bottom of Lake Okeechobee. The Coastal Petroleum Company controlled large areas of these deposits under lease from TIIF and yearned to dig them out. Their claim of right had considerable validity. The Florida courts had previously held the leases to be valid, giving the company the state's imprimatur to proceed. Furthermore, navigation was not an issue. Therefore, the question of stopping the project fell squarely upon environmental consideration. Environmentalists saw grave dangers lurking in the project, including a possible threat of saltwater intrusion into the lake's waters, which are a principal source of fresh water for southeast Florida. Would the federal government block the project by refusing to allow the mining operations to go on in navigable waters? The decision in the Zabel-Russell proceeding could be precedential in the Coastal Petroleum situation.

The CE ruling in the Zabel-Russell case next came under attack in the federal courts. On 10 May 1967, the Zabel-Russell interests brought suit against CE in the Tampa Federal District Court, claiming that the permit had been erroneously denied because denial was authorized under the Rivers and Harbors Act only when navigation would be hindered. During pretrial maneuverings, the two crucial legal positions crystallized. On the one hand, the landowners stipulated that environmental damage would occur, thereby removing any factual dispute as to the propriety of the denial if environmental factors were legitimate concerns of CE. On the other hand, CE admitted that "the proposed work would have no material adverse effect on navigation," thereby removing the factual basis of denial customarily relied upon by CE. Hence, the issue was formed: under the present state of the law, is it erroneous for CE to refuse because of adverse environmental effects to permit dredge-and-fill operations in privately owned bottoms under navigable waters?

On 17 February 1969, Federal District Judge Krentzman answered that question in the affirmative (43). The permit must issue. Krentzman was concerned, as had been the Florida Supreme Court before him, about the prospects of taking, or denying the use of, private property without a clear legislative authorization. Krentzman carefully studied the history of the Fish and Wildlife Coordination Act of 1958, and though he found it required multi-agency consultation about conservation factors, he did not find a clear congressional intention to add to the secretary's regulatory powers. Said Krentzman, "[T]he Rivers and Harbors Act of 1899 . . . even if said statute is read in pari materia with the U.S. Fish and Wildlife Coordination Act . . . does not vest the Secretary of the Army with discretionary authority to deny an application for a dredge and fill permit there under where he has found factually that the construction proposed under the application would not interfere with navigation." Having so decided the legal issues, Judge Krentzman ordered Colonel Tabb and Secretary Resor to issue a permit "in accordance with the application of plaintiffs." Krentzman restrained the execution of the order, however, while appeal was made to higher authority.

Here, we focus on the reasoning of this court (and of the Florida Supreme Court), because it in large measure epitomizes the crux of most environmental controversies. Between private rights of ownership—indeed, rights that civil libertarians might choose to defend—and conceptual and somewhat amorphous public rights, which has the superior call for legal protection? Note that this question is different from asking which *deserves* the greater legal protection. Both courts addressed the former question and gave the reply they thought dictated by existing law: "Property rights are better." To the latter question, Judge Krentzman said, "Advocates of conservation are both able and effective. The way is open to obtain a remedy for future situations like this one if one is needed and can be legally granted by the Congress." As shall be seen, Judge Krentzman was wrong about the existing state of the law. Those who are interested in strategies for future conflicts might ponder whether he did a poor job of legal craftsmanship or whether he approached the task with the wrong state of mind (in view of who was to review his opinion).

In appealing the decision of the U.S. Fifth Circuit Court of Appeals, CE's lawyers noted that the Rivers and Harbors Act of 1899 forbade any obstruction to navigable waters except as affirmatively authorized and took the position that any fill, whether materially adverse to navigation or not, could not be made until the ban was lifted. Moreover, argued CE's lawyers, the Fish and Wildlife Coordination Act "set a clear standard that the prohibition was not to be lifted, if to do so would adversely affect fish and wildlife."[5] That was the essence of the government's argument, although reference was made to two earlier federal cases (38) that arguably supported the view that permits could be denied even in situations where navigation was not to be adversely affected.

Countering the government's contention, the Zabel-Russell lawyers

5. Government's brief is filed with Fifth Circuit Court of Appeals, Case No. 27555, p. 34.

brought in a new line of argument which had been intended to solve an earlier, even more tumultuous, dispute over the control of sovereignty lands. Instead, it was to tangle the fate of the 11.5 acres of Boca Ciega Bay. Stated simply, the earlier fight was over which sovereign—the federal government or the states—controlled the exploitation of minerals, notably oil, lying beneath sovereignty lands at the margin of the oceans. Texas, California, and Louisiana, where oil had been found in plentiful supply, were the hot spots. Although the grant of statehood to these states was commonly assumed to have carried with it the right of ownership of the bottoms, subject to the commerce servitude, the U.S. government contested that assumption in several lawsuits, including one involving bottomlands off the California coast. A 1947 opinion of the U.S. Supreme Court announced that "the United States of America is now, and has been at all times pertinent hereto, possessed of paramount rights in, and full dominion and power over, the lands, minerals, and other things underlying the Pacific Ocean lying seaward of the ordinary low-water mark on the coast of California . . ." (39). This was a stunning blow to the coastal states and all holders of interests in sovereignty lands deriving from the states. Although the ruling applied directly only to California, the U.S. attorney general announced plans to press the theory everywhere in protection of the interest of the United States (35). Throughout the country, doubts arose about title to lands valued in terms of fabulous fortunes.

After heated debate, Congress enacted legislation (32) in 1953 to settle the confusion created by the California case. The solution, condemned as a great giveaway by many critics (36), was to convey to the states "all right, title, and interest of the United States" in sovereignty lands and in the natural resources found in them. The Submerged Lands Act, as it was named, in effect operated as a quitclaim deed releasing most or all of the interests of the United States in the lands, if any existed, to the various coastal states.

Sixteen years after the Submerged Lands Act became law, the Zabel-Russell case came along, testing just how far relinquishment of federal control really went. Arguing from the text of the statute, the landowners asserted that the states had been given full right to manage natural resources and, moreover, that the federal government retained rights only over navigation, flood control, and production of power. Furthermore, relying heavily on Judge Krentzman's earlier opinion, the landowners argued that the Fish and Wildlife Coordination Act had not expanded the scope of federal control. Therefore, according to that argument, regulation of conservation was vested in the state of Florida and not in the federal government through the army.

Another of the decision-swaying episodes that is not documented in the written records occurred at this point in the case. By this time the question of whether or not mining limestone in the bottom of Lake Okeechobee should be permitted under the Rivers and Harbors Act had come before CE. Because Florida authorities protested, CE had denied the permit and subsequently had been hauled into federal court a second time on charges of erroneously denying a permit. Realizing that the decision rendered in the Zabel-Russell case by the federal appeals court would control the disposition of the Okeechobee dispute, the plaintiff there, Coastal Petroleum Company, requested permission to file a brief as "friend of the court" in the Zabel-Russell proceedings. Permission was granted.

According to the Zabel-Russell lawyers, this action took place just after they had been formally notified that their case had been placed on the Fifth Circuit Court of Appeals' summary disposition docket without a hearing having been held. In the great bulk of cases this would mean an affirmance—that is, victory for the Zabel-Russell interests, since rarely will a lower federal judge be summarily reversed without hearing arguments. In view of this posture of the case, the Zabel-Russell lawyers opposed any tampering with the existing status of it. Nevertheless, the Coastal Petroleum brief was filed. Shortly after, according to the Zabel-Russell lawyers, the case was removed from the summary disposition docket and set for trial.

Whether or not the Coastal Petroleum brief actually changed somebody's mind about the case is not known to the Zabel-Russell lawyers; they believe that it did. Nevertheless, examination of the brief itself reveals no remarkable new arguments. Merely differing in emphasis from the Zabel-Russell brief, the Coastal Petroleum argument delved into the history of the Fish and Wildlife Act of 1958 to show that the act, when proposed, was virtually noncontroversial and received "*no discussion at all in either house. . . .* Not one person or one Representative said a *single word* about the purpose or content of the bill." Reciting as fact that 16 million acres lie under navigable waters in the state of Florida alone and that the nation has "multi-millions," Coastal Petroleum argued that "this routinized passage of what appeared to be an unremarkable bill, a bill which purported to be nothing but a Federal in-family-housekeeping statute, is eloquent testimony that no single Senator or Representative had any idea that the bill was intended to affect tens of thousands of private persons and multi-millions of acres"(1).

Issue was joined in oral argumentation in Jacksonville on 5 December 1969 before a three-judge panel of the U.S. Court of Appeals for the Fifth Circuit. The notes made by a nonparticipating CE lawyer reveal two impressions conveyed to him by the judges' demeanor. The first was that at least one judge appeared to favor conservation strongly. The other was that the court repeatedly questioned the lawyers about the scope of Congress's commerce power and the extent of its applicability to the dispute. This orientation should have been disquieting to the vested interests.

The court began its 27 July 1970 opinion (44) by saying, "It is the destiny of the Fifth Circuit to be in the middle of great, oftentimes explosive issues of spectacular public importance," and then ruled, "We reverse." Moving rapidly to the most fundamental question, the court examined whether or not Congress had the power to "protect wildlife in navigable waters." Supplying the requisite indicia of authority, which is "effect on interstate commerce," the court continued: "In this time of awakening to the reality that we cannot continue to despoil our environment and yet exist, the nation knows, if Courts do not, that the destruction of fish and wildlife in estuarine waters does have a substantial, and in some areas a devastating, effect on interstate commerce. . . . [D]redge and fill projects are activities which may tend to destroy the ecological balance and thereby affect commerce substantially. Because of these potential effects Congress has the power to regulate such projects."

Countering the argument that Congress had relinquished its power to the states in enacting the Submerged Lands Act, the court cited a section of the statute stating that the federal government specifically retained its "powers of regulation and control of said lands and waters for the constitutional purposes of commerce. . . ." Therefore, said the court, the right to control activities affecting commerce had not been abrogated and, to the contrary, remained in federal hands.

Gaining momentum, the court next confronted the argument that Congress, in enacting the Rivers and Harbors Act, had exercised its commerce power only so far as navigation was concerned and no further. In essence, the argument is a somewhat subtle one that is used by lawyers in differentiating between the existence of a source of power in the Constitution and an exercise of the power through legislation. Without an enabling statute giving it life, the constitutional power is dormant and unavailable to the executive in regulating the citizenry. Agreeing with the government's brief on that point, the court held that the Rivers and Harbors Act imposed an absolute ban on obstruction to navigable waters. Furthermore, not only had earlier cases shown that factors other than navigation can be considered by CE in denying permits (see footnote 3), but the Fish and Wildlife Coordination Act and administrative policies devised to implement it "unequivocally expressed [that] [t]he Secretary must weigh the effect a dredge and fill project will have on conservation before he issues a permit lifting the Congressional ban." With the utterance of that statement fell not only the claim of Zabel and Russell to be free to "sterilize" the bottom of their lands but also the claim of Coastal Petroleum Company to mine the bottom of Lake Okeechobee regardless of the effect on the state's water supply. No doubt, as Coastal Petroleum argued, plans to exploit other claims embracing multimillions of acres of submerged lands elsewhere were blunted as well.

One last forum was to be petitioned before this thirteen-year account came to an end: the Supreme Court of the United States. In preparation for the final bout, new lawyers familiar with Supreme Court practice were brought in to seek intercession by the high court on behalf of the landowners. Merely obtaining an audience with the court is always problematical, since it is literally impossible for nine justices to consider more than a small percentage of the cases pressed upon them. Pleading with the Court to issue a writ of *certiorari* to the Fifth Circuit Court of Appeals and bring the case up for review, the Zabel-Russell lawyers argued that their case was a good vehicle for resolving the important public issues involved. The argument was unconvincing. On 22 February 1971, the U.S. Supreme Court denied the petition for writ of *certiorari,* putting an end to legal recourse for obtaining a permit to add that particular 11.5 acres to the fills in Boca Ciega Bay (45). In reaction to the Court's action, Zabel-Russell lawyers reportedly said, "This is the end of the line. There is no more Zabel-Russell fill proposal" (2).

Aftermath

Although the full ramifications of the Zabel-Russell result have yet to be felt, several direct consequences are clear. Most direct, but ironically enough perhaps least important in the total scheme of things, the 11.5 acres of Boca Ciega Bay that once were destined for destruction have been rescued. Also, Coastal Petroleum Company has been halted, under authority of the reinvigorated federal law, in its plan to mine the bottom of Lake Okeechobee. Furthermore, CE purports to be more rigorously exercising its responsibilities, as redefined in the Zabel-Russell case, to insure that due consideration is routinely given to applications for the removal of the congressional ban against obstructions to the navigable capacity of the waters of the United States In a tone of some incredulity, the chief conservation protagonist reports that now *she* is asked to comment on the dredge-and-fill proposals as they come in.

The results of the Zabel-Russell case have been far-reaching. In 1967 Florida law was strengthened to require taking account of various environmental factors before bulkhead lines are set, before dredge-and-fill permits are issued, and before any of the remaining sovereignty lands are sold (14). In 1968 the so-called Florida public doctrine, which purportedly prohibited sales of sovereignty lands when contrary to the public interest, was raised to constitutional dignity in the new state constitution (5).

In view of the meaningless connotation that had previously been given to the Florida doctrine by the state supreme court, the people of the state were not satisfied with it, even as a constitutional statement, and modified the constitution in 1970. Sales of sovereignty lands are now authorized only when the sale would be in "the public interest" (6). Hence, a showing of public benefit to be derived from the sale must be made. Although no court interpretation has yet been given the new doctrine, presumably it requires much more than a mere showing that the public interest in remaining lands is not harmed, which was all the Florida Supreme Court required for a valid sale under the superseded doctrine.

Also, a section of the Florida Constitution first appearing in 1968 proclaimed that it is the "policy of the state to conserve and protect its natural resources and scenic beauty" (7). In a situation involving the construction of a nuclear power reactor on Biscayne Bay, the Florida Supreme Court rendered an opinion (28) attaching substantive meaning to that statement. This holding could signal a change in the judicial state of mind of the Florida court. What could easily have been passed off as mere froth, policy without sanction, was given substance by the court.

Acting to protect the remains of Boca Ciega Bay, the Florida legislature in 1969 enacted a law designating the bay as an aquatic preserve to be retained, insofar as possible, in an essentially natural condition so that its biological and aesthetic values may endure for the "enjoyment of future generations" (15). The next legislative move was to protect larger stretches of the Florida shore from exploitative developments. Noting that "unguided development of [Florida's] beaches and shores coupled with uncontrolled erosive forces are destroying or substantially damaging many miles of our valuable beaches each year," the legislature in 1970 created a construction setback rule (11) forcing evacuation and construction projects away from mean high water on much of coastal Florida. 1970 also saw TIIF given the authority to acquire submerged lands through condemnation and return them to the public domain for public use (12).

The same tempest that resulted in so many public-interest handholds in the previously obdurate body of private-interest Florida law was also at work nationally. Of a number of important changes made in federal law during the Zabel-Russell era, the 1969 addition of the National Environmental Policy Act (NEPA) is probably the most important in protecting the natural environment from unthinking exploitation. In enacting NEPA, Congress stated several purposes, including, "To declare a national policy which will encourage productive and enjoyable harmony between man and his environment; to promote efforts which will prevent or eliminate damage to the environment and biosphere and stimulate the health and welfare of man. . ." (24). NEPA's operative thrust is to mandate that environmental factors be considered in planning federal actions that significantly affect "the quality of the human environment." Already the law books are brimming with cases in which federal judges have insisted that NEPA's strictures be observed. The U.S. Fifth Circuit Court of Appeals' *Zabel* opinion says that issuing dredge-and-fill permits is a federal action of the sort that must conform to NEPA's requirements.

The dredges have been stilled in Boca Ciega Bay and they have been quieted over much of Florida and, presumably, the whole country—at least temporarily. However, while it is true that *Zabel* and related happenings have slowed and stilled dredges, they have not eliminated them. Although dredge-and-fill permits have been made difficult to obtain, they have not been outlawed. Furthermore, thousands of acres of bottomlands remain in private ownership stemming from sales made long ago under the early laissez faire laws that ignored the environment and pampered economic development. The upshot is that the ingredients for exploitation still exist: submerged lands in private ownership under a system of laws that will permit dredge-and-fill operations, given the satisfaction of designated conditions.

The principal effect of this set of circumstances may be to shift the strategic role over to economic vested interests. Forced from free exploitation into a regulated posture by the sword of public interest, the vested interests will now turn their wits and resources to "beating" the system. So long as money is to be made in creating dry land out of wet, someone will press to do it. So long as minerals lie under navigable waters, protection of the public's water supply notwithstanding, someone will want to dig them out. And, so long as a system of permitted uses exists without a master plan for environmental use and resource development, abusive projects will be approved.

One consequence of the *Zabel* opinion is bound to be the generation of many attempts to achieve that result. *Zabel* represents an important triumph of the public interest over vested economic interests. The public interest banner for the most part was carried by a doughty band of concerned citizens, joined early by a group of local officials (PCA) and late, under pressure of immense public outcry, by the agents of Congress. One cannot assume, however, that all is now well on the environmental front bcause federal protectors have been appointed. In a real sense, they were kicked into performing their protective role; they did not volunteer. Moreover, regulators are more urgently courted by the regulated than by countervailing interests and often reverse their role from regulator to protector. Who, then, will watch the appointed watchers? Perhaps the answer to this question is the cornerstone of all strategies for achieving environmental goals. The present answer is unsatisfactory, but clear. The duty of ceaseless vigilance falls to the private citizen concerned with protection of the environment.

References

1. Coastal Petroleum Company *amicus curiae* brief, Zabel v. Tabb, U.S.C.A. 5th Cir. No. 27555.
2. *Commercial Fisheries Review*, February 1971.
3. "Developing and Managing Estuaries." Statement adopted by the Atlantic States Marine Fisheries Commission, Portland, Me., 7 October 1966.
4. "Estuaries—America's Most Vulnerable Frontiers," p. 4. National Wildlife Federation, 1959.
5. Fla. Constitution (1968), Art. 10 §11.
6. Fla. Constitution (1968), Art. 10 §11, as amended 3 November 1970.
7. Fla. Constitution (1968), Art. 11 §7.
8. Fla. Laws 1917, Ch. 7303.
9. Fla. Laws 1955, Ch. 31182.
10. Fla. Laws 1957, Ch. 57–362.
11. Fla. Laws 1970, Ch. 70–230, adding Fla. Stat. §161.052.
12. Fla. Laws 1970, Ch. 70–353, amending Fla. Stat. §253.02.
13. Fla. Laws 1970, Ch. 70–358, adding Fla. Stat. §253.02.
14. Fla. Laws, Ch. 67–393, amending Fla. Stats. §§ 253.12; 253.122; 253.124; 253.126.
15. Fla. Laws, Ch. 69–342, adding Fla. Stat. §268.16(1).
16. Gies v. Fisher, 146 So. 2d 361 (Fla. 1962).
17. Holland v. Ft. Pierce Financing and Construction Co., 157 Fla. 649, 657 (1946).
18. Illinois v. Illinois Central Railway Co., 146 U.S. 387 (1892).
19. McQuigg, J. "The Economic Value of Preserving the Natural Shoreline." Address to the Bulkhead Seminar, Stuart, Fla., 21 May 1965.
20. Opinion and Decree upon Appeal from the Decree of Pinellas County Water and Navigation Control Authority, App. 80, Circuit Court of the Sixth Judicial Circuit for Pinellas County, Fla., Law No. 14, 419, 7 November 1961.
21. Pembroke and Pembroke v. Peninsular Terminal Co., 108 Fla. 46 (1933).
22. Pinellas County Water and Navigation Control Authority v. Zabel, 178 So. 2d 370 (Fla. DC–2, 1965).
23. Pub. Law 85–624, 16 U.S.C.A. § 662 (a).
24. Pub. Law 91–190, 42 U.S.C. §433-47.
25. Riparian Act of 1856, Fla. Laws 1856, Ch. 791.
26. Riparian Act of 1921, Fla. Laws 1921, Ch. 8537.
27. Rivers and Harbors Act of 3 March 1899, Ch. 425 §10, 30 Stat. 1151, 33 U.S.C.A. §403.
28. Seadade Industries, Inc., v. Florida Power and Light, 245 So. 2d 209 (Fla. 1971).
29. *St. Petersburg Independent*, 29 November 1966.

30. *St. Petersburg Times,* 5 May 1966.
31. State *ex rel.* Buford v. City of Tampa, 88 Fla. 196 (1924).
32. Submerged Lands Act, Pub. Law 83–31, 43 U.S.C. §1311 et seq.
33. Taylor, J., and Sploman, C. *Fishery Bulletin* 67 (1968):213, 237.
34. *U.S. Code Congressional and Administrative News* (1953), 1390.
35. *U.S. Code Congressional and Administrative News* (1953), vol. 2, 1422.
36. *U.S. Code Congressional and Administrative News* (1953), vol. 2, 1439 et. seq.
37. U.S. Constitution, Art. 1 §8.
38. U.S. *ex rel.* Greathouse v. Dern, 289 U.S. 352 (1933) and Miami Jockey Club, Inc., v. Dern, 86 F. 2d 135.
39. U.S. v. California, 332 U.S. 19 (1947).
40. Winters, J. W. Memorandum of 7 December 1966 to Board of Pilot Commissioners.
41. Zabel v. Pinellas County Water and Navigation Control Authority, 154 So. 2d 376 (Fla. DC–2, 1963).
42. Zabel v. Pinellas County Water and Navigation Control Authority, 171 So. 2d 376 (Fla. 1965).
43. Zabel v. Tabb, 269 F. Supp. 764 (1969).
44. Zabel v. Tabb, 430 F. 2d 199, 5th Cir. (1970).
45. Zabel v. Tabb, *cert. den.,* 91 S. Ct. 873 (1971).

10

Identification and Achievement of Quality Levels in Managing the Use of Natural Resources

John F. Timmons

Public interest in environmental quality has become aroused and focused upon our natural resources as the constituents of our deteriorating natural environment. This interest is manifested in mounting public discussions and pressures for action. Reacting to these pressures, state and federal administrations and legislatures are taking numerous actions designed to articulate and ameliorate environmental problems which are the causes of public concern.

In the process of formulating and implementing actions to improve the natural environment, important conflicts are surfacing. These conflicts arise from (a) the use of natural resources to produce an increasing flow of goods and services demanded by an increasing population in our affluent and technological society and (b) the management of natural resources (as inherent constituents of the natural environment) to guarantee a continued flow of desired goods and services in terms of higher qualities and quantities demanded. Ancillary conflicts are surfacing in terms of the nature and magnitude of environmental management costs and the incidences of these costs.

Implicit questions to be raised and answered in reconciling these conflicts are directed toward the meaning of quality, the desired levels of quality, and how the desired quality levels are to be achieved. These are the questions to which this paper is addressed. More precisely, the purpose of the paper is to suggest certain procedures whereby quality levels may be identified, measured, analyzed, and achieved in the management of natural resources as components of the natural environment within the national economy.

In pursuing this purpose, the problems inherent in managing the natural environment in terms of its constituent and interrelated natural resources are discussed. Methods are suggested for identifying, analyzing, and measuring qualities of resources within the environmental context of ecological, technological, and economic interrelationships. Approaches to achievement of particular quality levels are discussed. Throughout the paper, suggestions are made for further studies as part of the continuing search for ways and means of developing, analyzing, measuring, and achieving quality levels to provide knowledge foundations for natural resource and environmental quality policy formulation and management.[1]

Natural Resources and the Environment: Use and Management

Inasmuch as the term "environment" has many meanings—"social environment," "natural environment," etc.—and since each meaning is susceptible to various interpretations, the meaning and interpretation should be specified. "Environment" in this paper refers to the natural environment made up of the various natural resources—air, water, soil, minerals, sunlight, vegetation, wildlife, topography, and temperature. The term includes the intricate interrelationships between and among these living and nonliving resources which constitute ecosystems and biomes. Thus, the natural environment is exceedingly dynamic, undergoing continuous interactions and change but achieving states of stability and equilibrium characterized by varying degrees of fragility and vulnerability to exogenous interferences.

These interferences are necessary to man's existence in his efforts to satisfy his wants and are accelerated by man's increasing numbers, affluence, and applications of technology. The interferences are occasioned by man's use of natural resources in satisfying his demands directly (consumption goods and services) and/or indirectly (raw materials). The "and" is necessary because certain resources—air and water, for example—are consumed directly and are also used as raw materials to produce other demand-satisfying goods and services.

Complicating the resource use process by man in affecting (interfer-

1. This paper is Journal Paper No. J-7157, Project No. 1925, of the Iowa Agriculture and Home Economics Experiment Station, Ames.

ing with) equilibria of ecosystems and biomes through their vulnerabilities to exogenous interferences are the combined effects of (a) extracting resources from their ecological equilibrium and (b) inadvertently, albeit necessarily, injecting substances and changes into natural resources and consequently into the environmental ecosystems as an inherent part of the use process. These two types of effects are experienced both in satisfying direct demands (such as breathing air and cleansing with water) as well as in satisfying indirect demands (the production of effluents from processing raw resources).

Effects of man's use of natural resources upon the natural environment are further complicated by the consequences that the use of one resource has upon another resource and its ecosystem. The availability and choice of technology used in the transformation process becomes crucial. For example, the use of fossil fuels to produce wanted energy also produces unwanted smoke which affects air, in the transformation process of coal to kilowatts. Use of uranium to produce nuclear energy also produces heat which, when dissipated into water, affects the thermal quality of water and the ecosystem of which this affected water is a component. Use of soil to produce food also sends suspended silt into water and/or air because of the technological practices used in the transformation process. (More will be said about this particular transformation process in the discussion of identification and measurement of qualities.) Many other examples could be cited.

From this reasoning, certain important inferences may be drawn concerning the management of the natural environment through use of natural resources in satisfying man's demands for goods and services.

The quality of the natural environment is conditioned by the use of the natural resource components of that environment. Use of one resource affects other resources through domino or multiplier actions on the environmental ecosystems. Yet, man is forced to use natural resources in satisfying his wants. Since the linkage between environmental quality and man's use of natural resources is the resources themselves and since society can control man's actions in the use process, the management of the environment involves technological choice and institutional constraints in the use of resources.

Man's choice of technologies in using natural resources can enhance or maintain as well as deteriorate environmental quality. Policies and programs can be developed by society which limit, specify, or enlarge man's choice of resource management practices and which will yield the desired effect on environmental quality as deemed necessary by society. Initially, however, society must determine its objective function regarding the desired quality of environment in relation to other societal objectives, including appropriate trade-offs in optimizing achievement of all desired objectives.

Problems in Managing the Natural Environment through the Use of Natural Resources

Since man affects the quality of environment through his use of natural resources and since man's use of natural resources involves choices and decisions, the range and kinds of permissible choices in resource use become the central issues in managing the natural environment. In the process of providing and limiting these choices, numerous problems arise, including insufficient knowledge of what constitutes desirable levels of environmental quality and how to achieve such levels once a determination has been reached.

The Council on Environmental Quality in its first annual report in 1970 emphasized the lack of knowledge and the need for research in these words: ". . . environmental improvement will depend increasingly on knowledge yet to be obtained through research and measurement. Also needed will be refinements in predictions, setting of priorities, development of comprehensive policies and strategies, and strengthening of institutions at all levels of government" (1, p. 2).

Similarly, President Nixon, in his environmental message to Congress in 1970, stressed the role of education including research and training: "We need new knowledge, new perceptions, new attitudes. . . . Our educational system has a key role to play in this reform. We must train professional managers to deal with pollution, land planning, and all the other technical requirements of a high quality of environment. . . .

"The basic causes of our environmental troubles are complex and deeply imbedded. They include: our past tendency to emphasize quantitative growth at the expense of qualitative growth; the failure of our economy to provide full accounting for the social costs of environmental pollution; the failure to take environmental factors into account as a normal and necessary part of our planning and decision-making; the inadequacy of our institutions for dealing with problems that cut across traditional political boundaries; our dependence on conveniences, without regard to the environment; and more fundamentally, our failure to perceive the environment as a totality and to understand and to recognize the fundamental interdependence of its parts, including man himself" (5, p. vii).

Since environmental quality has become a major national concern and since the level of environmental quality to be achieved involves consideration of other national concerns, enhancement of environmental quality must necessarily be approached in conjunction with other national goals. Thus, improvement of the natural environment is joining and perhaps competing with economic growth and full employment as a major domestic goal. Conversely, deterioration of the natural environment is joining depression and unemployment as major domestic ills to be avoided or remedied.

However, economic growth has been defined and is measured in terms of annual percentage increase in the gross national product. And full employment has been defined and is measured in terms of the proportion of the labor force that is employed at a particular time. But there exists no well-defined and agreed-upon quality standard(s) of the natural environment which can serve as a viable national goal. Neither are there instruments for measuring and achieving environmental quality comparable to measures and means for economic growth and full employment.

Without this definition and means of measurement, environmental quality as a national goal and the means for its achievement remain obscure, ambiguous, and subjective. Also, it becomes difficult to visualize inherent and strategic interrelationships between environmental quality and other major policy goals, including trade-off options among the goals. For example, the meaning of environmental quality as a goal for a member of the Sierra Club is quite different from the meaning espoused by the employer and employees of a small factory who might be put out of business and out of work by the air and water quality standards supported by the Sierra Club members.

Also, the means for pursuing particular environmental quality standards are quite different in terms of motivation and consequences for people in different situations. For example, a monopolist producing chemicals can shift added pollution control costs of his product to consumers. But a farmer must bear pollution control costs himself, at least initially. Of course, the farmer can reason from his knowledge of economic principles that eventually his added costs will also be passed on to the consumer of his products. But this process will take time, and in the meantime he may go broke.

In either case, the consumer will bear the costs ultimately through higher prices. Then he, or more likely she (since women do most of the buying), will wonder whether she really wants improved quality of the environment as much as she did when she supported environmental resolutions as a prominent member of her local civic club. So may the owner of the small factory who can't stay in business. And so may his employees who face unemployment. And so may the farmer who faces increased costs of cleaning up the environment.

They will also wonder if there aren't trade-offs between levels of environmental quality and their own economic growth and opportunities for employment. For sooner or later, national goals must be evaluated and supported in terms of how they affect individual people who constitute society.

Thus, our apparent consensus in support of improving environmental quality today may well turn out to be a very fragile and uneasy confederation as the costs to people become more obvious. This is particularly true if today's support consensus is being forged from emotional appeals exemplified by the Ehrlichs and Paddocks. As with the Vogts and Osborns two decades ago, emotion and hysteria may well lead to reaction and loss of concern when dire doomsday predictions fail to materialize and when individuals are confronted with paying the costs. Concerns and efforts for environmental improvement must be founded upon much more substantial foundations of fact and logic.

Thus, as our states and nation proceed in meeting urgent needs for improving environmental quality, the costs of quality enhancement are likely to meet resistance from many of the same people who presently support environmental changes. As costs of environmental pollution controls press upon producers, as prices of products reflecting pollution control costs press upon consumers, as pollution control taxes press upon the taxpayer, and as pollution control measures restrict individual freedom in resource use, voluntary support and enthusiasm may well diminish—unless environmental improvement policies and programs are founded on and supported by facts and logic that are widely understood and accepted by citizens.

These issues will be and indeed are being decided in current legislative, executive, and judicial processes of government. However, support for and enforcement of these decisions rest with the general citizenry. Their support and compliance, in turn, depend upon how well public resource managers and citizens are informed regarding these very important and very complicated issues. How well public resource managers and people are informed, in turn, depends upon availability of relevant information and how well this information is used by policy makers and made available to citizens.

It becomes apparent that our ability to manage the natural environment through the use of natural resources rests heavily upon the identification and measurement of quality levels and upon the achievement of particular levels.

Identification and Measurement of Environmental Qualities

The Council on Environmental Quality has concluded that the identification and measurement of environmental and constituent natural resource qualities are crucial needs in the assessment of current environmental conditions and in laying the foundations for future environmental quality policy. The council's first annual report states: "Most important, the lack of measurement tools prevents an assessment at this time of the status and trends of the major environmental classes of the nation . . . environmental improvement will depend increasingly on knowledge yet to be obtained through research and measurement" (1, p. 1).

Traditionally, resource scarcity has been interpreted in terms of quantities of resources, i.e., gallons of water, depth of soil, barrels of oil, etc. Increasingly, however, we are realizing that scarcity of resources is largely a function of quality.[2]

The total quantity of water, for example, may be abundant or even superfluous, but we may not have available sufficient water of a particular quality to satisfy a particular use-demand. The water may be too salty, too hot, too toxic, etc., for a particular use. As a consequence, the use process may be made more costly in changing the quality, the use may be diminished, or the use may be precluded entirely even though there is an abundant quantity of water in the aggregate (7).

THE NEXT USE APPROACH TO UNDERSTANDING QUALITY LEVELS

Qualities of water may be the result of another use or they may be produced in the natural state. For example, one set of qualities within a given supply of water may satisfy a particular use but preclude another use. Furthermore, one use of water may leave a residue or an effluent in the water, which diminishes or precludes another use or which increases the cost of another use of the same water.

This situation would constitute pollution, which is a supply-related concept. In economic terms, environmental pollution means a change in a characteristic(s) of a particular resource supply such that additional costs, either monetized or nonmonetized, must be borne by the next use and the next user either (a) through diminishing or precluding the next use or (b) through forcing the next use to absorb more costs in cleaning up the residue left by the initial use or in developing a new source of supply. The next use encompasses a public good (including service) as well as private goods and services.

These events mean that the initial use did not absorb the full cost of its effluent or residue effect upon the resource it used, but instead

2. This realization is part of a much larger syndrome developing in our culture which holds that qualities are, within limits, more important than mere quantities. This syndrome is rejecting largeness and quantities in favor of qualities. For example, the largest building, the largest dam, the largest university, the largest gross national product, or the largest family which Americans have bragged about in the past because of efficiency, size, or other reasons, are currently under serious indictment.

shifted this cost to another use. The external effect may create a diseconomy in the form of an increased cost for another use or it may create an economy or benefit for another use. Of course, problems arise mainly when the externality is a diseconomy or an added cost, monetized or nonmonetized.[3]

What does this reasoning have to do with identifying quality standards for natural resources and the environment? It suggests two criteria—the next use test and the test of irreversibility.

The next use test holds that quality problems occur when the effluent or other effect of an initial use adversely affects the next use to which the resource may be put in meeting needs of people. If there are no adverse effects on any next use(s), then there is little cause for concern and no need for setting a quality standard.

On the other hand, if the initial use creates adverse effects (external diseconomies), monetized or nonmonetized, on the next use(s), then the quality standard should reflect the costs, monetized or nonmonetized, to the next use as well as benefits gained in the initial use. This general philosophy is implied in the National Environmental Policy Act of 1969 (Public Law 91-190, 91st Congress), which requires federal agencies to prepare environmental impact statements on all their activities affecting the natural environment. The Environmental Protection Agency is responsible for the review of these statements. Lack of well-defined environmental quality standards and their measurement is causing considerable confusion and problems in the preparation of impact statements.

This procedure is termed the next use approach for deriving and testing environmental quality standards and is currently being applied in studies on natural resources and environmental quality, as will be noted later in this section. For further discussion of this approach, see Timmons (7, 8, 9, 10, 11, 13, 14).

The second criterion, irreversibility, requires that the use of a resource or any component of the natural environment must not result in an irreversible state of quality. This criterion appears necessary in the formulation of quality standards in order to retain options for resource use that may not be apparent at the moment but may become viable through future technological developments and increases in demand. If

3. For example, a nuclear reactor in power generation uses water to disperse heat. If the increase in temperature adversely affects another use—fish reproduction and growth, for example—this effect is an externality of the power plant and it creates an external diseconomy. We call it thermal pollution. On the other hand, if the effect of heat dispersion by the power plant were to warm up the water so that the water would not freeze and hence would be more useful for transportation, to be sure an externality would be created; but this instance would constitute an external economy since the next use would be favorably affected.

irreversibility of resource quality is permitted, future use options are foreclosed. But such foreclosures must be evaluated in terms of their opportunity costs to other national goals, as indicated earlier.

Through application of these two criteria, two deductions may be made with important implications for policy and programs.

First, only the irreversible criterion may be used as the basis for formulating universal resource quality standards.

Second, the next use criterion means that quality standards will vary from area to area, from time to time, and from use to use, depending on the actual and potential existences of other (next) uses. This criterion seems to rule out national quality standards which do not take into consideration heterogeneities of use requirements and area and time differentials.

The latter deduction appears most likely to constitute the major concern for developing policy and programs concerned with natural resource and environmental quality.

APPLICATION OF THE NEXT USE APPROACH THROUGH PROGRAMMING

In an effort to develop and test procedures for application of the next use approach to environmental quality, two studies, by Edmond Seay and James Jacobs, have been completed in a western Iowa watershed using sediment and phosphates, respectively, as induced changes in water quality from agricultural land use practices within the watershed (2, 6).

In the Seay study, suspended sediment from gully and sheet erosion of crop and pasture lands was selected to typify nondegradable, diffuse-source agents affecting water quality. By parametrically changing the quality level constraints measured by milligrams of suspended silt per liter of water in the stream, using linear programming, least-cost estimates of achieving successively higher-quality standards were obtained. The program was constituted and run to yield solutions with the suspended sediment level initially set at 10,600 mg/1, decreased by 1,000 mg/1 increments down to 1,600 mg/1, and finally decreased to 300, 150, 75, and 37.5 mg/1 levels. Obtaining solutions in this manner made it possible to develop cost functions for the entire range of quality levels specified and to observe various activities (technological and use practices) enter and leave the optimal solutions for each quality level.

In this study, the first use was defined as agricultural cropping which generated 10,600 mg/1 suspended sediment into the stream. If no other use of the water required a higher level of quality (lower sediment load), then there was no apparent reason for raising the quality. However, if there existed other uses—next uses—of the water which required a higher quality (lower sediment load), then the quality needs of the other uses in relation to the first use were given further consideration. In order to test the first use effects on quality against possible next use quality requirements, three additional uses were synthesized: municipal water supply, warm-water fish habitat, and recreation (in the form of contact sports and aesthetics). For these three other uses, quality levels were specified as 150 mg/1, 75 mg/1, and 37.5 mg/1, respectively, based on available but insufficient data.

Results of the analysis, when the three synthesized uses were included and when the level of output of crops from the first use was maintained, showed that the cost of raising the quality level (lowering the sediment load) to that level required by these additional uses would amount to slightly over $9 million for the watershed with the use of the most efficient (lowest cost per unit of output) technological practices. "In every instance it was possible to achieve the most stringent quality standard of 37.5 mg/1 . . . it is somewhat surprising to find that not only could the most stringent standard be met but in fact it was possible to do so while maintaining a substantial part of the cropland in continuous row crops" (6, p. 78).

These are the kinds and measures of essential data required in determining environmental quality levels, but they are not sufficient. Next, we need to determine how the conflicts between the first and next uses may be reconciled in terms of alternative means involving all the uses. One alternative is for the first use to rearrange its technologies so that the quality level demanded by next uses could be met. This would involve consideration of other technological means for the first use to dispose of its effluent. In the case under consideration, a silting basin would be a possibility. A second alternative would be for the first use to bear the cost initially. In the case of the watershed, this cost would be the estimated $9 million. Shifting of this cost would depend upon the competitive position of the firms involved and the elapsed time required to adjust their level of output. A third alternative would be for the next uses to seek a new source of the natural resource. In the watershed case, a deep well, a fish-rearing pond(s), and a swimming pool, respectively, would be possibilities. A fourth alternative would be for the next uses to improve the quality to conform with their required quality needs. In the case under consideration, a treatment plant would be a possibility. A fifth alternative would be for first and next uses to join in providing the required qualities for each use. In the watershed case, one or any combination of these technological alternatives would be possibilities.

The process of choosing among these five alternatives is strategic in resource management. Analysis for making this choice involves locating the least-cost alternative in relation to providing the goods and services (from all relevant uses) demanded by society. Most of the input and output coefficients developed in the linear programs for each of the uses will be helpful in finding the least-cost technological means of achieving the quality needs for all of the uses, including trade-offs in producing the optimum mix of goods and services.

The Jacobs study builds on the results of the Seay study by taking sediment as the transport agent for phosphates within the same watershed. Like the Seay study, the Jacobs study synthesized three uses of water other than the first use (cropping): municipal treatment, warm-water fish habitat, and primary contact recreation. The estimated quality requirements for the three other uses expressed in conjoint terms of suspended sediment (as the transport agent) and available phosphorus were as follows: (a) 150 mg/l and .2 mg/l, (b) 75 mg/l and .09–.015 mg/l, and (c) 37.5 mg/l and .09–.015 mg/l, respectively.

Using these values as quality constraints in the programming model, parametrically changed, on suspended silt and associated phosphates delivered into the stream by the first use (cropping), beginning with 10,000 mg/l, the constrained levels were changed by increments of 1,000 down to 1,000 mg/l, with the remaining levels set at 500, 250, 150, 75, and 37.5 mg/l. The last three constraints represented the estimated levels required by the three synthesized next uses. "Since phosphorous losses are directly related to sediment, phosphorus constraints were computed by applying the sediment load to the phosphorus loss equation, using the E-value of 2, times the A/T ratio for that sediment load. These computed phosphorus constraints covered the range of phosphorus requirements specified for the next uses" (2, p. 106).

Results of the Jacobs study indicated that the most stringent requirements of other uses could be met at an estimated cost of $4.75 per acre annually under assumptions and with the estimated data used in the analysis. Since this study included two quality change agents, sediment and phosphorus, the programming results in terms of the methodology used are of special interest in dealing with more complex quality problems within and between water, air, and other resources. In this study, the result of "limiting phosphorus values indicates, based on the physical coefficients developed, at what level phosphorus becomes the constraining element in the various sediment levels. Thus, by comparing the sediment constraint and the corresponding limiting phosphorus value with the sediment and phosphorus requirements of a particular use, it is possible to determine which one is truly the limiting factor. For example, which factor is limiting for a warm fish habitat with sediment and phosphorus requirements of 75 mg/l and .05 mg/l, respectively? Observing the sediment constraint and the corresponding limiting phosphorus values, it is apparent that the sediment is the limiting factor with a D.R. (delivery ratio) of .20 while phosphorus is the limiting value for the two other D.R.'s. Another interesting observation is the decrease in the value of the dual activity (marginal cost) for phosphorus constraints over a given range" (2, p. 110).

Although the above studies, which are essentially methodological, are limited in their application to one resource—water—to two quality change agents—suspended sediment and phosphates—and to only four uses, the methods developed adhering to the next use concept of resource quality determination could, with appropriate remodeling, be extended to all quality change elements affecting water and to all resources and hence to the quality of the environment. This extension is conceived within the resource and environmental quality complex discussed earlier in this paper. Likewise, all relevant uses could be included. These extensions in applications of the proposed models and methods would constitute a research program of tremendous scope and magnitude. But such a program is essential in providing data foundations upon which consistent and interrelated environmental quality policies and programs may be formulated. The research activities within the program can be fashioned in a manner that provides comparisons and trade-offs among various resource and environmental quality levels, kinds and levels of goods and services produced, and alternative technologies.

Experience with developing and applying the models in the two studies reveals the serious dearth of physical and biological data. At the same time, the models serve an important role in suggesting the kinds and nature of physical and biological data required to satisfy data requirements of the models. Also, implicit directions are suggested for technological innovations necessary to increase the range of choice in the management of resource and environmental quality. These experiences also underscore the necessity of multidisciplinary research including the relevant physical, biological, and technological disciplines and economics. In fact, conclusions for policy making inferred from economic analysis are no better than the physical and biological data upon which the analysis is based. But the models used in making the analysis are necessary in specifying the kinds and measurement of data required from physical and biological sciences for purposes of generating decision-making data for use by administrators and legislators charged with managing the quality of the natural environment and its natural resources.

Achievement of Particular Levels of Environmental Quality

The achievement of a particular quality level, once the level has been determined, rests upon interrelated technological, economic, and institutional considerations. Some of the issues and possibilities within the economic and institutional dimensions are treated briefly in the following sections.

SOME ECONOMIC CONSIDERATIONS

Continuing with our watershed analysis, let us examine who might be expected to pay the costs if the next use were contact recreation carrying the most stringent quality requirement (i.e., 37.5 mg/l sediment), which would cost the watershed's agriculture $9.74 million annually, which would average $2,675 per farm operating unit annually.

There are several possible groups on whom these costs might fall, including: (a) initial use—farm operating units; (b) next uses—contact recreation, fishing, municipal water supply; (c) consumers of products and/or services produced by initial use and/or next uses; (d) taxpayers; and (e) combinations of the above.

Frequently, the assertion is made that the polluter—in this case the initial use, agriculture—should bear all the costs of his operations including any externally imposed costs on other uses. However, if there were not other (next) uses and if the soil and water resources remained within the reversible range, there would be no costs assignable against the initial use since no water quality standards would be violated. In this instance, the watercourse with its 10,500 mg/l suspended silt load, might be performing a beneficial use in diluting, disintegrating, and transporting the residues of the initial use.

Also, it is usually assumed that increased costs to a firm resulting from pollution abatement will be passed along to consumers in the form of higher prices for the products. However, for the agricultural entrepreneur, this option is not available since he tends to be a price taker, not a price maker, operating as he does in the most nearly perfectly competitive of all real-world markets.

Ultimately, however, higher costs of production caused by pollution control measures without product price increases would tend to force farmers, presumably marginal farmers, out of farming. Eventually, production would tend to decrease, which would tend to be accompanied by increases in product prices (depending upon price and income elasticities) which would indirectly reflect pollution control costs.

If pollution control measures result in reductions in the use of pesticides, fertilizers, and other production-increasing technologies, yields per acre and more particularly yields per man-hour would decrease, causing increasing per-unit output costs which would most likely be reflected in reduced production followed by increased prices to consumers.

Such consequences of setting and enforcing pollution control measures could be expected to result in reverberations beyond agriculture and the consumer. For example, industries providing technological inputs in the form of fertilizers and pesticides would be affected. Also, agricultural exports from the United States could be reduced, with effects on the terms of trade between the United States and other nations.

It should be noted that if one state legislated pollution control costs on its producers of a product that was also produced in other states where producers were not encumbered with such costs, the state with the legislation would discriminate against its own producers and tend to benefit producers in the other states. The same reasoning would apply among countries.

SOME INSTITUTIONAL ALTERNATIVES

In achieving particular levels of quality, three broad alternatives may be considered. One is that society would pay for environmental quality enhancement through public outlays. A second alternative is that citizens, as consumers, would pay for environmental quality enhancement through higher prices of products and services. (On the other hand, environmental quality deterioration could cost the consumers higher prices of products and services and reduced flow and/or reduced qualities of such products and services.) In either of the above alternatives, citizens would pay for environmental quality enhancement costs either as taxpayers or as consumers. A third alternative is that society would develop rules and conditions for resource use to which resource users would conform. Most likely, resource management will include elements of each of the three alternatives.

Within the third alternative, there exists a broad continuum of possibilities from which options may be fashioned. One option is to continue to provide individuals with the freedoms of using resources and the environment pretty much as they please in accordance with our traditional land property and use concepts. It is becoming increasingly obvious that this option is not conducive to managing land resources and the natural environment in the best interests of society. Another option, on the opposite end of the continuum, would shift the ownership of land (and the resources that go with each parcel of land) to public ownership. Although one-third of all land in the United States is already publicly owned, this approach does not appear to be socially acceptable, nor is there assurance that public ownership would produce the desired land resource use—for example, timber harvesting, grazing, and mining on public lands are practices that have been criticized.

The third option falls between the first two: land resource ownership vested in private and public entities but characterized by responsibilities and duties as well as rights and privileges. In developing this option as an integral part of our property system, the basic idea is that control over land resources, be it ownership or leasehold, would be exercised in the form of a trusteeship. This concept would apply to public and private ownership alike. It would consider the person or entity in control of a particular parcel of land as the trustee of the resources associated with this land on behalf of society, including both its present and future members. This form would emphasize responsibilities to society in the use of resources and the environment instead of the traditional concept of freedom to exploit and pollute.

This idea was implied by the English economist A. C. Pigou almost half a century ago, when he reasoned, "It is the clear duty of government, which is the trustee for unborn generations as well as for its present citizens, to watch over, and if need be, by legislature enactment, to defend the exhaustible natural resources of the country from rash and reckless spoliation" (4, p. 26).

The idea was also suggested by Aldo Leopold in his proposed "Land Ethic": "An ethical obligation on the part of the private owner is the only visible remedy for these situations" (3, p. 214).

The rights and responsibilities of trusteeship of resources would be defined, implemented, and enforced through resource development and environment control districts. Boundaries of these districts would be determined by the occurrence and flow of particular resources following natural boundaries of resources, such as watersheds, river basins, aquifers, soil areas, flyways, oil fields, and air-sheds. Thus, districts would cut across municipal, county, state, and even national boundaries.

These districts would be empowered to use the policy, tax, and eminent domain powers of government in setting, implementing, and enforcing resource use and environmental control practices. These districts would be responsible and responsive to the citizens of the district and nation in protecting their common interests in resources and environment. The districts would, in turn, hold resource users responsible to the citizens affected by land resource use and environmental effects.

The districts would set use and quality standards: "They would keep resource use within reversible limits. They would effect resource substitutability as needed. They would resolve the problems of competitive uses of a resource and competitive resources for a use. They would determine the application of technologies, use of credit and other instruments in the interest of the people of the district and, therefore, the people of the nation. Externalities would be internalized within the district. Resource educational programs would be carried out within the district concentrating on explaining resource problems common to the district along with remedial alternatives for solving these problems. Federal, state and local programs would be adapted to and administered through the districts" (12, p. 9). Also, district use and quality standards would be consistent from district to district through adherence to state, regional, and national guidelines established and enforced through national and state legislation and entities such as the current environmental protection agencies.

Research studies would concentrate on resource problems within districts to provide the informational foundations for education and action toward the improvement of resource and environmental quality.

As we face the challenge of reversing the trends toward resource exploitation and environmental pollution, serious consideration should be given to basic changes in property structures as foundations for future action. These changes are presented in terms of emphasizing responsibilities as well as rights in resource use. The proposed resource development and environmental control districts would develop the rules for using the specific land resource—soil, water, air, vegetation, wildlife, and minerals—within the districts. These rules of use would form the nature of the trusteeship in land with its rights, duties, and responsibilities.

Ideas of the trusteeship in land and the resource development and environmental control district are derived from and built upon our past heritage and experience in endeavoring to resolve our resource use and environmental problems for the future. Our society has gained rich experiences from the many forms of resource and service districts presently in existence. Our society has always held, in theory and in practice, that public interests transcend private interests subject to statutory guidelines. From these experiences, and in search for the means to deal with today's critical problems of resource use and the natural environment, further study should be given the trusteeship and district concepts along with other means for developing desired qualities of the natural environment and its natural resource components.

References

1. *Environmental Quality*. First annual report of the Council on Environmental Quality. Washington, D.C.: U.S. Government Printing Office, August 1970.
2. Jacobs, James J. "Economics of Water Quality Management: Exemplified by Specified Pollutants in Agricultural Runoff." Preliminary report, Project 425-40-24-09-1925. Department of Economics, Iowa State University, Ames, 1972.
3. Leopold, Aldo. *A Sand County Almanac*. New York: Oxford University Press, 1949.

4. Pigou, A. C. *The Economics of Welfare.* 4th ed. London: Macmillan and Co., Ltd., 1938.
5. President's message to Congress transmitting the first annual report of the Council on Environmental Quality, delivered August 1970. Washington, D.C.: U.S. Government Printing Office.
6. Seay, Edmond E., Jr. "Minimizing Abatement Costs of Water Pollutants from Agriculture: A Parametric Linear Programming Approach." Preliminary report, Project 401-44-48-06-1445. Department of Economics, Iowa State University, Ames, 1970.
7. Timmons, John F. "Economics of Water Quality." *Water Pollution Control and Abatement*, ch. 3. Ames: Iowa State University Press, 1967.
8. Timmons, John F. "Water Allocation: Supply and Demand Relationships." *Opportunities for Regional Research on Water Resources Problems.* Monograph No. 10, Agricultural Law Center. Iowa City: University of Iowa, 1968.
9. Timmons, John F. "Economic Aspects." *Agricultural Practices and Water Quality*, ch. 27. Journal Paper No. J-6469 of the Iowa Agriculture and Home Economics Experiment Station, Ames, 1970.
10. Timmons, John F. "Economics of Soil and Water Conservation." Journal Paper No. J-6470 of the Iowa Agriculture and Home Economics Experiment Station, Ames, 1970.
11. Timmons, John F. "Some Economic Considerations in Planning for Iowa's Future Needs for Water." Journal Paper No. J-6471 of the Iowa Agriculture and Home Economics Experiment Station. Iowa Academy of Science, Iowa City, 1970.
12. Timmons, John F., and Cormack, J. M. "Managing Natural Resources through Land Tenure Structures." *Journal of Soil and Water Conservation* 26, no. 1 (January–February 1971).
13. Timmons, John F., and Dougal, Merwin D. "Economics of Water Quality Management." Proceedings of the International Conference on Water for Peace. Washington, D.C.: Government Printing Office, 1967.
14. Timmons, John F.; Dougal, Merwin D.; and Baumann, E. Robert. *Physical and Economic Factors Associated with the Establishment of Stream Water Quality Standards.* Vols. 1 and 2. Ames: Iowa State University Engineering Research Institute, 1970.

Models for Analysis of Environmental Problems

The first paper in this section, by Edna Loehman, David Pingry, and Andrew Whinston, considers several aspects of the problems associated with the minimum-cost achievement of water quality goals. The model in the paper predicts water quality in a river as a function of flow and physical characteristics of a river and gives costs of treatment on site for polluters along the river and in regional treatment plants. Nonlinear programming can then be used to find the least-cost way to achieve given water quality standards. The paper also discusses the problems of achieving the minimum-cost regional solution through taxation and incentive systems. A system of finance is described which would provide incentives for regional treatment plants. An application of the programming and cost allocation model is presented for the West Fork White River in Indiana.

The paper by John Cumberland gives a model based on environmental-economic linkages. Cumberland develops an extension of input-output analysis which provides information on waste levels and costs associated with various levels of productive output for the economy. His model can be used to investigate the implications of various policy options in terms of environmental quality and costs. However, to implement his model requires detailed information on the wastes produced by each industry per unit output and cost for abatement. Such information is not now readily available. Information about industrial wastes could be obtained through a survey of industrial practices—for instance, through the Census of Manufacturers—but could be quite costly to collect.

The final paper in the book, by Howard Odum and Suzanne Bayley, presents a model which includes both economic and ecological systems. The premise of the paper is that ecological processes have values to man just as economic processes do, but our realization of their importance is limited due to the lack of common units of comparison. The authors propose that energy provides a common unit of comparison and show how to obtain "energy values" when both economic and ecological systems and their linkages are considered. Using their simulation model, energy values for various uses of resources can be computed. By converting energy values to money values, energy cost-benefit analyses could be performed for various resource uses to aid in decision making.

II

Cost Allocation for a Regional Pollution Treatment System

Edna Loehman, David Pingry, and Andrew Whinston

One of the central themes of economics is the analysis of resource allocation. In this paper[1] we consider several facets of a very specific resource allocation problem, that of the allocation of the waste disposal capacity of a river basin. Particular interest is focused on the problems of obtaining and financing an optimal basin solution for a given amount of necessary waste removal.

The first section of the paper presents a mathematical programming model of a river basin of the following form:

Minimize: The sum of the construction, operation, and maintenance costs of all treatment structures in a river basin.

Subject to the constraints: The required level of water quality is maintained under given institutional and physical constraints.

The solution to this programming problem will yield the lowest-cost combination of the treatment alternatives considered.

1. Research was supported by Resources for the Future and the Office of Water Resources Research under Contract 14-31-0001-3080. The opinions presented are the responsibility of the authors.

Assuming that the programming model mentioned above has been solved, the problem of how to implement and finance a basin-wide system remains. When the above problem is constrained to require uniform treatment by each polluter, the total basin treatment cost can be divided among polluters by having each polluter pay for his own required treatment. However, in the case where "joint" facilities such as pipes, flow augmentation, and regional plants are allowed, it is no longer obvious how to assign costs to individual polluters. In the second section of the paper we discuss previous pricing proposals with attention to shadow or marginal prices, and present a new method for cost allocation. These cost allocation and pricing mechanisms are discussed with regard to equity considerations and revenue-raising capability. The relationship between equity and "damage cause" is examined.

The last part of the paper gives an application of the programming and cost allocation model to the West Fork White River in Indiana.

Programming Model of Waste Treatment in a River Basin

A river has a certain amount of waste removal capacity and can be utilized at some levels for decomposition of organic wastes and dilution of some inorganic wastes with little or no effects on water quality. In the past, no attempt was made to ration or allocate this waste removal capacity, partly because relatively low levels of waste disposal did not overtax this capacity and partly because ownership of the water quality commodity was not well defined. We have recently become aware of the need to ration the use of our waterways as waste disposal sites due to increasing scarcity of the water quality commodity resulting from increasing concentrations of inorganic poisons and organic wastes. In many rivers, the waste removal capacity has been overloaded to such a degree as to interfere with alternative river uses such as consumption and recreation.

We have recognized that water quality is a public good whose amount is an issue to be decided by public choice. Two questions regarding public policy toward water quality now arise: (a) What should water quality be? (b) What policies should be adopted to achieve the desired water quality? The first question is a social choice problem which depends on the relative cost of additional water quality with respect to achieving other social goals. (It is clear that any degree of water quality can be achieved at the cost of giving up or altering some of our activities.) In a programming model such as the one presented in this section, the dual variables associated with the quality constraints measure the increase in treatment costs due to an increase in quality goals and so give some help in deciding what water quality should be on the basis of treatment cost. However, the main discussion of this paper concentrates on the second question, that of choosing policy to achieve a desired level of water quality.

The traditional response to the overloading of the waste disposal capability of a river basin is to require polluters to treat part of their wastes, usually in on-site treatment plants. The common practice is to require a fixed percentage of removal of pollutants before the effluent is dumped into the river. However, it has been pointed out in recent articles (1, 3, 4, 5, 11, 12) that this approach does not result in the lowest possible total expenditure for a given amount of waste removal in a river basin. Several alternative combinations of treatment arrangements based on a basin-wide point of view have been suggested. Among these proposals are: (a) nonuniform treatment levels (required treatment would depend on the polluter's location and type of pollutant); (b) regional treatment plants (effluent could be treated in regional plants rather than at the site of the polluter to take advantage of economies of scale); (c) bypass piping (effluent could be piped to various sites along a river rather than disposed of at the site of the polluter); and (d) flow augmentation (water could be stored to use in dilution of wastes).

The first three proposals alter either the pattern of effluent release, quality of effluent, or both. The last proposal increases the natural waste treatment capacity. The mathematical programming model presented here, when solved, will yield the least-cost combination of the above treatment alternatives to meet a given set of quality goals for a river basin. If a regional authority wishes to operate the most efficient (i.e., least-cost) waste removal system, it could find the optimal treatment combination by solving a programming problem of the general type presented at the beginning of this paper.

For the purpose of formulating a mathematical programming problem of a river basin, we model a river divided into sections. A new section is defined when one of the following occurs:

(a) Flow in the river is altered by effluent flow entering the river; incremental flow entering the river (groundwater, tributary flow, etc.); or the flow in the main channel being augmented or diverted.

(b) A change occurs in parameters describing the river's response to effluent.

For an illustration of a typical section k, see Figure 1.

For simplicity, we will only be concerned with organic wastes and their associated demand on the dissolved oxygen in a river. Therefore, the water quality will be measured at the end of each section in terms of the dissolved oxygen deficit. The value of this deficit is calculated using

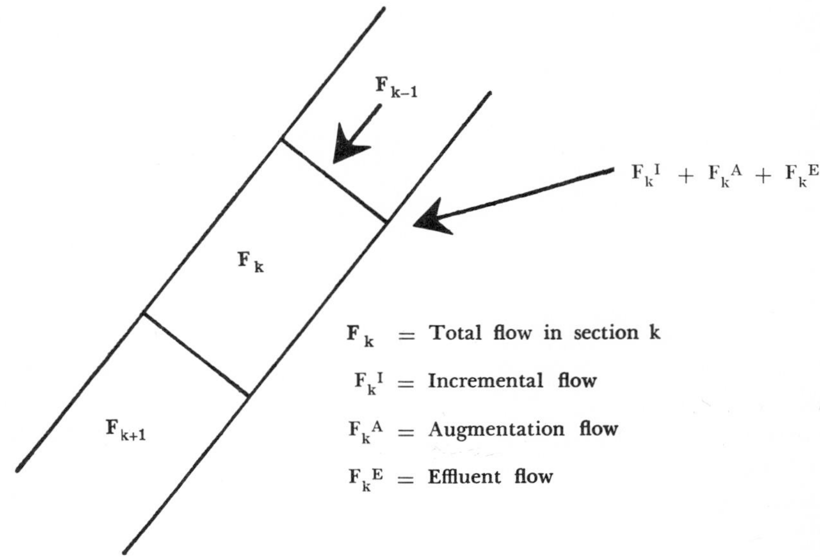

FIGURE 1. A typical river section.

the Streeter-Phelps (13) equations [1] and [2]. (Other types of wastes could be included in the model by adding other measures of water quality and other equations predicting effects in terms of these other measures.)

$$b_k = b_k^B C_{1k} \tag{1}$$

$$d_k = b_k^B K_k[C_{1k} - C_{2k}] + d_k^B C_{2k} \tag{2}$$

The notation is defined as follows: b_k^B is biological oxygen demand at the head of section k (mg/l), b_k is biological oxygen demand at the end of section k (mg/l), d_k^B is dissolved oxygen deficit at the head of section k (mg/l), d_k is dissolved oxygen deficit at the end of section k (mg/l) and

$$K_k = K_{1k}/\ (K_{2k} - K_{1k}) \tag{3}$$

$$C_{1k} = \exp(-K_{1k}t) \tag{4}$$

$$C_{2k} = \exp(-K_{2k}t) \tag{5}$$

$$t = \frac{X_k}{V_k} \tag{6}$$

where K_{1k} is rate of deoxygenation in section k (days^{-1}), K_{2k} is rate of reaeration section k (days^{-1}), X_k is length of section k (miles), and V_k is velocity of flow in section k (miles/day).

It will be assumed that the level of the flow velocity, V_k, and the reaeration parameter, K_{2k}, are functions of the volumetric flow F_k. It is also assumed that the reoxygenation and reaeration parameters, K_{1k} and K_{2k}, are related to the temperature. These relationships are written as:

$$V_k = VC_k (F_k)^{VD_k} \qquad [7]$$

$$K_{1k} = (K_{1k}^{20})\, \theta_1^{T_k - 20} \qquad [8]$$

$$K_{2k} = AK_k\, (F_k)^{BK_k}\, \theta_2^{T_k - 20} \qquad [9]$$

where AK_k, BK_k, VC_k, VD_k, θ_1, and θ_2 are parameters to be estimated for particular river sections and K_{1k}^{20} is the rate of reoxygenation at 20° Centigrade. The terms T_k and F_k are defined as:

$$T_k = \text{temperature in section k (°C)} \qquad [10]$$

$$F_k = \text{flow in section k (cfs).} \qquad [11]$$

As given in equations [1] and [2], b_k^B and d_k^B are in effect weighted averages of, respectively, the biological oxygen demands and dissolved oxygen deficits in the flows F_{k-1}, F_k^A, F_k^I and F_k^E. The values of d_k, $k = 1,n$ can be calculated by starting at section 1 and successively evaluating equations [1] and [2] using the quality information about all incoming flows and the parameters of the river sections.

These equations are the basis for the quality constraints of the programming model, which can be written

$$d_k \leqq d_k^* \qquad k = 1,s$$

where d_k^* is the given quality for a particular section.

This model, as described in detail in Graves, Pingry, and Whinston (5), allows for the following treatment alternatives: nonuniform treatment levels, treatment in regional plants, flow augmentation, and bypass piping.

The objective function of the programming model is the sum of the costs of the various structures necessary to provide the listed alternatives (C^{TP} refers to the cost of treatment plants; C^P, the cost of pipelines; and C^R, the cost of reservoirs). The programming model is given in the following form:

Minimize: $TC = C^P + C^{TP} + C^R$
Subject to: $d_k - d_k^* \leqq 0 \qquad k = 1,s \qquad [12]$
plus institutional and physical constraints.

This is a nonlinear programming problem where the policy variables to be chosen are: flow in pipes, water in reservoirs, treatment level at treatment plants, and location of treatment plants. The costs C^P, C^{TP}, and C^R can be written as a function of these variables.

The solution of this programming problem should give the best (least-cost) solution to meet given quality standards in a river basin.

In order to illustrate this programming technique we will solve a small example. The river of interest will be assumed to be eight sections long. The necessary information concerning river sections, parameters, and incremental and effluent flows is in Tables 1, 2, and 3.

For the purpose of this example it is assumed as an institutional constraint that each polluter is required to treat at a level of 50 percent removal before his effluent enters the regional system. The least-cost solution to the river basin problem [12] under these conditions is to combine all the effluent in a regional plant located at section 4 and treat at a level of 80.5 percent removal. The total cost of this system is \$240,730, of which \$66,480 is piping costs. This cost was obtained by using the cost functions from Frankel (2) and Linaweaver (8) for piping and treatment plants. The cost of augmentation flow was assumed to be \$5,000/cfs.

TABLE 1
RIVER SECTIONS DATA

k	X_k	K_{1k}^{20}	AK_k	BK_k	VC_k	VD_k	θ_1	θ_2
1	1.0	.15	2.55	–.197	.005	.765	1.02	1.05
2	1.0	.15	2.55	–.197	.005	.765	1.02	1.05
3	1.0	.15	2.55	–.197	.005	.765	1.02	1.05
4	1.0	.15	2.55	–.197	.005	.765	1.02	1.05
5	1.0	.15	2.55	–.197	.005	.765	1.02	1.05
6	1.0	.15	2.55	–.197	.005	.765	1.02	1.05
7	1.0	.15	2.55	–.197	.005	.765	1.02	1.05
8	1.0	.15	2.55	–.197	.005	.765	1.02	1.05

TABLE 2
INCREMENTAL FLOW DATA

Section No.	Flow (cfs)	BOD[a] (mg/l)	DO[b] (mg/l)
1	100.0	1.0	6.0
3	5.0	1.0	6.5
5	5.0	1.0	6.5
7	5.0	1.0	6.5

a. Biological oxygen demand concentration of flow.
b. Dissolved oxygen concentration of flow.

TABLE 3
EFFLUENT FLOWS

Section No.	Flow (cfs)	BOD[a] (mg/l)	DO[b] (mg/l)
2	60.0	380.0	0.5
4	60.0	380.0	0.5
6	60.0	380.0	0.5

a. Biological oxygen demand concentration of flow.
b. Dissolved oxygen concentration of flow.

The same problem was also solved allowing treatment only at each polluter as an institutional constraint. This resulted in a system which cost $409,820 and required treatment levels of 82.5 percent, 79.2 percent, and 68.5 percent at polluters 2, 4, and 6, respectively.

If uniform treatment only is allowed, the solution is a system which costs $447,971 and demands a level of treatment of 79 percent from each polluter.

In this particular example we see that savings of close to 50 percent can be made by considering the alternative of a regional plant. The savings from the economies of scale in the regional plant are greater than the cost of piping necessary to move the effluent from polluters 2 and 6 to section 4.

POLLUTION TAXES AND CHARGES IN PERSPECTIVE

In the previous section a model was presented to find a minimal treatment cost solution to a water quality problem. A solution to such a problem gives an efficient solution in terms of cost minimization. However, such a solution may be costly to implement and enforce unless each polluter accepts the regional solution and his share of its costs. We now consider the question of whether there are decentralized mechanisms in which decisions by individual polluters correspond to minimization of regional costs. The possibility of the decentralization of decision making is important in economics since enforcement costs are minimized when the social optimum can be achieved through individual decision making. In economics, taxes or charges of various types are often suggested as a decentralized means of making individual behavior correspond to a social optimum. Several taxation and charge schemes are discussed below.

Examination of the literature concerning the economics of water quality reveals the assumption that society has a right to a certain level of water quality, or that there is a socially optimum level of water quality. By implication, polluters should either be forced to treat waste material at a high enough level to maintain the quality required by society or pay the costs society incurs to maintain the required water quality. In this view, two types of tax schemes are discussed—those relating to enforcing a quality standard and those relating to raising revenue. The first type can be called an enforcement tax. One example of such a tax would be charging a polluter an extremely high tax (or fine) on wastes dumped above a certain level. Thus, above this level, the polluter would rather cease polluting than pay the fine. (To do this, he could either curtail production or build a treatment facility.) Below this level, the polluter is in effect given free rights to pollute. Such a tax would not be intended to raise any revenue.

Another enforcement-type tax would be a uniform tax per unit of waste and the tax would be computed so that a polluter would dump no more than a certain amount. This is illustrated in Figure 2. DD represents

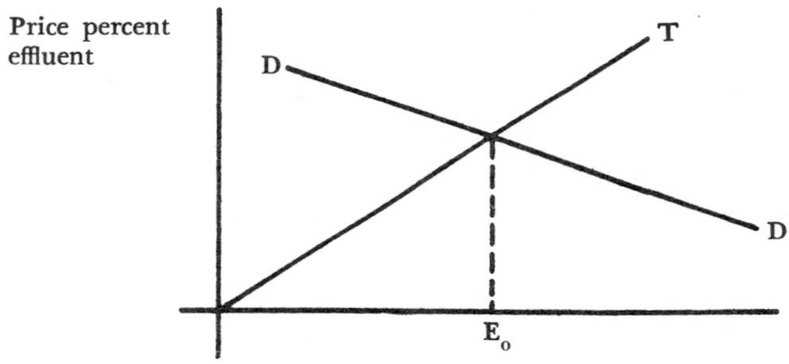

FIGURE 2

a polluter's demand to dump effluent as a function of the tax. If E_0 is the amount of effluent to be allowed under a quality standard, then the per unit tax which would result in E_0 is given by the slope of T. If the polluter should want to produce at a higher level than that corresponding to E_0, then again he would have to build waste treatment facilities. A related concept would be to view the service of waste disposal via a river as a public resource to be sold at a price. The price and amount sold is set to ration use of the service corresponding to the quality goals. In both these cases, the tax revenue collected is "gravy" since the tax-collecting agency does not construct treatment facilities; the taxes serve only to force achievement of the quality standards. Any treatment under these enforcement tax systems would be at an individual level and would be paid for individually. Because of the individual emphasis, such tax systems would not result in minimizing regional treatment costs.

The second type of tax scheme would be for the purpose of raising revenue for treatment purposes. For instance, a polluter could be charged for waste disposal according to the social cost of his pollution, and revenues collected could be used either to alleviate the damages or for treatment. Again, this may not lead to the least-cost regional solution, since it is always easier and cheaper to treat wastes before they enter a stream than to remove them from the stream once they are there. Alternatively, revenue could be raised through charging the polluter for his use of a public or joint waste treatment facility. It would not be necessary for the charge to be collected by a governmental agency in this case. A contractual agreement could be formed among several polluters to operate a joint facility such as a regional treatment plant or reservoir. The charge for use of the facility would be based on cost. The advantage of this system is that the least-cost regional treatment system could be obtained on a voluntary basis. However, in this case, there would first have to be some sort of enforcement mechanism, either legal or through enforcement taxes, to give incentives to polluters to have wastes treated in the joint facility rather than dumping them. If enforcement taxes were used as incentives, then the treatment charges would have to be lower than the tax; otherwise polluters would pay the tax rather than treat their wastes in the regional facility. The charges would also have to be low enough for the polluters to choose the joint treatment alternative rather than treating their own wastes individually. The problem is complicated by the need to cover full costs of building and operating the joint facility from the charges.

It is possible that a proposed tax could fall into both of the above categories as it affects polluters. For example, suppose a uniform effluent charge of five cents per mg/d is to be levied on effluent per unit BOD concentration to pay for treatment costs. Because of differing manufacturing processes, locations, and other parameters, the cost of removing waste material may vary for polluters. For this reason one polluter may have an on-site BOD removal cost of four cents per mg/d and another an on-site BOD removal cost of six cents per mg/d. In this case the second polluter would pay his effluent charges since his marginal removal cost is more than the cost of dumping it in the river, and the first polluter would treat his own waste. This is not inconsistent with the least-cost regional solution since the first polluter can remove his wastes himself more cheaply than in a regional plant; such a situation can arise when a polluter is so far from a regional plant that piping costs overcome possible economies of scale.

Here we see that the tax has served two purposes. In the case of the first polluter, he has been forced to treat his own wastes. In the case of the second polluter, revenue has been raised to defer the cost of treatment undertaken by the "government" or tax-collecting unit. However, it is clear that unless treatment plant sizes and charges are based on the least-cost regional solution, the result of such charges generally may not cover costs of the facilities. That is, in the above example, if a treatment plant were designed to treat wastes of both the first and second polluter and the charge set accordingly at five cents per mg/d, then the plant would in fact be too large since the first polluter would do his own treatment rather than use the plant at that charge.

The determination of charges for the purpose of quality enforcement is generally based on two criteria: equity between polluters, and quality resulting from implementation of charges meeting quality goals. Johnson (6) determines several types of effluent charges which meet the second criterion. The methods used are called least-cost, single effluent charge, and zoned effluent charge.

The least-cost method proposed by Johnson seeks to find the set of effluent charges which will result in the minimization of the sum of the taxation costs incurred by the individual polluters, subject to the constraint that the quality goals are met. This approach could possibly result in a different effluent charge for each polluter.

The second approach seeks to impose a single effluent charge in terms of dollars/lbs. to all polluters, again subject to the constraint that the quality goals are met. Another approach, the zoned method, divides the polluters among regions and assigns a single effluent charge to each region to minimize the total taxation cost over the region. Actually, all of these methods are variants of the zoned method, since the single charge method treats the entire basin as one zone and the least-cost method in effect assigns each polluter to a zone. In all cases the least-cost solution is sought, given the constraints on the charges and the quality requirements. Johnson's charges are all examples of enforcement taxes. His cost minimization criterion is a way of determining how polluting rights are to be distributed and is thus an equity criterion. It would also be possible to devise other methods of assigning effluent charges. For example, instead of zones the polluters could be divided with respect to type, each type being assigned an effluent charge. Assigning the same charge for each type gives another equity criterion.

As already mentioned, there is no reason to assume that the revenue obtained from a uniform effluent charge would exactly meet the cost of treatment. Also, an enforcement-type tax would not generally result in minimizing basin treatment costs. For these reasons, the revenue collection type of tax has recently become more interesting since the thrust has been to reduce total basin costs significantly through the use of treatment alternatives such as bypass piping, regional plants, and flow augmentation. Each of these alternatives creates problems of joint funding and operation of facilities. In such a case the revenue necessary for the operations of these joint facilities must be obtained from the polluters concerned. Charges of the revenue collection variety are usually based on three criteria: equity between polluters, quality goals maintained, and revenue sufficient to cover costs incurred by tax-collecting unit.

Graves, Hatfield, and Whinston (3) have constructed a pricing scheme in their paper on bypass piping. Their scheme is based on an equity criterion of charging polluters according to damages. The scheme is not self-enforcing and so would have to be preceded by some enforcement mechanism to give incentives to meet the quality goal through bypass piping. The minimum-cost piping arrangement is first solved, subject to meeting the quality goals and conservation of flow constraints. The dual variables associated with the flow conservation constraints measure the marginal cost of extra effluent flow from an individual polluter to the least-cost basin solution. Suppose each polluter were charged according to the dual variable per unit effluent. This would lead to a total charge of

$$TP_k = \frac{\partial \hat{TC}}{\partial \hat{F}_k^E} \hat{F}_k^E.$$

(F_k^E denotes the optimal effluent flow from polluter k from solution of the least-cost programming problem, TC is the least-cost solution, and the partial derivative is evaluated for the least-cost solution.) The notation is that introduced in the first section of this paper. Total revenue from this charge would be:

$$\sum_{k=1}^{n} \frac{\partial \hat{TC}}{\partial \hat{F}_k^E} \hat{F}_k^E = \sum_{k=1}^{n} TP_k \qquad [13]$$

which in general would not equal TC. The expression in [13] is only guaranteed equal to TC for all values of F_k^E, k = 1,n if the least-total-cost function is linear homogeneous in the effluent flows.

In the five-polluter example in Graves, Hatfield, and Whinston (3), the least-cost solution is $55,577. The total revenue collected using an effluent charge equal to the value of the dual variables associated with the flow consistency constraints is $179,499. In terms of the notation above:

$$TC = \$55{,}577$$

$$\sum_{k=1}^{5} TP_k = \$179{,}499$$

or

$$TC < \sum_{k=1}^{5} TP_k.$$

In Graves, Hatfield, and Whinston, the revenue is forced to equal cost by redefining the total payment of polluter j:

$$TP_j^* = (TP_j / \sum_{k=1}^{n} TP_k)\, TC.$$

This automatically gives:

$$\sum_{k=1}^{n} TP_k^* = TC.$$

This cost allocation method is based on achieving the quality goals at least cost, the costs are covered from the revenues, and there is an equity criterion. The equity criterion is based on the assumption that polluters causing the same marginal damage will pay the same per unit effluent charge, where marginal damage is defined to be the increase in the basin solution cost due to an extra unit of effluent.

Although the above is one type of equity criterion, it is clear that there are other types, such as the same charge per unit for the same type of pollutant, or the same charge for polluters in the same zone. The notion of what is meant by "equity" must be further examined. Equity is included as a criterion for both revenue and enforcement taxes. Its importance is due both to our ideas of fairness and to the difficulty of enforcing and collecting the tax or charge when it is not felt to be equitable by those who will be charged. In general, the notion of equity is based on two principles: polluters who cause more damage should pay more, and polluters who cause equal damage should pay the same.

The problem which is evident from these requirements is that of interpreting "damage." The proposal to charge polluters of the same type the same amount per unit weight makes the implicit assumption that polluters who dump equal weights of effluent of the same composition are causing equal damage. However, this assumption may be false—for instance, when the flows (hence concentrations) of their effluents differ. The location of a polluter also determines how much damage he will cause. A polluter located in an area of high water quality (and/or high flow) will do considerably less damage than the same polluter located where water quality is poor (and stream flow is low). Damage also depends on what is located downstream from a polluter; there will be much less damage if a pulp mill is located downstream than if a municipal water plant is located downstream. Under closer examination it is not at all clear that any measure of effluent composition alone reflects pollution damage. In an economic sense, the only measure of damage that is really relevant is the amount of additional cost necessary to maintain desired quality goals due to the existence of polluter k. If polluter k dumps a certain effluent but causes no additional treatment cost to the system (i.e., quality constraints are not violated), then his existence is irrelevant as far as any treatment cost scheme is concerned.

Graves, Hatfield, and Whinston recognized cost in this way as a reflection of damage through their use of the dual variables of the programming model to generate equitable shares of the total basin costs. The problem associated with this measurement of damage, as with any sort of marginal concept, is that this information is only "local" in nature. Since the relationship between the optimal basin solution and the flows from the individual polluters is nonlinear, the marginal cost at the optimum solution of an additional unit of flow from polluter i is no reflection of the marginal cost of earlier units. It is also no reflection of the added cost to meet the standards if effluent from a polluter were to be increased by more than one unit. Thus, the equity criterion used by Graves, Hatfield, and Whinston is not completely satisfactory.

Incremental Cost Allocation Scheme

In the preceding sections of this paper we have indicated several faults associated with the pricing and cost allocation systems presented in the literature. These faults can be summarized as follows: (a) failure of revenue collected to meet total costs of treatment; (b) failure of some pricing systems to be based on the most efficient (least-cost) combination of treatment methods; and (c) failure of pricing schemes to satisfy acceptable equity criteria.

In this section we present a cost allocation system which we feel adequately deals with these problems. This approach takes as given the present composition of polluters in the river and the given quality goals and attempts to allocate the costs of a basin-wide system. Both the costs of individual polluters and the joint costs of using regional treatment plants are considered in the allocation scheme.

After an optimal solution to a basin pollution problem, such as that described earlier, has been obtained, it is not at all clear what part of the cost of that system of dams, treatment plants, and pipelines can be attributed to the fact that a particular polluter is in the basin. That is, when several polluters are present, it is not always clear who was responsible for violating the quality constraints, and hence the exact damage cost attributable to any one polluter is not well defined. If we could measure the cost that an individual polluter causes to the system, then we would have some basis upon which to decide what his contribution to the total cost of the abatement system should be. We will now describe a way of allocating the total system costs to polluters based on the idea of each polluter paying the incremental cost he causes to the system.

Consider a basin with only two polluters, designated 1 and 2. Denote the least-cost solution to the basin problem of formula [12] by C(1,2). The incremental cost caused by polluter 1 being in the basin, given that polluter 2 is in the basin, is defined to be:

$$IC(1) = C(1,2) - C(2)$$

where C(2) is the cost of polluter 2 treating his own waste. Both the values of C(1,2) and C(2) can be computed using the programming model in the previous section.

A logical tax based on each polluter paying his social cost would then appear to be to charge polluter 1 IC(1) and polluter 2 IC(2), where

$$IC(2) = C(2).$$

We note that

$$IC(1) + IC(2) = C(1,2)$$

which means that the total cost of the basin project has been covered by this tax scheme. However, the following question now arises: what if the polluters are considered in reverse order? Consider the following definitions of $IC^*(1)$ and $IC^*(2)$:

$$IC^*(1) = C(1)$$
$$IC^*(2) = C(1,2) - C(1).$$

If polluter 1 is charged $IC^*(1)$ and polluter 2 is charged $IC^*(2)$, the total cost of the basin system is covered as before, but the charge to each polluter differs in these two schemes. As an example, consider a case where if either of the polluters are alone in the basin the quality goals are met without treatment, and if they are both in the basin the goals are violated. Assume that the optimal solution when both are present is to build a reservoir for flow augmentation at a cost of C(1,2) = \$100. The values of C(1) and C(2) are both zero since the standards are met if either polluter is absent. If the first calculation of incremental cost is used, the charges for polluters 1 and 2 are:

$$IC(1) = \$100$$
$$IC(2) = \$0.$$

If the second calculation is used, the charges are:

$$IC^*(1) = \$0$$
$$IC^*(2) = \$100.$$

Polluter 1 would clearly prefer the second cost allocation over the first allocation, and by the same token polluter 2 would prefer the first allocation. Since either ordering of the polluters is equally plausible, we may average all the possible incremental costs which each polluter could cause to obtain a cost allocation of

$$\begin{aligned}\rho(1) &= \tfrac{1}{2}\, IC(1) + \tfrac{1}{2}\, IC^*(1) \\ &= \tfrac{1}{2}\,(100) + \tfrac{1}{2}\,(0) = 50\end{aligned}$$

and

$$\begin{aligned}\rho(2) &= \tfrac{1}{2}\, IC(2) + \tfrac{1}{2}\, IC^*(2) \\ &= \tfrac{1}{2}\,(0) + \tfrac{1}{2}\,(100) = 50.\end{aligned}$$

The sum of the payments from the polluters covers the total basin cost of $C(1,2) = \$100$. However, the equity problem has been taken care of by considering all possible orders of the polluters, in this case (1,2) and (2,1), and averaging over possible definitions of incremental cost for each polluter.

This approach is easily extended to a case of three polluters where there are six possible orders for calculating incremental costs for each polluter. For example, considering polluter 1, the following orders are possible:

Order 1:	(1 2 3)	polluter 1 before polluters 2 and 3
Order 2:	(1 3 2)	
Order 3:	(2 1 3)	polluter 1 after polluter 2
Order 4:	(3 1 2)	polluter 1 after polluter 3
Order 5:	(2 3 1)	polluter 1 after polluters 2 and 3
Order 6:	(3 2 1)	

Corresponding to each of these orders is a way of defining incremental cost for polluter 1 (the subscripts denote the order under consideration):

$$\begin{aligned}IC_1(1) &= C(1)\\ IC_2(1) &= C(1)\\ IC_3(1) &= C(1,2) - C(2)\\ IC_4(1) &= C(1,3) - C(3)\\ IC_5(1) &= C(1,2,3) - C(2,3)\\ IC_6(1) &= C(1,2,3) - C(2,3).\end{aligned}$$

For polluter 2, the following incremental cost definitions are possible:

$$\begin{aligned}
IC_1(2) &= C(1,2) - C(1)\\
IC_2(2) &= C(1,2,3) - C(1,3)\\
IC_3(2) &= C(2)\\
IC_4(2) &= C(1,2,3) - C(1,3)\\
IC_5(2) &= C(2)\\
IC_6(2) &= C(2,3) - C(3).
\end{aligned}$$

And for polluter 3:

$$\begin{aligned}
IC_1(3) &= C(1,2,3) - C(1,2)\\
IC_2(3) &= C(1,3) - C(1)\\
IC_3(3) &= C(1,2,3) - C(1,2)\\
IC_4(3) &= C(3)\\
IC_5(3) &= C(2,3) - C(2)\\
IC_6(3) &= C(3).
\end{aligned}$$

Giving each of the possible orders equal weight, the average incremental cost for each polluter is obtained:

$$\rho(i) = \frac{1}{6} \sum_{j=1}^{6} IC_j(i) \qquad i = 1,2,3.$$

Note that

$$\sum_{i=1}^{3} \rho(i) = C(1,2,3)$$

so that total costs would be covered by charging each polluter the amount $\rho(i)$.

Generalizing to the case of n polluters where there would be n! orderings, the cost allocation formula is given by

$$\rho(i) = \frac{1}{n!} \sum_{j=1}^{n!} IC_j(i) \qquad i = 1, \ldots, n \qquad [14]$$

where $IC_j(i)$ is the incremental cost due to i in ordering j. Also,

$$\sum_{i=1}^{n} \rho(i) = C(1,2, \ldots, n).$$

This cost allocation scheme is discussed in Loehman and Whinston (10). In another Loehman and Whinston paper (9) there is a theoretical development of the cost allocation method described. It is demonstrated that formula [14] is a unique formula which satisfies the following axioms: (a) Charges for the use of the basin treatment system must cover costs. (b) A user's charges are based only on the incremental cost caused by the user. (c) The user's charge is independent of the ordering or labeling of the users. (d) If a user's incremental costs increase by λ, then his charge will increase by λ. The equity properties of this scheme are evident from axioms b–d.

The following example illustrates cost allocation for the three-polluter case. Suppose the costs of treatment to meet the quality goals are given as follows:

$$\begin{aligned} C(1,2,3) &= 70 \\ C(1,2) &= 40 \\ C(1,3) &= 60 \\ C(2,3) &= 50 \\ C(1) &= 30 \\ C(2) &= 40 \\ C(3) &= 40 \end{aligned}$$

$$\rho(1) = \frac{1}{3}(30) + \frac{1}{6}(40 - 40) + \frac{1}{6}(60 - 40) + \frac{1}{3}(70 - 50)$$

$$= \frac{30}{3} + 0 + \frac{10}{3} + \frac{70}{3} = \frac{60}{3} = 20$$

$$\rho(2) = \frac{1}{3}(40) + \frac{1}{6}(40 - 30) + \frac{1}{6}(50 - 40) + \frac{1}{3}(70 - 60)$$

$$= \frac{40}{3} + \frac{15}{3} + \frac{5}{3} + \frac{10}{3} = \frac{60}{3} = 20$$

$$\rho(3) = \frac{1}{3}(40) + \frac{1}{6}(60 - 30) + \frac{1}{6}(50 - 40) + \frac{1}{3}(70 - 40)$$

$$= \frac{40}{3} + \frac{15}{3} + \frac{5}{3} + \frac{30}{3} = \frac{90}{3} = 30.$$

Note that

$$\rho(1) + \rho(2) + \rho(3) = 70 = C(1,2,3).$$

Applications of Pricing Scheme

In the last section we presented an alternative cost allocation mechanism to be used for regional treatment systems. In this section we apply the scheme to some small examples and to the West Fork White River.

Examples using three polluters located on the river are given below to illustrate use of the programming model in the cost allocation scheme. The effluent data for these polluters are given in Table 4.

TABLE 4
EFFLUENT DATA (EXAMPLES 1, 2, AND 3)

Polluter (Section)	Flow (cfs)	BOD (mg/l)	DO (mg/l)
2	60.0	380.0	0.5
4 (5)[3]	60.0	380.0	0.5
6	60.0 (120.0)[2,3]	380.0	0.5

NOTE: Superscripts 2 and 3 denote alterations to Table 4 for examples 2 and 3 in Tables 5 and 6.

In solving the programming models, the least-cost solution to the basin problem for Example 1 is to construct a regional plant at section 4 and pipe the effluent from 2 and 6 to this plant to be treated. Flow augmentation does not enter this solution. The cost is $240,730.

We now wish to divide the total cost of the regional system, in this case the cost of the plant and pipes, between the three polluters using the cost allocation method explained in the last section. This necessitates the calculations of C(2), C(4), C(6), C(2,4), C(2,6), and C(4,6). These calculations appear to be straightforward. However, when the situation is examined more carefully, it is not so clear how to define C(G) where G is a subgroup of the total group of users N. For example, assume that we wish to calculate C(2). What do we assume about polluters 4 and 6? Are they nonexistent? Are they treating at some uniform level? Are they dumping their effluent with no treatment? An infinite number of assumptions could be made concerning the behavior of the polluters not in the coalition to be examined.

The only restraint on the behavior of the polluters outside of the group G being considered is that they are treating in a manner which will allow the polluters in G to gain feasibility of the basin problem (i.e., the quality constraints can be satisfied for some level of treatment of wastes from G). For example, if the polluters outside of the coalition G are assumed to be dumping all wastes directly into the stream, it is very likely that several sections of the river will violate the quality constraints no matter what the polluters in G do. One procedure which can guarantee the feasibility of the problem is to find the least-cost solution to the basin problem, C(N), and assume that all polluters outside of G are required to treat their effluent to the same level as they did in the solution for C(N).

The term C(G) can now be interpreted as the least cost the polluters in G must pay to maintain the quality goals, given that the other polluters in the basin are treating on site at the same level required for the least-cost base solution. The polluters in G can make use of flow augmentation, regional plants, and piping. In the special case where G contains only one polluter, flow augmentation and piping are the only alternative methods available. In certain cases, some coalitions of polluters may receive no savings over on-site treatment; this occurs if they are so far apart that piping costs overwhelm any economies of scale gained from a regional plant, and flow augmentation is relatively more expensive than treatment. The best possible alternative for these polluters is to treat on site. In such a case, the cost to the coalition would be just the sum of the individual on-site costs, or

$$C(G) = \sum_{i \epsilon G} C(i).$$

The cost allocation of the solution to Example 1, given the above cost definition, can now be determined by using the treatment required in the solution for C(2,4,6) to determine the values of C(2), C(4), C(6), C(2,4), C(2,6), and C(4,6). These results are presented in Table 5. Using the formulas of the previous section, the cost allocation for this example is:

$$\begin{aligned} \rho(2) &= 165 \\ \rho(4) &= 92 \\ \rho(6) &= -19. \end{aligned}$$

Since $\rho(6)$ is negative, it indicates a subsidy for polluter 6. The reason for the subsidy for polluter 6 is that adding him to the other coalitions actually reduces their total costs, since they can then pipe their effluent down to section 6 where the flow is greater, which reduces the necessary treatment levels. The relatively high cost which polluter 2 must pay reflects his location upstream where the total flow is lower.

TABLE 5
SUB-COALITION COSTS ($1,000)

		Example 1	Example 2
C (2)	=	226.2	252.9
C (4)	=	139.6	129.9
C (6)	=	42.3	117.3
C (2,4)	=	286.1	290.6
C (2,6)	=	158.5	284.5
C (4,6)	=	103.8	202.3
C (2,4,6)	=	240.7	300.0
C* (2,4,6)	=	408.1	500.1

NOTE: C* (2,4,6) denotes the cost when each polluter must treat on site, i.e., no regional treatment is allowed. C* (2,4,6) = C (2) + C (4) + C (6).

In order to examine the cost allocation system in more detail we consider the second example from Table 4 where the effluent flow from polluter 6 is doubled but the other data are the same as in Example 1. The costs of the subcoalition solutions are also presented in Table 5. The cost allocation for this example is:

$$\rho(2) = 171$$
$$\rho(4) = 69$$
$$\rho(6) = 60.$$

We note that polluter 6 has a greatly increased share. Polluter 2's cost share is reduced, as he is now able to take advantage of economies of scale made available because of polluter 6's increased volume. Since

TABLE 6
SUB-COALITION COSTS ($1,000)

Example 3		
C (2)	=	249.5
C (5)	=	58.6
C (6)	=	148.3
C (2,5)	=	194.4
C (2,6)	=	309.8
C (5,6)	=	187.7
C (2,5,6)	=	291.1
C* (2,5,6)	=	456.4

NOTE: C* (2,5,6) denotes the cost when each polluter must treat on site, i.e., no regional treatment is allowed. C* (2,5,6) = C (2) + C (5) + C (6).

polluter 6 would have higher on-site treatment costs if he had to treat his wastes to the level required outside a coalition, his share in the final allocation of costs is increased.

In order to see the effects of location on the cost shares we consider a further alteration of our basic example. Assume that polluter 4 is relocated in section 5. The data in Table 4 for Example 3 now apply. To indicate the relocation, we simply relabel polluter 4 as polluter 5. The subcoalition costs are given in Table 6. Since piping costs are reduced by the relocation of polluter 4 to section 5, we note the reduction in total basin costs. The cost allocation for this particular example is:

$$\rho(2) = 167$$
$$\rho(5) = 11$$
$$\rho(6) = 113.$$

The programming model and cost allocation system as proposed have been applied to the West Fork White River in Indiana. The West Fork White River has its source near the Indiana-Ohio border and flows southwesterly for 371 miles through the state of Indiana. At this point it joins the East Fork White River and flows to the Ohio River.

The major city on the West Fork White is Indianapolis, a city with a population of over 600,000, which is 234 miles from the mouth. Two minor cities, Anderson and Muncie, are upstream from Indianapolis. The concentration of population and industry around these three cities causes the major portion of the pollution problem in the West Fork White.

For the purpose of this analysis we have chosen a length of the West Fork White which runs from the headwaters above Muncie to Spencer below Indianapolis; the area is shown in Figure 3. There are thirteen major polluters, described in Table 7. The part of the river described is 172.8 miles long and is divided into 62 sections based on information about polluters, incremental flow, and river parameters. The sections range in length from .1 miles to 6.2 miles. The incremental flows and section parameters necessary for the implementation of the model are given in Tables 8 and 9.

For the purpose of this application we assume that all polluters are already treating on site at a level of 80 percent removal (secondary treatment). The basin solution in this case will contain only advanced (tertiary) waste treatment necessary to achieve required standards. The quality standards assumed will be 5 mg/1 for every section.

The least-cost solution for tertiary treatment for the West Fork White River is to build a regional plant for polluters 40 to 46 at section 46 treating at the 95 percent level. The rest of the polluters, except for 6 and 16, remain treating on site at 80 percent removal. Polluters 6 and 16 must treat on site at levels of 93 and 86 percent, respectively. They are not close enough neighbors to use a regional plant, since the piping costs would exceed any gains from economies of scale. The cost of the basin solution is \$2,013,296. Of this amount, \$1,587,054 is for the regional plant at section 46; \$208,577 is for the pipeline from polluter 40 to the regional plant; and the rest is divided between polluters 6 and 16 in amounts of \$158,068 and \$59,597, respectively.

Since the only joint facility is between polluters 40 and 46, the costs for any coalition, except those including both 40 and 46, will be separable into the sum of costs for each individual polluter. That is,

$$C(G) = \sum_{i \in G} C(i)$$

if both 40 and 46 are not in G

$$C(G) = C(40,46) + \sum_{i \in G-40-46} C(i)$$

if both 40 and 46 are in G.

The cost allocation resulting is that each polluter except 40 and 46 pays the on-site treatment costs (at the 80 percent level for all except polluters 6 and 16, at the 93 percent level for polluter 6, and at the 86 percent level for polluter 16). For polluters 40 and 46 the allocated costs are:

$$\rho(40) = \frac{1}{2} C(40) + \frac{1}{2} [C(40,46) - C(46)]$$

$$= \frac{1}{2} (\$1,013,415) + \frac{1}{2} [\$1,795,631 - \$988,081] = \$910,482$$

and

$$\rho(46) = \frac{1}{2} C(46) + \frac{1}{2} [C(40,46) - C(40)]$$

$$= \frac{1}{2} (\$988,081) + \frac{1}{2} [\$1,795,631 - \$1,013,415] = \$885,148.$$

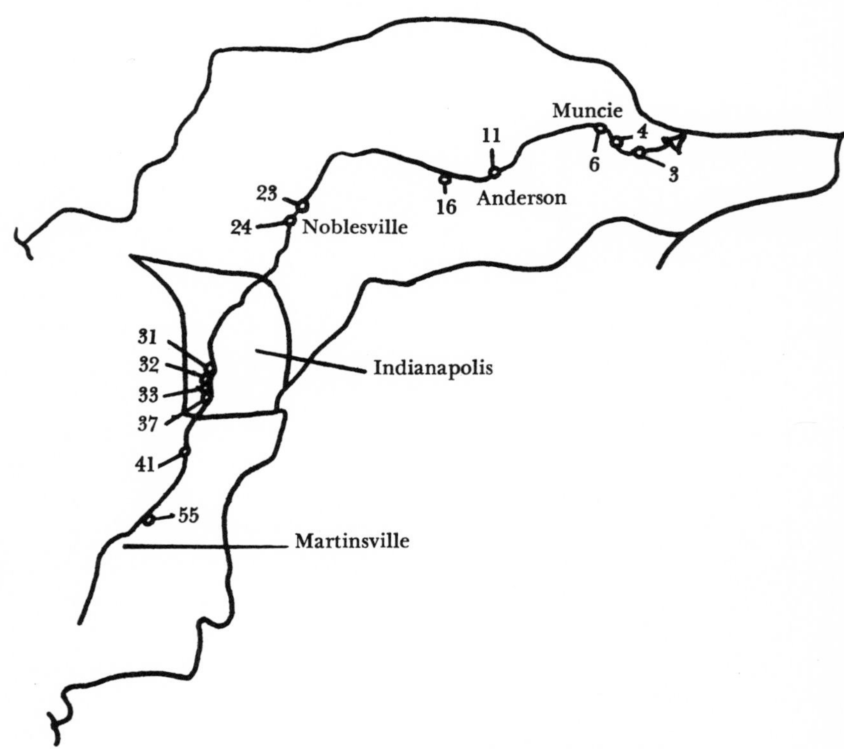

FIGURE 3. West Fork White River, location of polluters.

In this particular example many joint facilities were not required for the solution. This is due to the fact that we assumed that 80 percent on-site treatment was already taking place uniformly in the basin. If this restrictive assumption were not made, the solution would include much more extensive use of joint facilities. We would then also expect the total basin expenditure to be much lower than in the above example due to the economies of more shared facilities.

Note that by the allocation scheme above, rights to pollute have in effect been assigned. For the above West Fork White example, all polluters except 6, 16, 40, and 46 are required to treat at only the 80 percent level while 6, 16, 40, and 46 are required to treat at a higher level. Both pollution rights and cost shares are allocated according to damage caused to the basin in terms of cost of achieving the quality standards. This is one way to allocate costs and rights which is equitable in the sense that those who cause equal basin costs are charged equally. However, from the polluter's own point of view it may not seem equitable. For instance, polluters 6 and 16 could say that their higher levels of treatment benefit the rest of the polluters by allowing them to treat only 80 percent. By this reasoning, polluters 6 and 16 could feel that some of their costs should be borne by the other polluters. This question of equity cannot be finally answered by any analytical means. The economist's job is merely to present some schemes which have various equity properties so that society can choose among them.

TABLE 7
POLLUTER DATA

Description	Polluter No. (k)	Location	Flow (cfs)	BOD (mg/l)	DO (mg/l)
Industry	4	Muncie	.27	40.00	4.00
Municipal T.P.	6	Muncie	20.83	322.00	3.00
Industry	11	Anderson	.30	298.00	0.00
Municipal T.P.	16	Anderson	24.40	200.00	2.00
Municipal T.P.	26	Moblesville	.78	270.00	2.00
Industry	35	Indianapolis	13.20	20.50	6.50
Industry	36	Indianapolis	.93	19.00	8.30
Industry	37	Indianapolis	13.00	20.00	2.30
Municipal T.P.	40	Indianapolis	195.00	450.00	2.60
Industry	41	Indianapolis	10.00	20.00	2.00
Combination of several polluters	42	Indianapolis	61.00	30.44	4.00
Municipal T.P.	46	Indianapolis	185.00	450.00	3.90
Municipal T.P.	56	Martinsville	.93	300.00	0.00

TABLE 8
INCREMENTAL FLOW DATA

k	Flow (cfs)	BOD (mg/l)	DO (mg/l)
1	52.00	2.92	2.30
2	6.10	2.63	6.70
4	−21.20	−0.00	−0.00
5	1.00	214.00	1.00
7	30.30	9.80	3.70
9	4.00	23.20	5.60
10	6.40	13.20	2.40
14	3.00	5.50	5.20
15	72.00	7.70	5.40
19	44.00	7.18	5.80
20	−35.00	−0.00	−0.00
22	23.00	12.10	5.60
27	16.10	6.90	6.40
28	13.00	5.00	6.50
30	14.00	5.00	5.90
32	−214.00	−0.00	−0.00
33	28.00	5.00	7.90
34	21.00	10.62	6.20
35	5.80	12.40	6.60
39	5.00	9.30	7.50
42	1.00	1.00	6.00
44	8.00	13.90	6.00
46	8.00	5.00	3.90
48	9.00	5.00	6.00
50	10.00	23.20	1.00
52	21.00	16.70	1.60
53	33.70	8.00	8.30
55	6.00	13.70	2.10
57	14.00	5.00	6.00
58	35.00	5.00	8.00
59	38.00	5.00	6.00
61	71.00	5.00	7.00
62	25.00	5.00	7.00

COST ALLOCATION OVER TIME

In the previous sections we have considered the cost allocation problem in terms of a given set of polluters and effluent flows. We now consider the use of the cost allocation procedure for a basin with changing numbers of polluters and changing effluent flows.

Assume, for example, that there are two sets of polluters, N^1 and N^2. N^1 is the set of all original polluters in a river basin currently operating joint facilities under the administration of a basin authority. The set N^2 consists of all the polluters who wish to join the existing basin organization. An increase in the flow from a polluter in N^1 can be handled by considering it as coming from a polluter in N^2. Let $C(N^1, N^2)$ denote the least cost of treatment to meet the standards after the addition of the polluters N^2 into the basin. N^2 will thus add the amount

$$C(N^1, N^2) - C(N^1)$$

to total basin costs. At this point it must be decided how N^2 should be treated in relation to the original members of the basin system. Suppose cost shares to N^1 are reallocated by allocating the cost $C(N^1, N^2)$ to members of $N^1 \cup N^2$ as if they had both entered into a coalition agreement at the same time. This approach would have one of two effects on the cost allocated to the members of the original system. It is possible that the economies of scale available because of the additional effluent flow from the entering polluters would lower the cost shares of some of the existing polluters. It is also possible that the degree of treatment necessary because of the additional polluters would result in more costs than gains from economies of scale and would cause the original polluters N^1 to pay a larger cost share than before. Treating members of N^1 and N^2 the same in cost allocation could thus lead to a situation which we would feel to be inequitable.

It is also probable, because of stepwise procedure used when groups of polluters enter the basin at different times, that the least-cost solution will not correspond to the least-cost solution that would result if they all entered the basin together. This is because the least-cost solution of the system including the latecomers may not include structures already built by the early-comers. It is also possible that one cannot enlarge an existing plant and still take advantage of returns to scale. For example, it is difficult to see how a pipeline could be enlarged by a certain quantity of flow capacity. It is only possible to expand pipe capacity by laying new pipe, and then any economies of scale have been lost. In this sense latecomers impose a cost on the current members of the basin system.

It would seem that an equitable restriction on latecomers would be forcing them to cover any additional costs incurred by the basin system. This could be implemented by dividing the additional costs caused by polluters N^2 among the members of N^2 using the cost allocation technique. In other words, the amount $C(N^1)$ would be divided among N^1 in the amounts previously calculated and the amount $C(N^1, N^2) - C(N^1)$ would be divided among the polluters in N^2, again using the incremental cost scheme. This solution to the problem, however, does not enable the polluters in N^1 to take advantage of possible economies of scale introduced by the polluters in N^2 which they would have had available had both groups arrived at the same time.

The questions of allocating costs over time and how effluent charges should change as new polluters are added to a river have not even been

TABLE 9

RIVER SECTION DATA[a]

k	X_k	K_{1k}^{20}	AK_k	BK_k	VC_k	VD_k
1	5.600	.115	6.45000	—.249	.0445	.550
2[b]	.100	.100	6.45000	—.249	.0445	.550
3	6.200	.103	6.45000	—.249	.0445	.550
4	1.900	.100	6.45000	—.249	.0445	.550
5	3.600	.100	6.45000	—.249	.0445	.550
6	3.700	.600	6.45000	—.249	.0445	.550
7[b]	.100	.115	6.45000	—.249	.0445	.550
8	3.200	.630	6.45000	—.249	.0445	.550
9	2.800	.630	6.45000	—.249	.0445	.550
10	3.000	.630	6.45000	—.249	.0445	.550
11	4.300	.623	6.45000	—.249	.0445	.550
12	1.900	.308	.03980	.538	.0125	.728
13	1.000	.308	2.76000	—.117	.0650	.471
14[b]	.100	.102	6.45000	—.249	.0445	.550
15	2.400	.304	2.76000	—.117	.0650	.471
16	3.400	.805	2.76000	—.117	.0650	.471
17	4.000	.805	2.76000	—.117	.0650	.471
18	5.000	.788	2.76000	—.117	.0650	.471
19[b]	.100	.104	6.45000	—.249	.0445	.550
20	3.000	.600	2.76000	—.117	.0650	.471
21	2.500	.600	2.76000	—.117	.0650	.471
22	.500	.100	2.76000	—.117	.0650	.471
23	3.300	.100	.03720	.403	.0045	.775
24	5.100	.100	3.27000	—.140	.0640	.448
25	1.200	.275	3.29000	—.140	.1400	.685
26	.800	.300	3.29000	—.140	.0140	.685
27[b]	.100	.103	6.45000	—.249	.0445	.550
28	2.900	.300	3.29000	—.140	.0140	.685
29	5.800	.100	3.29000	—.140	.0140	.685
30	5.000	.100	3.29000	—.140	.0140	.685
31	4.800	.100	.14100	.183	.0056	.715
32	5.400	.095	.14100	.183	.0056	.715
33	5.000	.091	.00334	.645	.0023	.780
34[b]	.100	.096	6.45000	—.249	.0445	.550
35	1.800	.093	.00334	.645	.0023	.780
36	.500	.093	.00334	.645	.0023	.780
37	.300	.093	.00334	.645	.0023	.780
38	1.800	.092	.00331	.619	.0007	.935
39	.700	.092	.00331	.619	.0007	.935
40	.700	.201	.00331	.619	.0007	.935
41	.200	.201	.00331	.620	.0007	.935
42[b]	.100	.940	6.45000	—.249	.0445	.550
43	.800	.201	.00331	.619	.0007	.935
44	2.400	.175	3.55000	—.197	.0050	.765
45	2.300	.175	3.55000	—.197	.0050	.765
46	1.600	.213	3.55000	—.197	.0050	.765
47	2.300	.213	3.55000	—.197	.0050	.765
48	3.300	.225	3.55000	—.197	.0050	.765
49	4.000	.225	3.55000	—.197	.0050	.765
50	4.000	.308	3.55000	—.197	.0050	.765
51	4.400	.308	3.55000	—.197	.0050	.765
52	2.600	.308	3.55000	—.197	.0050	.765

TABLE 9—*Continued*

k	X_k	$K_{1k}{}^{20}$	AK_k	BK_k	VC_k	VD_k
53[b]	.10	.100	3.55000	—.197	.0050	.765
54	1.20	.310	3.55000	—.197	.0050	.765
55	2.80	.298	.03730	.403	.0445	.775
56	4.40	.284	5.50000	—.233	.0660	.438
57	4.70	.204	5.50000	—.233	.0660	.438
58	4.90	.238	5.50000	—.233	.0660	.438
59	5.00	.244	5.50000	—.233	.0660	.438
60	5.00	.244	5.50000	—.233	.0660	.438
61	5.00	.182	5.50000	—.233	.0660	.438
62	5.00	.182	5.50000	—.233	.0660	.438

a. Parameters same as in Table 1.
b. Tributaries.

considered by previous tax schemes. However, as discussed above, handling such questions under the incremental cost scheme presents no problem.

The incremental cost scheme for effluent charges presented in this paper is based on least-cost treatments; it satisfies certain equity properties based on each polluter paying for the costs he causes; and finally, it can be extended to deal with dynamic situations which are, after all, realistic.

References

1. Deininger, R. A. "Water Quality Management; Economically Optimal Pollution Control Systems." Ph.D. dissertation, Northwestern University, Evanston, Ill., 1964.
2. Frankel, R. J. "Economic Evaluation of Water Quality; An Engineering-Economic Model for Water Quality Management." SERL Report No. 65-3, University of California, Berkeley, January 1965.
3. Graves, G. W.; Hatfield, G. B.; and Whinston, A. "Water Pollution Control Using By-Pass Piping." *Water Resources Research* 5, no. 1 (February 1969).
4. Graves, G. W.; Hatfield, G. B.; and Whinston, A. "Mathematical Programming for Regional Water Quality Management." *Water Resources Research* 8, no. 2 (April 1972).
5. Graves, G. W.; Pingry, David E.; and Whinston, A. "Water Quality Control: Nonlinear Programming Algorithm." *Revue Française d'automatique, informatique, et de Recherche operationnelle* 2 (October 1972):49–78.
6. Johnson, Edwin L. "A Study in the Economics of Water Quality Management." *Water Resources Research* 3, no. 2 (1967).
7. Kneese, Allen V. *The Economics of Regional Water Quality Management*. Baltimore, Md.: John Hopkins University Press, 1964.
8. Linaweaver, F. P., and Clark, C. S. "Cost of Water Transmission." *Journal American Water Works Assn.* 56, no. 12 (1964).
9. Loehman, E., and Whinston, A. "An Axiomatic Approach to Cost Allocation for Public Investment." *Public Finance Quarterly* 2, no. 1.

10. Loehman, E., and Whinston, A. "A New Theory of Pricing and Decision-Making in Public Investment." *Bell Journal of Economics and Management Science* 2, no. 2 (Autumn 1971):606–25.
11. Loucks, D. P.; Revelle, C. S.; and Lynn, W. R. "Linear Programming Models for Water Pollution Control." *Management Science* 14, no. 4 (December 1967).
12. Schaumberg, G. W. *Water Pollution Control in the Delaware Estuary.* Harvard University Water Program, Harvard University, Cambridge, Mass., May 1967.
13. Streeter, H. W., and Phelps, E. B. "A Study of the Pollution and Natural Purification of the Ohio River." *U.S. Public Health Bulletin,* no. 146, February 1925.

12

A Model of Economic-Environmental Relationships

John H. Cumberland

For those working on problems of environmental analysis, the current surge of interest in environmental quality is both a source of satisfaction and a source of concern. We can feel gratification in the fact that our apprehensions about environmental issues are now widely shared by the general public and by elected officials. However, we must also be candid about the serious limitations in our understanding and concerned about the lack of information on environmental processes.

The data and analyses required for intelligent decision making and improved resource allocation in the field of environmental improvement do not exist in adequately comprehensive and precise form at this time. This paper[1] deals with one type of model which is intended to provide one step along the long and difficult path ahead in achieving more ade-

1. The author, while assuming full responsibility for errors, gratefully acknowledges the participation of graduate students who have worked on this project in recent years in the Bureau of Business and Economic Research of the University of Maryland. Significant contributions have been made, especially by Charles S. Gibson, Jr., Robert J. Korbach, and Bruce N. Stram. The author is also grateful to Edna Loehman and J. Richard Conner of the University of Florida, Food and Resource Economics Department, who suggested preparation of this paper and offered valuable comments on an earlier draft. Research on this paper was supported by the U.S. Department of the Interior, Office of Water Resources Research, Contract No. 1431-0001-389-B007.

quate understanding of environmental-economic linkages, assessing the current situation, examining data requirements, and identifying opportunities for future improvements in environmental management.

The Problem

It has been widely recognized that both production and consumption processes involve flows, not only of economic inputs and outputs, but also of vast quantities of unpriced residuals, wastes, and pollutants (1). Some unpriced inputs are extracted from the environment and residuals of materials and energy are emitted into the environment outside of market structures. From the viewpoint of the profit-maximizing firm, internal costs are minimized if residuals are emitted into the common property resources of air and water. Too often also, individuals maximize consumer satisfaction by discharging wastes or otherwise misusing common property resources. The existence of the resulting economic externalities creates an opportunity for improvement of welfare through the use of taxes, subsidies, regulations, or other control measures to close the gap between social cost and private cost.

The fact that environmental pollution results directly from the economic processes of production and consumption, and the fact that generation of residuals, wastes, and pollution is therefore a direct function of the level of economic growth and activity, have profound implications for economic theory. This relationship between the level of economic activity and the magnitude of environmental problems suggests a list of essential characteristics which must be included in an economic model capable of analyzing environmental relationships.

First, because different economic activities have different environmental characteristics, the model should be highly disaggregated down to a level which distinguishes between different environmentally significant activities. Second, because pollution treatment processes may change the form of residuals, but cannot eliminate matter, a general interdependence model is needed which is capable of revealing how alternative waste management policies affect environmental quality. Third, because environmental, technological, and economic relationships change over time, the model should have dynamic characteristics. Fourth, because environmental change is essentially a spatial phenomenon which is strongly influenced by local characteristics, the model should be capable of disaggregation by region. Fifth, because the model must be solidly based upon environmental realities, it should contain submodels indicating the relationships between pollutants and ecological systems. Finally, because environmental improvement is only one of many public goals,

and resources available for achieving goals are limited, the model should permit derivation of systems of social accounts and benefit-cost estimations which compare the benefits and costs of alternative expenditure programs.

While the model presented in this paper falls short of achieving all of these objectives, it is suggested as a beginning step toward improved understanding of economic-environmental relationships.

The Model

The proposed model of economic-environmental relationships is based upon extension of conventional interindustry input-output models to include materials-energy balances and benefit-cost relationships within a general systems approach. The complete model is shown in Figure 1.[2] Figure 2 presents a reduced form version of the model and emphasizes a comprehensive accounting system for measurement of total emissions, wastes, and pollutants. The interindustry model with conventional final demand sectors which drive the system is shown in Figure 3.

The model is designed to account for all economic and environmental flows, with computer programs written to meter and to print out measurements of these flows at significant points. Initially, the model will use the 360 activity sectors of the U.S. Department of Commerce, Office of Business Economics (OBE) Interindustry Sales and Purchases model. The emissions to be identified include approximately thirty types of liquid, airborne, and solid wastes in a classification system (shown in the Appendix), which is designed to account for all wastes, additively, in terms of weight, and to include energy emissions in the form of heat, noise, and radioactivity.

In operation the model, which can be regional or national, estimates the gross residuals (by type) produced as a function of the output level of each activity. The flow of these residuals is traced as they are discharged into the environment or into treatment processes or recycling. Treatment processes are observed also to emit residuals, since matter in most cases cannot be created or destroyed. The emission of residuals into the environment directly or after treatment is evaluated in terms of the damages or costs resulting from the impact of these residuals upon environmental and ecological receptors. The costs of alternative methods for treating wastes and improving treatment processes are evaluated for each activity and residual. The resulting benefit-cost ratios serve as a guide for determining priorities and allocating resources for the improvement of environmental management.

2. Figures 1, 2, and 3 are displayed in the Appendix.

The general structure of the model is defined by a set of equations which can be computed by stages (3). In the first stage of the analysis, gross economic outputs are estimated for any set of final demands in the input-output model, using conventional matrix multiplication as follows:

$$[X] = [I-a]^{-1} \cdot [Y]$$

where [X] is a vector of gross outputs, $[I-a]^{-1}$ is the inverse of the identity matrix minus the matrix of input coefficients, and [Y] is a vector of final demand elements.

The input-output (I-O) stage, shown in Figure 3 in detail, is represented as the upper lefthand box (labeled A) in Figure 2, and is divided into two separate boxes (inputs and outputs) at the top of Figure 1. The final demand sectors of this model, households, capital formation, and government, are assumed to be the exogenous groups whose purchasing decisions drive the model and determine the activity levels of the other sectors.

In the second stage of operations the gross residuals and net emissions to the environment are estimated for each gross output. Gross residuals are estimated by multiplying the matrix of gross outputs from stage 1 by a matrix of gross residual coefficients, as follows:

$$[GR] = [X]\ [GRC]$$

where [X] is a vector of gross outputs, and [GRC] is a matrix with:

$$GRC(I,J) = \frac{GR(I,J)}{X\ (I)}$$

where GRC(I,J) is the gross residual coefficient relating residual J to gross output of industry I, and GR(I,J) is the amount of gross residual J produced by industry I; I = 1,n, and J = 1,m.

Net emissions to the environment are similarly calculated:

$$[NE] = [X]\ [NEC]$$

where [NE] is a vector and [NEC] is a matrix. The components of [NEC] (net environmental emission coefficient relating residual J to gross output of industry I) are computed as:

$$NEC(I,J) = \frac{NE(I,J)}{X\ (I)}$$

where NE (I,J) is the amount of net emission to environment of pollutant J by industry I; I = 1,n, and J = 1,m.

Finally, in the third stage of the analysis, the benefits and costs of applying alternative treatment processes to each residual from each sector are estimated. The benefits are computed as the incremental damages avoided by reducing the net emissions from each sector. The costs involved are the additional inputs needed in each treatment process, as measured by changes in the social accounts derived from the input-output model. One advantage of using a disaggregated model is that it offers the possibility of attributing benefits and costs to the particular industries and activities affected. The use of the interindustry approach also estimates all of the total indirect as well as direct effects of impacts upon benefits and costs, though the significance of aggregating estimates of benefits and costs from more than one sector may be open to question.

Movements towards Pareto optimality would be identified in those instances where alternative combinations of final demand and net benefits over costs of alternative waste treatment processes satisfied the conditions:

$$Y_{t+1} \geqq Y_t$$

and

$$B_{t+1} - C_{t+1} \geqq B_t - C_t$$

where Y is the matrix of final demand, B is benefits from pollution abatement, C is cost of pollution abatement, and t is the base period, provided that any losers could be sufficiently compensated out of gains so as not to be left worse off than in the base period.

A series of trial printouts, using the OBE industry classification and the emission classification system described above, is shown in Tables 1 through 12. Definitions of the variables and an explanation of the tables are given in the next section.

Demonstration of the Model

Tables 1 through 12 have been printed out, using hypothetical data to test the program and the model.[3] Descriptions of the tables and definitions of the notations are as follows:

TABLE 1

The coefficients presented in Table 1 represent the technological relationships between potential industrial waste loadings (by type) to the environment, and their market value outputs.

The first row of this table shows the gross amount of each pollutant produced by industry 1601 per unit of output in that same industry. The key below the table identifies industry 1601 as broadwoven fabric mills and fabric finishing plants. The key also identifies the pollutant types. For the purposes of this demonstration, the units of output are in mone-

3. Material for this section was prepared by Bruce N. Stram in order to provide a format for data collection by the EQUIPS effort; see EQUIPS-MABET (4).

TABLE 1

GROSS RESIDUAL COEFFICIENTS, INDICATING GROSS RESIDUAL, BY TYPE, IN THOUSANDS OF POUNDS, GENERATED BY $1 MILLION OF GROSS OUTPUT, 1963

OBE	1	2	3	4	5	6	7	8	9	10	11
1601	.00	.00	79.70	32.80	81.50	.00	.00	.000	.00	.00	.000
2402	.00	.00	518.00	467.00	2,040.00	.00	.00	.000	.00	.00	.000
3701	202.00	.00	.00	700.00	.00	15.40	89.20	.298	2.66	.98	.182
3804	294.00	74.00	.00	.00	.00	.00	.00	.000	.00	.00	.000

POLLUTANTS

1 = Particulate matter
2 = Hydrogen fluoride
3 = Suspended solids
4 = BOD
5 = Dissolved solids
6 = Lube oils
7 = Acids
8 = Soluble metals
9 = Emulsions
10 = Coke plant chemicals
11 = Fluorides

INDUSTRIES

1601 = Broadwoven fabric mills and fabric finishing plants
1804 = Apparel made from purchased materials
2402 = Paper mills, except building paper
2404 = Envelopes
2601 = Newspapers
3701 = Blast furnace and basic steel products
3804 = Primary aluminum
3901 = Metal cans
4005 = Metal doors, sash and trim
5402 = Household refrigerators and freezers

tary terms, and $1 million has been selected as the unit. The pollutant units are in thousands of pounds; thus, the coefficients are dimensioned in thousands of pounds per million dollars. These coefficients may be calculated directly from the data, and together with other sets of coefficients, represent the basic analytical tools of the environmental model.

The coefficients for the gross amount of pollutants (gross residual) are calculated as follows: the amount of a particular type of gross residual thrown off by a given industry in the base year is divided by the amount of gross output, again for the base year, in that same industry. In matrix notation we have:

$$GRC(I, J) = \frac{GR(I, J)}{X(I)}$$

where GR(I, J) is the amount of gross residual of type J produced by industry I, in thousands of pounds, X(I) is the gross output in industry I in millions of dollars, and base year is 1963. These coefficients thus represent, in summary form, the technological relationships that existed in the base year between the various types of pollutants and the output of the industry in question.

It should be noted that for the purposes of the model, gross residual has been defined as that waste, or pollutant material, which *cannot* be recovered at a profit. It follows from this definition that the short-run profit-maximizing firm (of the classical economics) would simply desire to get rid of this material as cheaply as possible, i.e., dispose of it to the environment. Thus, gross residual is, in a potential sense, the amount of pollutant that would be loaded upon the environment in the absence of voluntary restraints or legal standards.

TABLE 2

The coefficients presented in Table 2 represent the technological relationships between actual industrial waste loadings (by type) to the environment, and their market-valued outputs.

This table is very similar to Table 1. Here the gross residual quantities have been replaced by net waste coefficients. Under this concept, net waste is defined as the sum of the amount of gross residual that is discharged untreated and the amount of gross residual that "escapes" treatment processes and does not meet prospective standards.

Thus, while Table 1 furnishes information on gross residual, or that amount of waste which potentially could be loaded upon the environment, Table 2 provides information on net waste, or that part of the gross residual that is actually loaded upon the environment. In matrix notation, the net waste coefficient is:

TABLE 2

NET WASTE COEFFICIENT, INDICATING NET WASTE, BY TYPE, IN THOUSANDS OF POUNDS, GENERATED BY $1 MILLION OF GROSS OUTPUT, 1963

OBE	1	2	3	4	5	6	7	8	9	10	11
1601	.00	.00	30.50	15.20	38.90	.00	.00	.000	.00	.000	.000
2402	.00	.00	69.30	63.30	277.00	.00	.00	.000	.00	.000	.000
3701	35.30	.00	.00	47.90	.00	10.60	50.50	.278	9.60	.334	.177
3804	14.70	.00	.00	.00	.00	.00	.00	.000	.00	.000	71.000

POLLUTANTS

1 = Particulate matter
2 = Hydrogen fluoride
3 = Suspended solids
4 = BOD
5 = Dissolved solids
6 = Lube oils
7 = Acids
8 = Soluble metals
9 = Emulsions
10 = Coke plant chemicals
11 = Fluorides

INDUSTRIES

1601 = Broadwoven fabric mills and fabric finishing plants
1804 = Apparel made from purchased materials
2402 = Paper mills, except building paper
2404 = Envelopes
2601 = Newspapers
3701 = Blast furnace and basic steel products
3804 = Primary aluminum
3901 = Metal cans
4005 = Metal doors, sash and trim
5402 = Household refrigerators and freezers

$$NWC(I, J) = \frac{NW(I, J)}{X(I)}$$

where NW(I, J) is the amount of net waste of type J produced by industry I in thousands of pounds, X(I) is gross output in industry I in millions of dollars, and base year is 1963. The net waste coefficient, like the gross residual coefficients in Table 1, reflects, in part, the technological relationship between an industry's monetary output and its generation of pollutants. It also reflects the nature of the various abatement technologies. Thus, these coefficients, which may be calculated directly from the data, represent one of the basic analytical tools of the model.

TABLE 3

The cost coefficients presented in Table 3 represent the average abatement expenditures, by industry, required to transform and reduce the gross residuals (Table 1) to the net waste levels (Table 2).

This table indicates the abatement expenditures, in coefficient terms (i.e., thousand dollars of cost per million dollars of output) associated with the treatment of the gross residual. It is this treatment which causes the net waste coefficients and totals (Tables 2 and 5) to differ from the gross residual coefficients and totals (Tables 1 and 4).

TABLE 3
COST COEFFICIENTS, INDICATING THE COST OF ABATING TO 1963. NET WASTE LEVELS (THOUSAND DOLLARS OF COST PER MILLION DOLLARS OF OUTPUT)

OBE	1	2	3	4
1601	.00	.000	2.32	.657
2402	.00	.000	43.60	4.560
3701	16.00	10.200	43.30	7.000
3804	5.07	.507	.00	.000

COSTS
1 = Air pollution abatement, fixed costs
2 = Air pollution abatement, operating costs
3 = Water pollution abatement, fixed costs
4 = Water pollution abatement, operating costs

INDUSTRIES
1601 = Broadwoven fabric mills and fabric finishing plants
1804 = Apparel made from purchased materials
2402 = Paper mills, except building paper
2404 = Envelopes
2601 = Newspapers
3701 = Blast furnace and basic steel products
3804 = Primary aluminum
3901 = Metal cans
4005 = Metal doors, sash and trim
5402 = Household refrigerators and freezers

These treatment expenditures were generally not available for each pollutant separately; therefore, they were aggregated over air pollution abatement and water pollution abatement for each industry shown.

For both air and water pollution abatement, the costs are broken into capital (fixed costs) and annual (operating costs). The capital costs represent replacement value rather than amortized value. In the basic worksheets, cost data, both fixed and operating, are requested not only for each pollutant, but also for each treatment process where more than one may apply. Thus, the worksheets will generate a much more detailed cost table than is available for this demonstration.

The cost coefficients are generated in a manner similar to that employed to compute both the gross residual and net waste coefficients. The cost coefficients may be represented as:

$$CC(I, J) = \frac{C(I, J)}{X(I)}$$

where C(I, J) is abatement expenditure of type J by industry I in thousands of dollars, X(I) is gross output in industry I in millions of dollars, and base year is 1963. These coefficients reflect the pollution abatement technology in 1963.

TABLE 4

Table 4 provides information, by pollutant type, on the gross residuals stemming from four industries in 1963.

Given Table 1, the levels of gross residual can be projected for any dollar value of industrial production. A computer program suitable for calculating such a projection has been developed, and the results of the calculations are given in Table 4.

The gross residual levels in Table 4 were generated by actual monetary gross output levels for 1963. Thus, these gross residual figures correspond (except for rounding errors) to the "actual" pollution levels in 1963. Forecasted gross output levels for any year may be employed at this stage to yield projected gross residuals; however, 1963 output data were used for this demonstration in order to verify the validity of the program. In matrix notation, gross residual may be represented as:

$$GR(I, J) = GRC\ (I, J) \cdot X\ (I)$$

where GRC(I,J) is gross residual coefficient for industry I and pollutant J (see Table 1), and X (I) is gross output of industry I projected or estimated for any year or set of assumptions.

It should be noted that any use of the gross residual totals, which employ the gross residual coefficients for their formation, must be pre-

TABLE 4

GROSS RESIDUAL BY INDUSTRY, 1963, IN THOUSANDS OF POUNDS

OBE	1	2	3	4	5	6	7	8	9	10	11
1601	0	0	836,850	344,400	855,750	0	0	0	0	0	0
2402	0	0	2,617,454	2,359,751	10,308,120	0	0	0	0	0	0
3701	4,040,000	0	0	14,000,000	0	308,000	1,784,000	5,960	53,200	19,600	3,640
3804	579,180	145,780	0	0	0	0	0	0	0	0	0

POLLUTANTS

1 = Particulate matter
2 = Hydrogen fluoride
3 = Suspended solids
4 = BOD
5 = Dissolved solids
6 = Lube oils
7 = Acids
8 = Soluble metals
9 = Emulsions
10 = Coke plant chemicals
11 = Fluorides

INDUSTRIES

1601 = Broadwoven fabric mills and fabric finishing plants
1804 = Apparel made from purchased materials
2402 = Paper mills, except building paper
2404 = Envelopes
2601 = Newspapers
3701 = Blast furnace and basic steel products
3804 = Primary aluminum
3901 = Metal cans
4005 = Metal doors, sash and trim
5402 = Household refrigerators and freezers

dicted on the existence of the same, or very similar, technology level as existed in the "base year." For instance, a gross residual projection for 1970 which employs the 1963 gross residual coefficients implicitly assumes that the waste-generating aspects of production remain relatively constant between those years. In a sense, this use of a base year "freezes" the technology to that of the same year. Thus, while projections from the base year coefficients are very useful, caution must be exercised in their usage. This is so because technology, and the coefficients themselves, may change over time.

In the basic worksheets, requests have been made for data estimates for future years. This information would enable the continued updating of the gross residual coefficients, and an explicit recognition of changes in production and abatement technologies.

TABLE 5

Table 5 provides information, by pollutant type, on the net waste stemming from four industries in 1963.

The net waste totals in this table were calculated from the net waste coefficients in Table 2 in a manner analogous to the computation of the gross residuals of Table 4. In matrix notation, net waste may be represented as:

$$NW\ (I, J) = NWC\ (I, J) \cdot X\ (I)$$

where NWC (I, J) is the net waste coefficient for industry I and pollutant J (see Table 2), and X(I) is gross output of industry I projected or estimated for any year or set of assumptions.

As with Table 4, the coefficients for net waste "freeze" the technology to that in existence in the base year. Data requested on the basic worksheets will permit estimation of net waste coefficients for future years, and thus an explicit recognition of technology change.

TABLE 6

Table 6 provides information on the total fixed and operating costs required by four industries to reduce the gross residual to net waste.

The abatement expenditure totals in this table were calculated from the cost coefficients developed in Table 3. Although the table represents abatement expenditures for 1963, the base year, the model concept will enable abatement costs to be projected to any year for which an estimate of gross output is available. In matrix notation, the abatement expenditure of industry I for abatement type J is:

$$C\ (I, J) = CC\ (I, J) \cdot X\ (I)$$

where CC (I, J) is the cost coefficient of industry I for abatement type J

TABLE 5

Net Waste by Industry, 1963, in Thousands of Pounds

OBE	1	2	3	4	5	6	7	8	9	10	11
1601	0	0	320,250	159,600	408,450	0	0	0	0	0	0
2402	0	0	350,173	319,855	1,399,661	0	0	0	0	0	0
3701	716,000	0	0	958,000	0	212,000	1,010,000	5,560	192,000	6,680	3,540
3804	28,959	0	0	0	0	0	0	0	0	0	139,870

Pollutants

1 = Particulate matter
2 = Hydrogen fluoride
3 = Suspended solids
4 = BOD
5 = Dissolved solids
6 = Lube oils
7 = Acids
8 = Soluble metals
9 = Emulsions
10 = Coke plant chemicals
11 = Fluorides

Industries

1601 = Broadwoven fabric mills and fabric finishing plants
1804 = Apparel made from purchase materials
2402 = Paper mills, except building paper
2404 = Envelopes
2601 = Newspapers
3701 = Blast furnace and basic steel products
3804 = Primary aluminum
3901 = Metal cans
4005 = Metal doors, sash and trim
5402 = Household refrigerators and freezers

(see Table 3), and X (I) is gross output of industry I projected or estimated for any year or set of assumptions.

TABLE 7

This table gives explicit recognition to the linkages between industry output and the demands for intermediate outputs (materials) required to satisfy that demand. Thus, industries create pollution by satisfying two types of demands for their products: final demands and intermediate demands. The table makes explicit the *potential* pollutant impact of various consumption goods.

TABLE 6
EXPENDITURES FOR ABATEMENT, 1963, IN THOUSANDS OF DOLLARS

OBE	1	2	3	4
1601	0	0	24,360	6,898
2402	0	0	220,311	23,042
3701	320,000	204,000	666,000	140,000
3804	9,988	999	0	0

COSTS
1 = Air pollution abatement, fixed costs
2 = Air pollution abatement, operating costs
3 = Water pollution abatement, fixed costs
4 = Water pollution abatement, operating costs

INDUSTRIES
1601 = Broadwoven fabric mills and fabric finishing plants
1804 = Apparel made from purchased materials
2402 = Paper mills, except building paper
2404 = Envelopes
2601 = Newspapers
3701 = Blast furnace and basic steel products
3804 = Primary aluminum
3901 = Metal cans
4005 = Metal doors, sash and trim
5402 = Household refrigerators and freezers

Table 7 illustrates some of the benefits obtained by "tying" the basic model to an economic input-output model of the U.S. economy. Table 7 shows the gross residuals (by type) generated by the delivery of goods to final demand by industry, per million dollars of final demand.

This can best be explained through an example. Industry 2404, envelopes, sells some of its output to final consumers such as households. In order to produce these envelopes, industry 2404 must purchase raw materials (intermediate outputs) from other producers such as industry 2402, the paper pulp industry. In meeting this intermediate demand, the paper pulp industry generates some gross residual. In a like manner,

TABLE 7

Gross Residual Coefficients, Indicating Gross Residual, by Type, in Thousands of Pounds, Generated by Gross Output Resulting from Delivery of $1 Million of Product to Final Demand, by Industry, 1963

OBE	1	2	3	4	5	6	7	8	9	10	11
1804	1.414	74.550	12.358	2.354	90.255	8.871	1.940	11.239	.030	.335	.123
2404	14.406	33.053	.947	4.827	105.710	18.166	2.233	12.934	.042	.306	.142
2601	9.984	.032	110.666	133.768	434.861	.752	4.53	.015	.130	.048	.009
3901	109.427	.087	7.005	384.259	27.250	8.316	48.168	.161	1.436	.529	.098
4005	74.550	12.358	2.354	90.255	8.871	1.940	11.239	.038	.335	.123	.023
5402	33.053	.447	4.827	105.710	19.166	2.233	12.934	.043	.386	.142	.026

Pollutants

1 = Particulate matter
2 = Hydrogen fluoride
3 = Suspended solids
4 = BOD
5 = Dissolved solids
6 = Lube oils
7 = Acids
8 = Soluble metals
9 = Emulsions
10 = Coke plant chemicals
11 = Fluorides

Industries

1601 = Broadwoven fabric mills and fabric finishing plants
1804 = Apparel made from purchased materials
2402 = Paper mills, except building paper
2404 = Envelopes
2601 = Newspapers
3701 = Blast furnace and basic steel products
3804 = Primary aluminum
3901 = Metal cans
4005 = Metal doors, sash and trim
5402 = Household refrigerators and freezers

other industries that are direct suppliers to the envelope industry also create some gross residual. Each of these industries, in turn, can only increase its production by increasing purchases from its direct suppliers. Thus, the structure of both production and waste generation exhibit "backward linkages." The input-output table furnishes an explicit definition of these linkages.

In Table 7, the amount of gross residual, by type, generated by all these indirect stages of production necessary to produce \$1 million of industry 2404 delivery to final demand, is summed. In matrix notation the calculation is as follows:

$$\text{GRC}^* (\text{K, J}) = \sum_{\text{I}=1}^{\text{N}} \text{GRC (I, J)} \cdot \text{X}^* (\text{I, K})$$

where GRC* (K, J) is the amount, in thousands of pounds, of gross residual of type J generated by production, both direct and indirect, resulting from the delivery of \$1 million of output by industry K to final demand, GRC (I, J) is the gross residual coefficient for industry I and pollutant type J, and X* (I, K) is the total amount of production in industry I required to produce one dollar of output in industry K.

The gross residual coefficient for the industry delivery to final demand does not include the gross residual generated by the production processes of the delivering industry itself. In this demonstration run of the basic model, the gross residual generated by the indirect production has been summed over the four industries shown in Tables 1–6 only. In the full implementation of the model, the summation process will be carried over all industries.

TABLE 8

This table, like Table 7, draws on the input-output structure of the U.S. economy. The table makes explicit the *actual* pollutant impact of various consumption goods.

In matrix notation the calculation is as follows:

$$\text{NWC}^* (\text{K, J}) = \sum_{\text{I}=1}^{\text{N}} \text{NWC (I, J)} \cdot \text{X}^* (\text{I, K})$$

where NWC* (K, J) is the amount, in thousands of pounds, of net waste of type J generated by production, both direct and indirect, resulting from the delivery of one dollar of output by industry K to final demand, NWC (I, J) is the net waste coefficient for industry I and pollutant type J, and X*(I,K) is the total amount of production in industry I required to produce \$1 million of output in industry K.

TABLE 8

NET WASTE COEFFICIENTS, INDICATING NET WASTE, BY TYPE, IN THOUSANDS OF POUNDS, GENERATED BY GROSS OUTPUT RESULTING FROM DELIVERY OF $1 MILLION OF PRODUCT TO FINAL DEMAND, BY INDUSTRY, 1963

OBE	1	2	3	4	5	6	7	8	9	10	11
1804	.023	6.903	.000	.349	6.332	1.252	1.336	6.363	.035	1.210	.042
2404	.026	5.307	.000	.718	7.555	2.566	1.537	7.322	.040	1.392	.048
2601	1.729	.000	14.889	15.884	59.164	.517	2.464	.014	.468	.016	.039
3901	19.079	.000	.966	26.730	3.741	5.724	27.270	.150	5.184	.180	.179
4005	6.903	.000	.549	6.332	1.252	1.336	6.363	.035	1.210	.042	.097
5402	5.307	.000	.718	7.555	2.565	1.537	7.322	.040	1.392	.048	1.128

POLLUTANTS

1 = Particulate matter
2 = Hydrogen fluoride
3 = Suspended solids
4 = BOD
5 = Dissolved solids
6 = Lube oils
7 = Acids
8 = Soluble metals
9 = Emulsions
10 = Coke plant chemicals
11 = Fluorides

INDUSTRIES

1601 = Broadwoven fabric mills and fabric finishing plants
1804 = Apparel made from purchased materials
2402 = Paper mills, except building paper
2404 = Envelopes
2601 = Newspapers
3701 = Blast furnace and basic steel products
3804 = Primary aluminum
3901 = Metal cans
4005 = Metal doors, sash and trim
5402 = Household refrigerators and freezers

TABLE 9

This table, like 7 and 8, draws on the input-output structure of the U.S. economy. The table makes explicit the actual cost of expenditure involved in abating the pollutants generated by production resulting from the purchase of consumption goods.

In matrix notation the calculation is as follows:

$$CC^*(K,J) = \sum_{I=1}^{N} CC(I,J) \cdot X^*(I,K)$$

where CC*(K,J) is the amount, in thousands of dollars, of expenditure presently involved in abating the pollution generated by production resulting from the delivery of one dollar of output by industry K to final demand, CC (I,J) is the cost coefficient for industry I and pollutant type J, and X*(I,K) is the total amount of production in industry I required to produce $1 million of output in industry K.

TABLE 9

COST OF ABATEMENT COEFFICIENTS, INDICATING COST OF ABATEMENT IN THOUSANDS OF DOLLARS, ASSOCIATED WITH GROSS OUTPUT RESULTING FROM DELIVERY OF $1 MILLION OF PRODUCTS TO FINAL DEMAND, BY INDUSTRY, 1963

OBE	1	2	3	4
1804	.097	2.863	1.370	5.646
2404	1.126	2.365	1.485	6.665
2601	.763	.498	11.410	1.316
3901	8.646	5.509	23.965	3.847
4005	2.663	1.370	5.646	.903
5402	2.366	1.485	6.669	1.057

COSTS

1 = Air pollution abatement, fixed costs
2 = Air pollution abatement, operating costs
3 = Water pollution abatement, fixed costs
4 = Water pollution abatement, operating costs

INDUSTRIES

1601 = Broadwoven fabric mills and fabric finishing plants
1804 = Apparel made from purchased materials
2407 = Paper mills, except building paper
2404 = Envelopes
2601 = Newspapers
3701 = Blast furnace and basic steel products
3804 = Primary aluminum
3901 = Metal cans
4005 = Metal doors, sash and trim
5402 = Household refrigerators and freezers

TABLE 10

This table, like Tables 7, 8, and 9, draws on the input-output structure of the U.S. economy. The table would show, as a coefficient, the pollution generated by production resulting from purchases of $1 million by a given final demand sector, such as households.

$$GRCF(L,J) = \sum_{I=1}^{N} GRC(I,J) \cdot XF(I,L)$$

where GRCF(L,J) is the amount, in thousands of pounds, of gross residual of type J generated by production resulting from $1 million of purchases by final demand sector L, GRC(I,J) is the gross residual coefficient for industry I and pollutant type J, and XF(I,L) is the total amount of production in industry I resulting from purchases of one dollar by final demand sector L.

Tables similar to this could also be calculated to obtain net waste coefficients and cost coefficients for a given final demand sector:

$$NWCF(L,J) = \sum_{I=1}^{N} NWC(I,J) \cdot XF(I,L)$$

$$CCF(L,J) = \sum_{I=1}^{N} CC(I,J) \cdot XF(I,L).$$

TABLE 11

This table would show the amount of expenditure (for each industry and pollutant type) necessary to meet prospective emission and/or treatment standards.

$$CA(I,J) = CAC(I,J) \cdot X(I)$$

where CA(I,J) is the additional amount of expenditure by industry I on pollutant type J that would be necessary if that industry were to meet prospective emission and/or treatment standards, CAC(I,J) is the coefficient indicating the additional amount of expenditure on pollutant type J in thousands of dollars per million dollars of output in industry I that would be necessary if that industry were to meet prospective emission and/or treatment standards, and X(I) is production in industry I in millions of dollars. The additional cost coefficients, CAC(I,J), would be determined on the basis of information supplied from the basic worksheets.

TABLE 10A

GROSS RESIDUAL COEFFICIENT, INDICATING GROSS RESIDUAL, BY TYPE, IN THOUSANDS OF POUNDS, GENERATED BY PRODUCTION RESULTING FROM $1 MILLION OF PURCHASES BY SELECTED FINAL DEMAND SECTORS, 1963

Sector	1	2	3	4	5	6	7	8	9	10	11
1	4.028	.109	6.749	17.603	20.977	.274	1.588	.005	.047	.017	.003
2	212.145	6.519	3.442	648.314	12.430	14.199	82.242	.275	2.453	.904	.168
3	85.398	2.886	58.478	296.304	169.490	5.636	32.647	.109	.974	.359	.067
4	7.679	.362	2.694	23.899	9.657	.476	2.756	.009	.002	.030	.006
5	6.300	.203	2.735	21.402	10.152	.419	2.426	.008	.072	.027	.005

POLLUTANTS

1 = Particulate matter
2 = Hydrogen fluoride
3 = Suspended solids
4 = BOD
5 = Dissolved solids
6 = Lube oils
7 = Acids
8 = Soluble metals
9 = Emulsions
10 = Coke plant chemicals
11 = Fluorides

SECTORS

1 = Personal consumption expenditures
2 = Gross private fixed capital formation
3 = Gross exports
4 = Federal government purchases
5 = State and local government purchases

TABLE 10B

Net Waste Coefficient, Indicating Net Waste, by Type, in Thousands of Pounds, Generated by Production Resulting from $1 Million of Purchases by Selected Final Demand Sectors, 1963

Sector	1	2	3	4	5	6	7	8	9	10	11
1	.650	.000	1.381	1.809	3.519	.189	.889	.005	.171	.006	.108
2	33.852	.000	.556	44.611	1.823	9.773	46.561	.256	8.851	.308	6.418
3	13.493	.000	8.315	23.959	25.580	3.880	18.483	.102	3.514	.122	2.834
4	1.163	.000	.442	1.832	1.425	.328	1.560	.009	.297	.010	.353
5	1.000	.000	.419	1.652	1.453	.288	1.374	.008	.261	.009	.199

Pollutants

1 = Particulate matter
2 = Hydrogen fluoride
3 = Suspended solids
4 = BOD
5 = Dissolved solids
6 = Lube oils
7 = Acids
8 = Soluble metals
9 = Emulsions
10 = Coke plant chemicals
11 = Fluorides

Sectors

1 = Personal consumption expenditures
2 = Gross private fixed capital formation
3 = Gross exports
4 = Federal government purchases
5 = State and local government purchases

TABLE 10C

COST OF ABATEMENT COEFFICIENTS, INDICATING COST OF ABATEMENT, IN THOUSANDS OF DOLLARS, GENERATED BY PRODUCTION RESULTING FROM $1 MILLION OF PURCHASES BY SELECTED FINAL DEMAND SECTORS, 1963

Sector	1	2	3	4
1	.294	.162	1.233	.183
2	15.199	9.449	40.191	6.484
3	6.054	3.753	19.524	2.985
4	.519	.315	1.547	.240
5	.449	.279	1.390	.214

COSTS
1 = Air pollution abatement, fixed costs
2 = Air pollution abatement, operating costs
3 = Water pollution abatement, fixed costs
4 = Water pollution abatement, operating costs

SECTORS
1 = Personal consumption expenditures
2 = Gross private fixed capital formation
3 = Gross exports
4 = Federal government purchases
5 = State and local government purchases

TABLE 12

This table would draw on the input-output structure of the U.S. economy. The table indicates the results of an estimation process which yields the amount of additional expenditure necessary to meet prospective standards associated with the production, in all industries, resulting from $1 million of delivery to final demand by a given industry. These figures could also be taken as an estimate of the percentage increase (expressed in tenths of percents) in the price of the good delivered to final demand, resulting from the additional expenditures necessary to meet standards.

$$CAC^*(K,J) = CAC(I,J) \cdot X^*(I,K)$$

where CAC*(K,J) is the additional expenditure coefficient expressing the amount of additional expenditure of type J, in thousands of dollars per million dollars, necessary so that the pollution generated by production resulting from $1 million of delivery to final demand by industry K is abated to meet prospective emission and/or treatment standards, CAC(I,J) is the amount of additional expenditure of type J, in thousands of dollars, necessary in order that industry I meet prospective emission and/or treatment standards, and X*(I,K) is the total amount of production in industry I required to produce one dollar of output in industry K.

TABLE 13

This table (not displayed in this book) is the basic control table for the model. As previously indicated, the model explicitly recognizes the neces-

TABLE 11

ADDITIONAL COST COEFFICIENTS, INDICATING ADDITIONAL COST OF ABATEMENT, IN THOUSANDS OF DOLLARS, REQUIRED PER $1 MILLION OF OUTPUT, TO MEET PROSPECTIVE STANDARDS, 1963

OBE	1	2	3	4
1601	.00	.00	3.56	1.050
2402	.00	.00	27.50	5.720
3701	5.78	11.20	57.20	5.000
3804	.00	.00	1.02	1.113

COSTS

1 = Air pollution abatement, fixed costs
2 = Air pollution abatement, operating costs
3 = Water pollution abatement, fixed costs
4 = Water pollution abatement, operating costs

INDUSTRIES

1601 = Broadwoven fabric mills and fabric finishing plants
1804 = Apparel made from purchased materials
2402 = Paper mills, except building paper
2404 = Envelopes
2601 = Newspapers
3701 = Blast furnace and basic steel products
3804 = Primary aluminum
3901 = Metal cans
4005 = Metal doors, sash and trim
5402 = Household refrigerators and freezers

sity of a materials balance. Since matter cannot be destroyed or created (except for insignificant amounts in nuclear reactions), none of the gross residual materials disappear but must be disposed of in some way.

Thus in Table 13 the gross residual is allocated into exhaustive and mutually exclusive final disposition categories. The total weight of the materials entered into these categories should equal the total gross residual generated (as shown in Table 4). Tables for the final disposition of gross residual and gross residual generated are developed independently in the worksheets. Hence, an essential cross-check is provided. At every level of aggregation it can be determined whether the final disposition items do indeed account for all gross residual. Table 13 is derived directly from the worksheets.

TABLE 14

In a sense this table (not displayed in this book) is the final output of the model. It shows the total material emitted to the environment by production processes and by external contractors who treat industrial wastes.

This total material includes not only gross residual discharged untreated and gross residual escapements from treatment processes, but also treatment residuals. Many treatment processes simply collect gross resid-

TABLE 12

NAL COST COEFFICIENTS INDICATING ADDITIONAL COST OF ABATEMENT, IN THOUSANDS OF DOLLARS, FOR WASTE MATERIALS GENERATED BY PRODUCTION RESULTING FROM DELIVERY OF $1 MILLION TO FINAL DEMAND, BY INDUSTRY, 1963

OBE	1	2	3	4
1804	.033	.903	3.649	9.083
2404	.406	.787	12.602	2.210
2601	.282	.547	8.664	1.516
3901	3.121	6.048	31.260	3.319
4005	.728	1.411	7.501	.968
5402	.903	3.649	9.083	.938

COSTS

1 = Air pollution abatement, fixed costs
2 = Air pollution abatement, operating costs
3 = Water pollution abatement, fixed costs
4 = Water pollution abatement, operating costs

INDUSTRIES

1601 = Broadwoven fabric mills and fabric finishing plants
1804 = Apparel made from purchased materials
2402 = Paper mills, except building paper
2404 = Envelopes
2601 = Newspapers
3701 = Blast furnace and basic steel products
3804 = Primary aluminum
3901 = Metal cans
4005 = Metal doors, sash and trim
5402 = Household refrigerators and freezers

ual and alter its form, but still eventually release this material to some environmental medium. Although the treatment process, by altering its form, renders the gross residual less harmful, the processed material (the terminology for this material is "treatment residual") is still very likely to have some effect.

CRITIQUE OF THE MODEL

The economic-environmental approach proposed here represents an effort to combine traditional economic analyses of general interdependence systems within a broader set of environmental systems, while retaining benefit-cost criteria as a guide to efficiency in resource allocation. The model permits forecasting of economic-environmental relationships, and permits the evaluation of alternative programs for achieving both economic and environmental objectives.

The system of social accounts embodied in the value-added rows and final demand columns of the interindustry submodel is supplemented with a new set of social accounts for residuals, wastes, and pollutants, which is designed to be comprehensive but nonduplicative. The total set of social accounts is intended to permit the evaluation of trade-offs between economic development and environmental quality resulting from alternative programs.

However, despite these significant advantages, the model must be recognized as only a tentative first step toward the design of the vastly improved economic models which are needed for environmental management. The model has a number of limitations which need to be overcome.

One significant limitation of the model is that it measures only those environmental externalities which can be structured in terms of emissions of wastes and pollutants. It fails to measure, at this stage of its development, such important factors as visual, psychological, demographic, and aesthetic aspects of environmental quality. Methods are needed for extension of the model into these areas.[4]

The model, in its present form, is based upon interindustry techniques, using linear homogenous relationships, with all of the problems which have been associated with such models. More work is needed on the introduction of nonlinear, nonhomogenous relationships in the model.[5]

The use of national base period data to derive linear relationships limits the ability of the model to explore scale economies, changing technologies, alternative treatment methods, and other options for improving environmental management. Adjustment of base period coefficients to reflect alternative treatment methods, regional differences, recycling, and changing proportions of waste to be treated would increase the flexibility of the model.

The model as it now stands is not an optimizing model, since it does not reflect changes in prices resulting from alternative environmental management practices, and it does not provide for feedback into the model. The current model emphasizes emissions of residuals, alternative treatment loops, and associated benefits and costs. Conceptually the model also deals with withdrawals from the environment on the input side. Added emphasis and disaggregation on the input side would have several advantages. Detailed accounting for inputs of potentially toxic materials, such as mercury, cadmium, and arsenic, and complete accounting for the flow of such materials could provide an early warning system for environmental hazards. Expansion of the environmental input components could

4. For proposals concerning extension of input-output models to include a wider range of externalities, see Bergmann (2).

5. Russell and Spofford (6) have shown that a general solution to the problem can be derived using programming methods and assigning shadow prices to the cost of emissions.

also provide information on current and projected requirements for land use, water use, and other critical natural resource demands associated with alternative economic development patterns.

The model as it now stands permits an approximation of dynamic relationships through the use of comparative statics. The feasibility of more explicitly dynamic approaches should be explored.

Major emphasis is needed in expanding the section of the model which deals with the impact of environmental emissions upon human society and upon other ecologies. Clearly the multidisciplinary participation of specialists in public health, ecology, biology, and other fields is essential in this phase of the study, especially in order to estimate benefits. These relationships should be analyzed on a regional basis, recognizing the nature of geographic differences in the absorptive capacity of alternative regional environments. The development of regional social indicators could be useful in this regard (5).

The model as it now stands enumerates emissions as though they were simple additives. It does not explicitly account for synergistic effects, such as when sunlight, acting upon a mixture of emissions, causes smog. Additional programs are needed for identifying those cases where the total effect of a combination of emissions differs from the sum of the individual emissions.

Some Policy Implications

The basic concepts of the model and its schematic representation in Figure 1 suggest the range of alternative options open for reducing pollution and improving environmental quality. The conventional task of public sector economics is to assess goals, to examine the range of alternative policy measures available, to estimate the benefits and costs of each, and to evaluate the control measures (taxation, subsidization, and direct regulation) available for implementing the preferred policies. The usual remedy applied in instances of gross pollution is to switch the flow of gross residuals from the untreated loop through the treatment loop. While this may have advantages in changing the form and state of the residuals, the model indicates that residuals once generated cannot be destroyed or eliminated, but only transformed.

The efficiency and structure of treatment loops can be improved as another policy option, but the total weight of emissions remains the same. Another policy option is to change the geographic location of the production and consumption process in response to different absorptive and assimilative capabilities of environmental reception at alternative locations. This option emphasizes the need for regionalizing the model.

Advanced regional-industrial planning could design industrial complexes with activities clustered for maximum productive use of wastes on a total systems basis.

Eventually programs for improving environmental quality must be found which are more fundamental than improvement of treatment. One such option is illustrated by the "residual reduction process" box in Figure 1, which symbolizes actions such as using cleaner inputs, reducing wear, corrosion, and obsolescence, improving efficiency of production and consumption processes, and developing improved technology. Even more fundamental is the recycling option, which will become increasingly essential, both to avoid release of residuals and to reduce the necessity for more withdrawals of resources from the environment. Converting wastes into usable by-products is a variant of recycling.

Major policy differences and basic philosophical gulfs exist between those who look for environmental solutions from recycling and technological advances and those who advocate the more fundamental alternatives suggested by this environmental model. The more basic approach requires not only closing some of the environmental loops in the model, but also drastic reduction in the total dimensions of the production-consumption processes which are embodied in the total model. In the view of the environmental fundamentalists, equilibrium can be achieved in the long run only by limiting or reducing population size and by de-escalating the magnitudes of production and consumption.

The resolution of this conflict between the concepts of the technologists and ecologists will be a major global issue for all societies which make up what we are beginning to recognize as the single environmental system of the planet Earth. The economic-environmental model discussed in this paper is offered as a modest step toward understanding and evaluating the environmental options among which we must now choose.

Appendix

Emission Classification System[6]

I. Gases and airborne material (weight/unit of time, tons/year preferred)
   - A. Particulate matter
     1. Hydrocarbons
     2. Other
   - B. Gases

6. This system is based on EQUIPS-MABET (4) Model Description and Worksheet Instructions, processed 23 September 1970.

1. Hydrocarbons
2. Sulfur oxides
3. Carbon monoxide
4. Carbon dioxide
5. Nitrogen oxides
6. Other

C. Radionuclides (by type, weight/unit of time, and curies)
D. Thermal (in BTU's)
E. Sound in decibels and frequencies (EPNDB units)
F. Other

II. Liquids and waterborne material (weight/unit of time, tons/year preferred)
   A. BOD materials (by type, where possible)
      1. Suspended solids
         a. Hydrocarbons
         b. Other
      2. Dissolved materials
      3. Other[7]
   B. Non-BOD materials
      1. Suspended solids
         a. Hydrocarbons
         b. Silt
      2. Other
      3. Chemicals and dissolved material
         a. Agricultural chemicals
            1) Fertilizers
               a) Phosphates
               b) Nitrates
               c) Potassium
               d) Other
            2) Nonfertilizers
               a) Insecticides
               b) Other
         b. Nonagricultural chemicals
            1) Metal salts
            2) Inorganic acids
            3) Inorganic bases
            4) Other
   C. Radionuclides (by type, weight/unit of time, and curies)

7. This category includes material (such as oil) which may be released to a water receptor and will be carried away by the water receptor but will not dissolve or become suspended.

D. Thermal (in BTU's)

III. Solid materials (tons/year)
   A. Garbage
   B. Rubbish, trash
   C. Ashes
   D. Other (please specify if possible)
   E. Radionuclides (by type, weight, and curies, if possible)

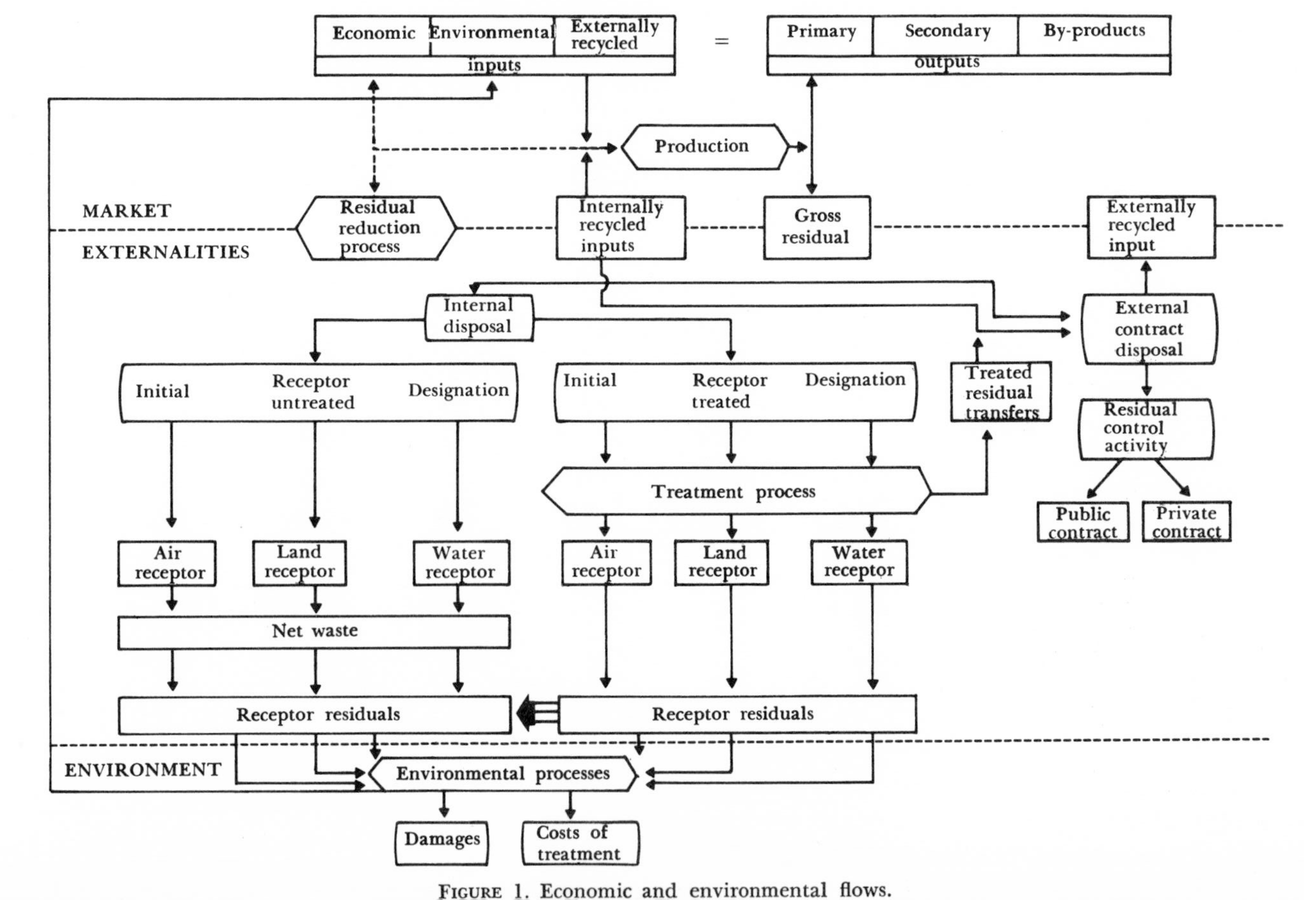

FIGURE 1. Economic and environmental flows.

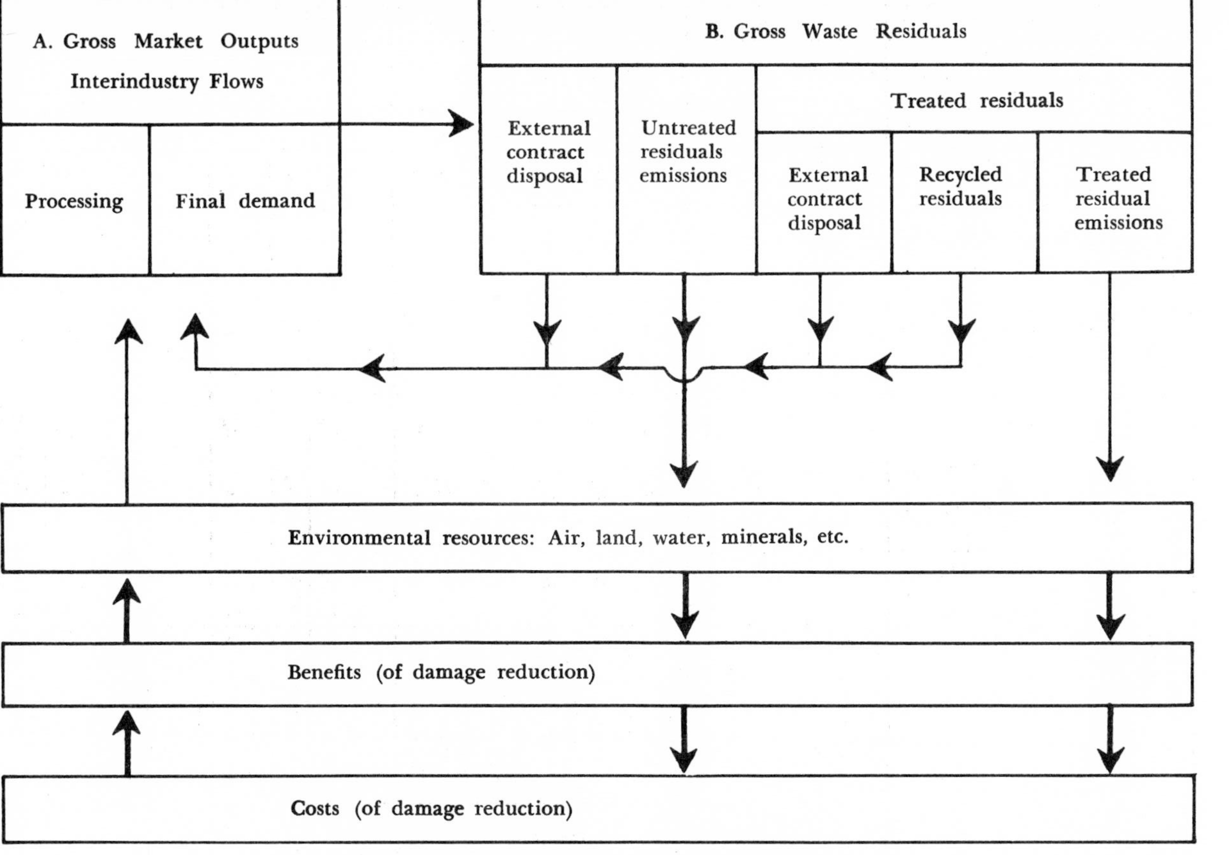

FIGURE 2. Economic and environmental flows.

	Purchasing sector / Producing sector		Intermediate sale: Agriculture	Manufacturing	Service	Trade	Other	*Total intermediate*	Final demand: Household	Capital formation	Government	Total final demand	Total purchases by regional economy	Total exports	Gross regional product Total purchases from regional economy	Environmental balance
			1	• 2	j	•	n	w	C	I	G	Y	D	E	X	B
Intermediate purchases	Agriculture	1	x_{ll}	•	x_{ij}	•	x_{ln}	w	C_l	I_l	G_l	Y_l	D_l	E_l	X_l	B_l
	Manufacturing	2	•													
	Services	i	x_{il}		x_{ij}	•	x_{in}	w_i	C_i	I_i	G_i	Y_i	D_i	E_i	X_i	B_i
	Trade	•	•													
	Other	n	x_{nl}		x_{nj}		x_{nn}	W_n	C_n	I_n	G_n	Y_n	D_n	E_n	X_n	B_n
	Total intermediate	u	u_l	•	u_j	•	u_n	u_w	C_u	I_u	G_u	Y_u	D_u	E_u	X_u	B_u
Value-added	Wages and salaries	L	L_l		L_j		L_n	L_w	C_L	I_L	G_L	Y_L	D_L	E_L	L	B_l
	Other household income	R	R_l		R_j		R_n	R_w	C_r	I_r	G_r	Y_r	D_r	E_r	R	B_r
	Regional personal income	H	H_l		H_j		H_n	H_w	C_h	I_h	G_h	Y_h	D_h	E_h	H	B_h
	Business savings	F	F_l		F_j		F_n	F_w	C_f	I_f	G_f	Y_f	D_f	E_f	F	B_f
	Government receipts	T	T_l		T_j		T_n	T_w	C_t	I_t	G_t	Y_t	D_t	E_t	T	B_t
	Value-added	V	V_l		V_j		V_n	V_w	C_v	I_v	G_v	Y_v	D_v	E_v	V	B_v
	Total sales by regional economy	S	S_l		S_j		S_n	S_w	C_s	I_s	G_s	Y_s	D_s	E	X	B
	Total imports	M	M_l		M_j		M_n	M_w	C_m	I_m	G_m	Y_m	M			
	Total sales to regional economy	Z	Z_l		Z_j		Z_n	Z_w	C	I	G	Y	D			
	Environmental benefits	(+)Q														
	Environmental costs	(−)C														
	Environmental balance	A	A_i		A_j		A_n	A_w	A_o	A_i	A_g	A_y	A			

Figure 3. Regional interindustry model including environmental factors. Source: John H. Cumberland, "A Regional Interindustry Model for Analysis of Development Objectives," *Regional Science Association Papers* 17:68 (1966).

References

1. Ayres, Robert U., and Kneese, Allen V. "Production, Consumption, and Externalities." *American Economic Review* 59, no. 7 (June 1969):282–97.
2. Bergmann, Barbara. "Assessing the Impact of Alternative Economic Outcomes on Social Objectives." Fifth International Conference on Input-Output Techniques, Geneva, Switzerland, 11–15 January 1971.
3. Cumberland, John H. "Application of Input-Output Techniques to the Analysis of Environmental Problems." Fifth International Conference on Input-Output Techniques, Geneva, Switzerland, 11–15 January 1971.
4. Cumberland, John H.; Gibson, Charles S., Jr.; Korbach, Robert J.; Gerhardt, Paul; Hibbs, James R.; and Stram, Bruce N. EQUIPS-MABET (Environmental Quality Information and Planning System-Materials Balance Externality Trace). September 1970.
5. Olson, Mancur. *Towards a Social Report*. Washington, D.C.: Government Printing Office, 1969.
6. Russell, C. S., and Spofford, W. O. "A Quantitative Framework for Residuals Management Decisions." In *Environmental Quality Analysis: Theory and Method in the Social Sciences*, edited by A. V. Kneese and B. T. Bower. Baltimore: Johns Hopkins University Press, 1972.

13

A Model for Understanding the Relationships of Money, Energy, and Survival Value

Howard T. Odum and Suzanne Bayley

At the root of the current concern over decision making and environmental quality is the basis for value. What are the ultimate criteria for value and what are their relationships to money, energy, and survival? For systems of nature that do not have money, what are the measures of value? For the newly emerging systems of man and nature in which money is only involved with man and not paid to nature, what are the means for the correct decisions about relative values of alternatives? In this paper the quantitative relationships of flows of energy and money are considered with the help of an energy-money unit model, and an analog simulation test is made to indicate its stability. Common roots of ecological and economic concepts are sought in basic laws of energetics and natural selection. Finally, suggestions are made for energy cost-benefit analysis and for stabilizing the economies of man during periods of changing energy basis.

The Reward Loop Energy Model

A generalized energy model for ecological and other systems has been developed at some length in previous papers (4) and summarized in a recent book (5). Shown in Figure 1a is one version of this unit model drawn with an energy systems language whose symbols are defined and mathematically translated in Figure 2. The model in Figure 1a shows the flow of usable potential energies from sources such as the sun passing through the plants on the left to the consumer animals and microorganisms on the right. Work is done along this path accompanied by dispersal of heat as required by the first and second laws of thermodynamics. In the diagram heat passes out through the heat sinks indicated by grounded arrows. The work done along the path increases the energy value of all units, services, or products downstream so that it has the facility to stimulate more inflow with multiplicative amplifier actions when fed back upstream as shown by the feedback arrow. Since the energy value of a process with two interacting energy flows depends on them both, a unit of reactant has higher energy value when it is scarce because it is then the limiting factor in facilitating another power flow.

The model is subject to additional laws, especially the criteria of survival from the theory of Lotka's (3) maximum power principle, summarized as follows: a system such as that in Figure 1a in competition with alternatives wins by maximizing its input power and utilization for useful purposes, where useful values are defined as those which facilitate system survival.

A corollary of power maximization is that the work done by a downstream consumer unit must stimulate as much new upstream energy flow as it drains, if it is to avoid weakening the competitive position of the system. By this reasoning, there is a retention of ultimate energy value in the closed loops of a surviving system with as much new amplifier power being developed as there is potential energy dispersed into heat. The reward-loop model suggests a concept of energy value that is based on energy but does not decrease with energy degradation.

It may help at this point to define an energy quality ratio as the ratio of the potential energy that a flow releases when it acts at its actual site of use (often in interaction with other flows) and the potential energy that it contains in itself without other energy flows. The flow from the consumers returning to the plants (to the left in Figure 1a) has a small energy value, but interacting with the plants and more solar energy facilitates a large energy input flow.

It was proposed in the earlier writings that value to any system and value to man are ultimately related to survival and maximizing useful power, since natural selection eliminates those patterns and programs which do not maximize power. In systems in which man plays a programmatic role, this hypothesis implies that those cultures and patterns surviving are continuously adjusted by natural selection to consider as most valuable those flows with maximum power. In other words, value was identified over the long range with high power and high quality ratios of

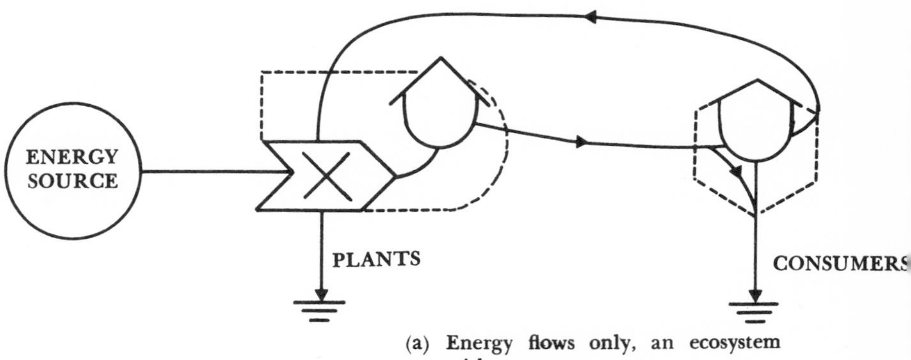

(a) Energy flows only, an ecosystem without man.

ENERGY

$

$

FARMS

CITY

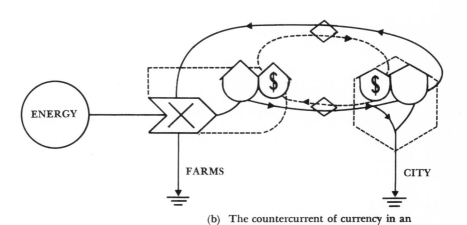

(b) The countercurrent of currency in an energy value loop, a human system.

FIGURE 1. A constant value loop in a productive and consumptive system.

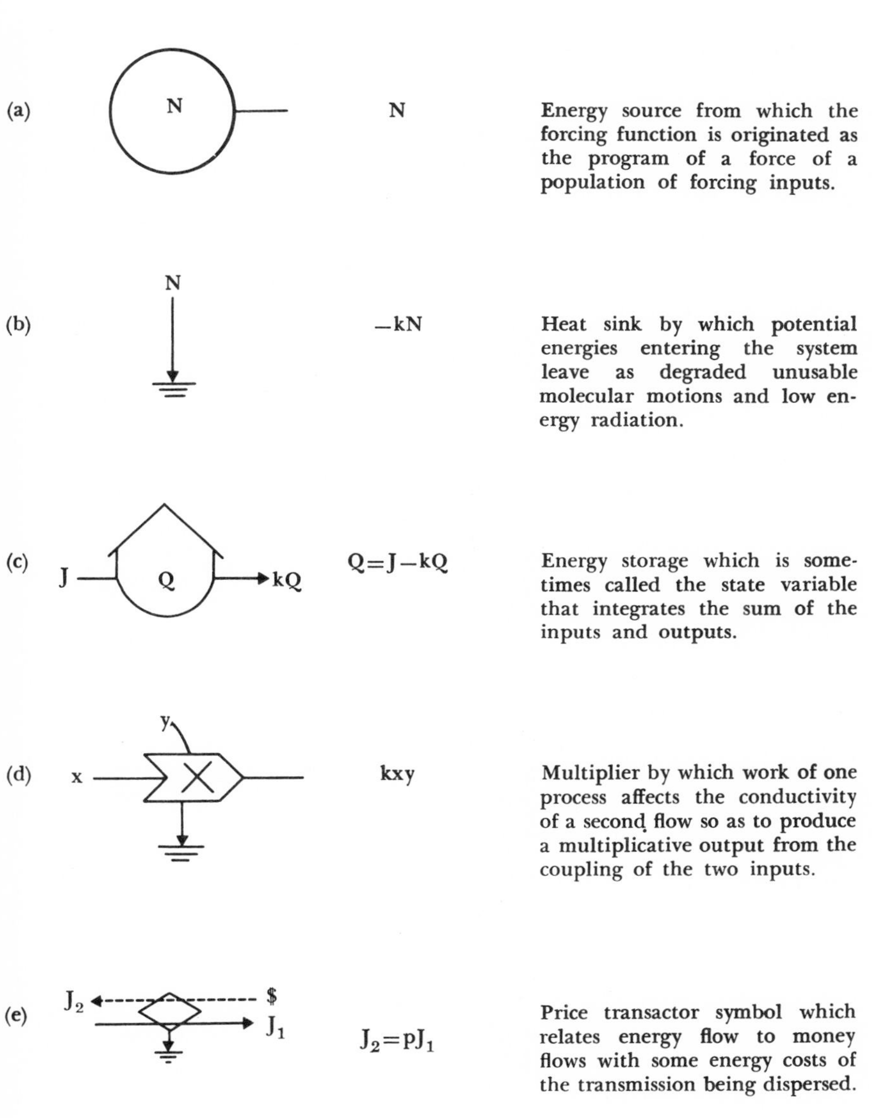

(a)
N
N
Energy source from which the forcing function is originated as the program of a force of a population of forcing inputs.
(b)
N
−kN
Heat sink by which potential energies entering the system leave as degraded unusable molecular motions and low energy radiation.
(c)
J
Q
kQ
Q=J−kQ
Energy storage which is sometimes called the state variable that integrates the sum of the inputs and outputs.
(d)
y
x
kxy
Multiplier by which work of one process affects the conductivity of a second flow so as to produce a multiplicative output from the coupling of the two inputs.
(e)
J2
$
J1
J2=pJ1
Price transactor symbol which relates energy flow to money flows with some energy costs of the transmission being dispersed.
(f)
Combinations
Cluster of modules that make up production processes.

FIGURE 2. Energy symbols used in energy diagrams.

power flows. These principles and premises include the environmental systems generally, whether man and money are involved or not. There is likely to be lag in the responses of man's programming when changes are rapid.

Money in the Energy Model

Systems with man and money are recognized to have the same kind of power flows, reward feedback loops, and increasing energy quality ratios downstream of the simpler ecosystems, except that there is a countercurrent of currency that moves around the value circle in opposite direction to the potential energy. As shown in Figure 1b, money circulates with price transactions (small diamond symbol) as an accounting system that serves to adjust automatically the coupling of feedback work to that of the downstream flow so as to maximize the productive system. There are, of course, various factors in more complex economic systems that may also control prices, such as governmental programs and international trade agreements, but our consideration here is for the most macroenergetic-macroeconomic properties.

Considered as a whole, there is a characteristic ratio of total money flow rate to total power flow in the system (Figure 1b), but within the system the ratio of money to energy flow is not constant but increases downstream. Here the energy flow is not considered for its energy content alone. If, instead of considering the energy of the flow as it is alone, one considers the energy quality ratio as the energy value the pathway ultimately develops, then there is a constant energy value within the circle and the ratio of money to ultimate energy flow is constant. Since some use energy in the restricted manner, calculating the values alone, and others consider energy the flow produced in its interaction, there is opportunity for confusion. Earlier efforts to relate money and value to work, such as those by Ricardo (8) or by the Technocrats (1), may not have generated acceptance because of the confusion of these two kinds of energy values produced by the same feedback flow. A systems diagram is probably required to make the two meanings clear, and the energy circuit diagram models (Figure 1) may be helpful for clarification.

In this paper we carry the theory further by showing that the model is consistent with elementary economics equations for price, supply, and demand. Or conversely, when the elementary equations of supply and demand are energy-translated, common multiplier relationships found in equations for ecological producer-consumer models emerge. The energy circuit language helps to link the independent work of these fields that deal in different ways with the same system.

Equations for a Purchase Pathway

The energy diagrams may be regarded as a conceptual way to represent a set of differential equations, and the terms of those equations become the pathways of the models written in this network language. In Figures 3 and 4 details of an economy of production and consumption are represented with both energy and money flows. The two diagrams are equivalent ways of representing the equations in energy language. The outside energy source (I) enables agriculture (Q_1) to produce special energy needs which are consumed by labor (Q_2). Labor through its work makes possible further production of agriculture. The money system which flows counter to the work and energy is equivalent in this diagram to the capital for agriculture (M_1) and the stock of capital and wages of cities and labor (M_2).

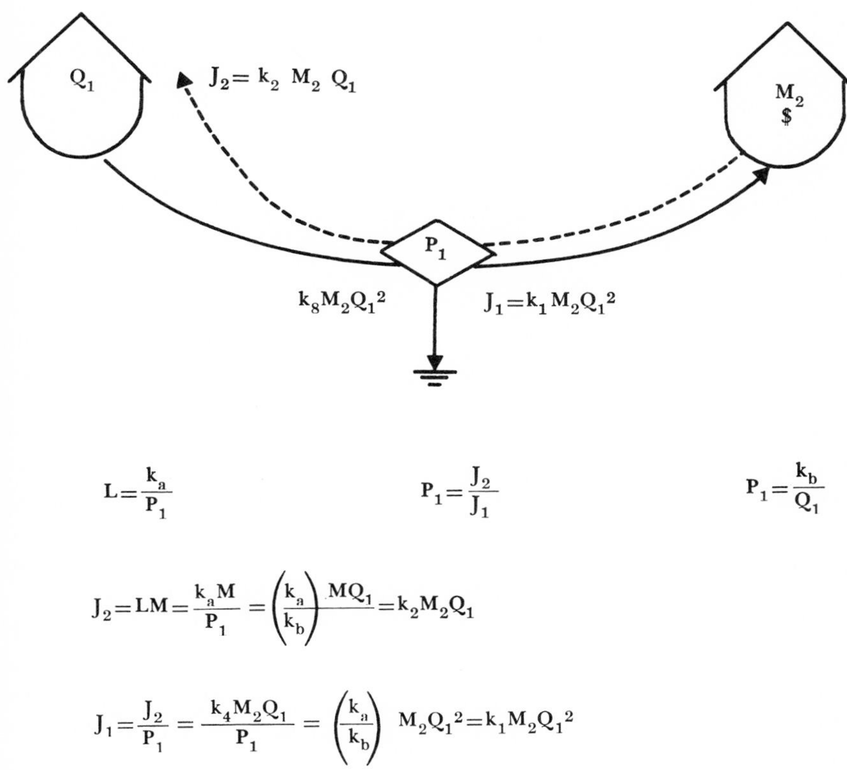

Q_1
$J_2 = k_2 M_2 Q_1$
M_2
$
P_1
$k_8 M_2 Q_1{}^2$
$J_1 = k_1 M_2 Q_1{}^2$
$L = \frac{k_a}{P_1}$
$P_1 = \frac{J_2}{J_1}$
$P_1 = \frac{k_b}{Q_1}$
$J_2 = LM = \frac{k_a M}{P_1} = \left(\frac{k_a}{k_b}\right) MQ_1 = k_2 M_2 Q_1$
$J_1 = \frac{J_2}{P_1} = \frac{k_4 M_2 Q_1}{P_1} = \left(\frac{k_a}{k_b}\right) M_2 Q_1{}^2 = k_1 M_2 Q_1{}^2$

FIGURE 3. Equations for the money-energy relationship of the model during a purchase of goods (Q_1) with money from stock (M_2).

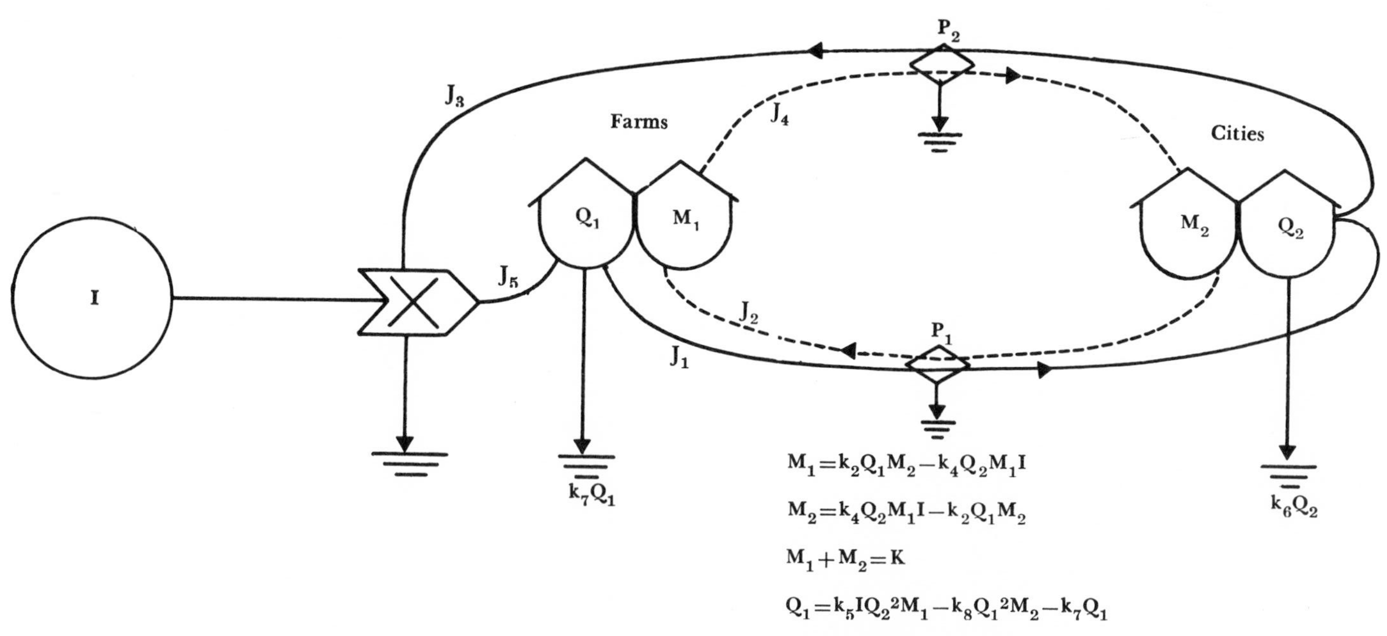

$$M_1 = k_2Q_1M_2 - k_4Q_2M_1I$$

$$M_2 = k_4Q_2M_1I - k_2Q_1M_2$$

$$M_1 + M_2 = K$$

$$Q_1 = k_5IQ_2{}^2M_1 - k_8Q_1{}^2M_2 - k_7Q_1$$

$$Q_2 = k_1Q_1{}^2M_2 - k_3IQ_2{}^2M_1 - k_6Q_2$$

FIGURE 4. **Production and consumption model** with money and energy flows drawn and equations for the model.

As given by equations in Figure 3, the flow of money in a purchase pathway is shown proportional to the money storage (M) depending on a conductivity (L) which is controlled by its price coupling to available goods to purchase. The equations for the transactor symbol involve the ratio of the two flows, money and energy (J_2/J_1) as price (P_1), and price is given as inversely proportional to quantity of available goods (supply and demand effect). Together when substituted, one finds that the collective action has the flow of energy proportional to the product of the upstream energy storage (Q_1) and the downstream money storage (M_2). These check intuitively with the individual person's programming, which finds him buying nothing if there are no goods to buy or if he has no money.

If the expressions are correct, then the energy flow becomes proportional to the square of the energy storage driving the flow. If one raises the energy levels, the ratio of money circulation to energy circulation decreases. However, if the energy source decreases, there is an inflationary increase in money per unit of work.

Analog Computer Simulation

In Figures 3 and 4 the implied mathematical equations for each pathway are written on the diagrams even though this is not necessary and is already implied by the conventions defined in the energy circuit language. A network energy diagram is really one large differential equation, but it may be represented as a set of smaller equations expressing the rate of change associated with each storage unit (tank symbol). The set of equations may be expressed in standard analog computer diagramming as in Figure 5, in which the flows of the terms are indicated by the lines that are also the wires connecting the mathematical operating hardware. The pathways in the analog diagram (Figure 5) move voltage which is manipulated according to the equations, thus adding, subtracting, multiplying, integrating, etc. Therefore, Figure 5 is yet another statement of the same model and is a wiring diagram for patching the analog computer. To illustrate the operation of the production-consumption operation, some values have been invented for stock levels and usual flow rates in a simplified microcosm of a solar-based economy. Referring to letters in Figure 4, stocks are: Q_1, $2.5 \times 10^3 g/m^2$; Q_2, $200 g/m^2$; M_1, $\$10/m^2$; and M_2, $\$10/m^2$ when flow rates are: J_1, $2.5 g/m^2/day$; J_2, $0.1¢/m^2/day$; J_3, $2 g/m^2/day$; and J_4, $0.1¢/m^2/day$. For each pathway, if the stocks and flows are known, the coefficients are established. One may solve the expression for the coefficient in terms of the stocks and flows in existence at the same time. In scaling, initial coefficients used are: k_1, 10^{-7}; k_2, 10^{-13}; k_3, 2×10^{-10}; k_4, 2×10^{-14}; k_5, 2×10^{-8}; k_6, 10^{-2}; k_7, 10^{-2}; and k_8, $10.^{-2}$

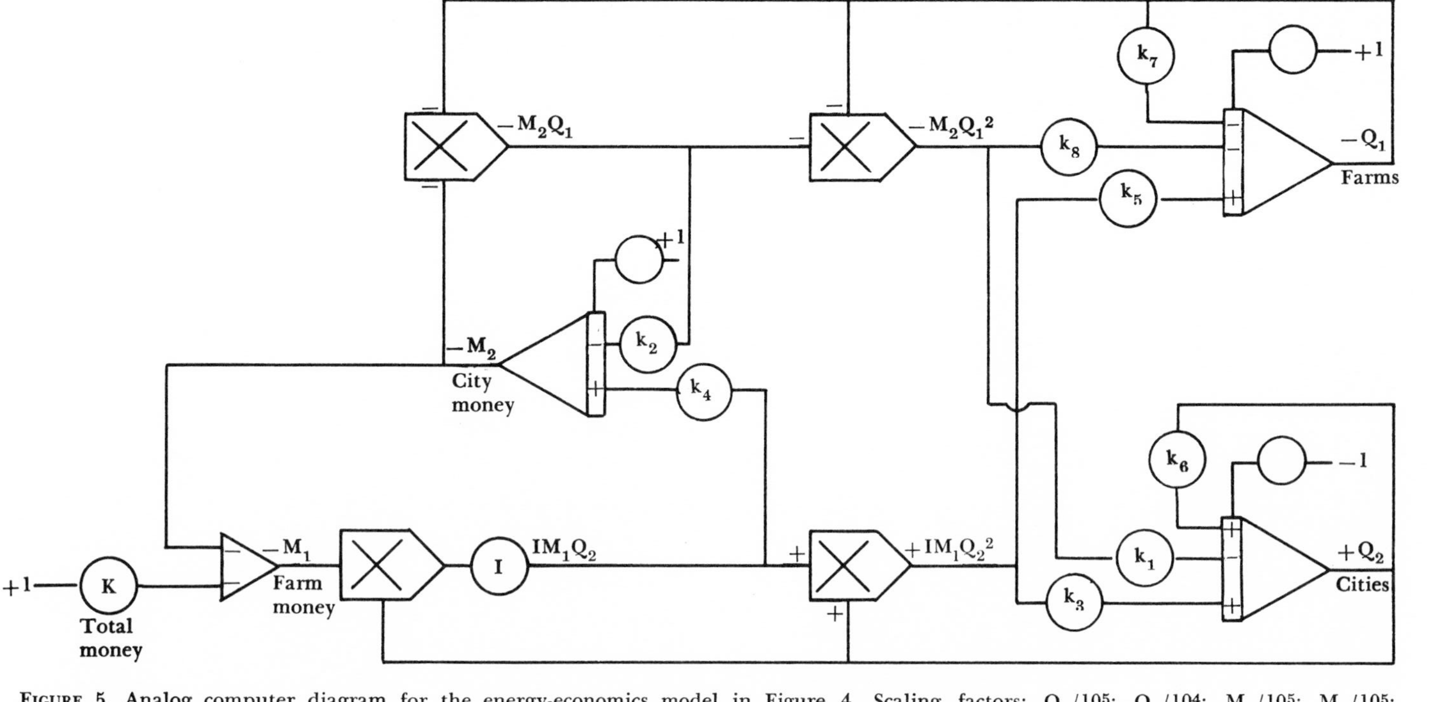

FIGURE 5. Analog computer diagram for the energy-economics model in Figure 4. Scaling factors: $Q_1/10^5$; $Q_2/10^4$; $M_1/10^5$; $M_2/10^5$; $I/10^4$; $K/10^5$.

With the coefficients calculated, the model is thus made quantitative for a particular set of numerical relationships. The analog computer provides an easy means for observing the temporal consequences of these relationships, starting with some arbitrary initial conditions. The analog wiring diagram is in Figure 5, and in Figure 6 are some computer graphical records of the simulation showing the drift of the system from the arbitrary initial state to a steady state pattern. The model is stable in a fairly narrow range of parameters. The model in Figure 5 is given the pot adjustments listed in the legend to Figure 6, with the graphs of Figure 6 exemplifying the model's performance with time. Notice the adaptation period of about twenty years and a sharp curve in the first two years when money is being redistributed. The simulation begins with an equal distribution of money between M_1 and M_2, but changes rapidly to a steady state with money mainly in the storage next to the energy source. The model is very stable.

Money Flow as a Function of the Square of Goods Available

Since price is made inversely proportional to the available goods (a hyperbolic relationship), then the flow of goods becomes a function of the product of the money available to purchase and of the stock of goods for purchase. The flow of money is then proportional to the product of the supply of money for purchase and the square of the stock of goods available. Thus, rising levels of energy accelerate the money flows proportionately more rapidly. The simulation shows the model becoming more unstable with rising levels of energy and stocks.

The model with money, transactions, and prices behaves like the previously studied models for production and consumption in natural systems which lack the money transactions. The exercise suggests that much larger and more detailed models may be constructed containing moneyed and nonmoneyed pathways for the study of macroenergetics and macroeconomics together. The model in Figure 5 has its value flows represented either by money or by the energy and work flows to which the money is a countercurrent. Since the equations given in elementary basic economics texts are included in the model along with the driving energy relationships, we hope the model shows how to generalize value concepts of money and energy and man and environment. The basis for money flows as a measure of value is thus established in the more general energy flows.

Uses of the Energy-Money Models

If these principles are correct, we need to implement more complex versions of these models into the macroeconomics and macroenergetics

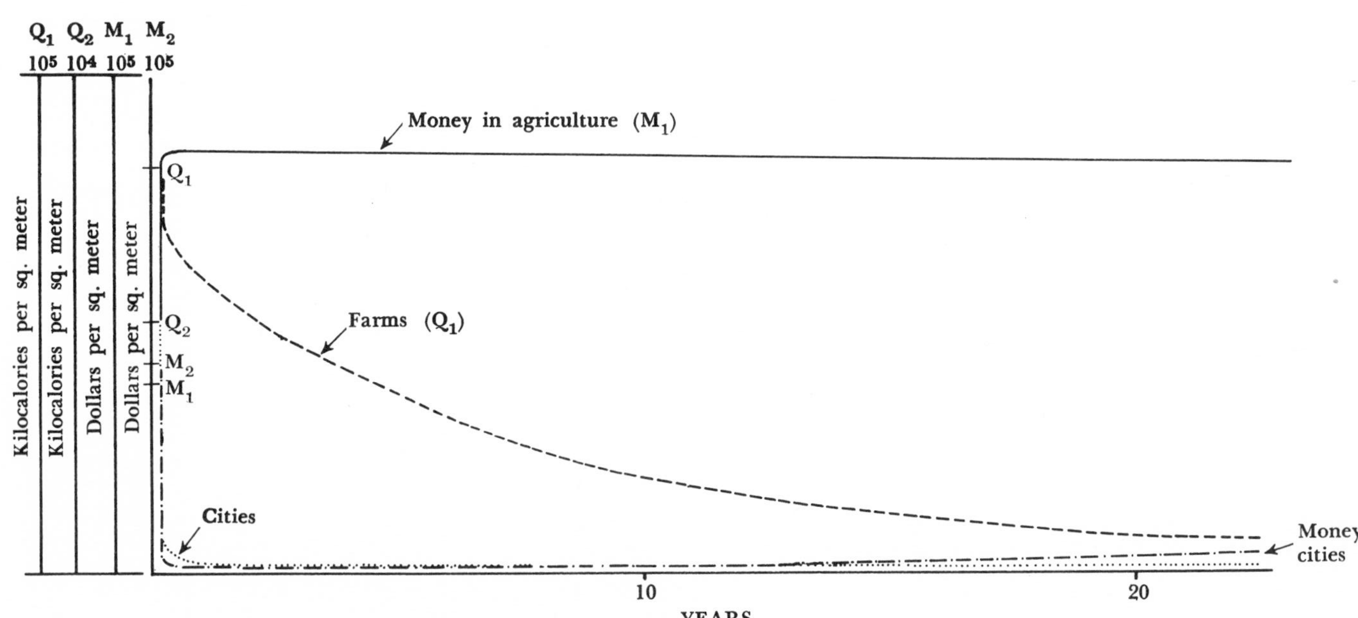

FIGURE 6. Graphical record of simulation model in Figures 4–6. Pot settingsare: k_1, .01; k_2, .1; k_3, .25; k_4, .025; k_5, .25; k_6, .0001; k_7, .0001; k_8, .1. Initial conditions are: Q_1, .91; Q_2, .56; M_2, 5; K, .97; I, .99.

of national and international decision making. It is the changing inputs of energy, forcing functions, and uses of lands and waters in moneyed and nonmoneyed sectors that are producing an expanding economy. Possibly inherent in these changes are such properties as inflation. If energies and forcing functions are changing and the decisions are made on the basis of incomplete money models, there can be no rational planning. As shown in Figure 7, only part of the useful work is accompanied by money. The current system of national policy advising is thus incomplete. The assumptions of growth as good for survival may be correct only for the recent period of history in which energy availability has expanded (I in Figure 5). If energy deliveries become more constant, then survival will require adaptation to no growth. Many aspects of our regard of money, value, and nature are so deeply ingrained in our culture that we may need institutional changes to alter them.

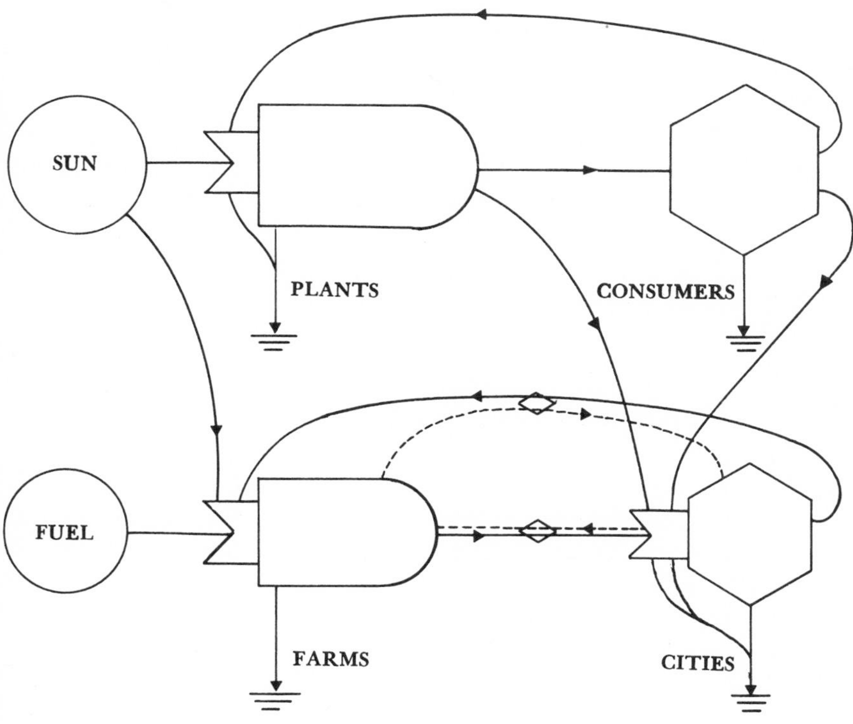

FIGURE 7. Model of man and nature showing the currency circle in only part of the whole system of energy and value that supports us now.

An Energy Standard for Currency

One possible change would be to put the currency on an energy basis. Something like this has been suggested before, but without a clear idea of the countercurrent relationship of currency and energy in value loops. For example, the magazine *Technocracy* (1) describes a net energy certificate for services to individuals. However, to make currency reflect the overall true energy values in the whole system would require the money supply to be maintained in a constant ratio to the total energy flows put into the system from the environment or from traditional fuels. This would keep the ratio of money to energy constant, thus making the money maintain constant value with time and place. This ratio for various countries is plotted by Gambel (2); see also Odum (5, p. 184). The process of establishing the energy standard would dramatize and orient the public to the true causal bases for their power and survival. It might even forestall some ill-advised national ventures not oriented to true capabilities. Energy inputs may be placed on an equivalent basis of similar concentration by converting to kilocalories of energy in food-fuel equivalents available to society. Fuels deep in the land, under the sea, or oils dispersed in rock have much less net energy value after the energies required to concentrate and transport have been subtracted from the total available energy. Similarly, solar energy is very dilute per volume and a high percentage of it must be fed back into the apparatus, whether this work is done by a green plant or by some photometric cells. Solar energy should be multiplied by its conversion efficiency under the situation of other inputs to get its equivalent value to other energy sources as an input to the economy on which the energy standard is calculated.

Extending Money Coverage to the Ecosystems

In order to provide money flow recognition for all the environmental energy inputs and drains, an environmental authority should be established, as shown in Figure 8, which will receive tax money from all human systems in proportion to the energy values derived from nature. This authority should use the received money to buy those natural services, recycled materials, etc., for the human systems so as to reward natural and artificial feedback systems and therefore maximize the survival of the natural system. This system would put the environmental sectors in perspective and allow money to be a correct measure of the total value, since money would circulate among all value cycles in the planet. Something like this is done now in areas where environmental royalties are

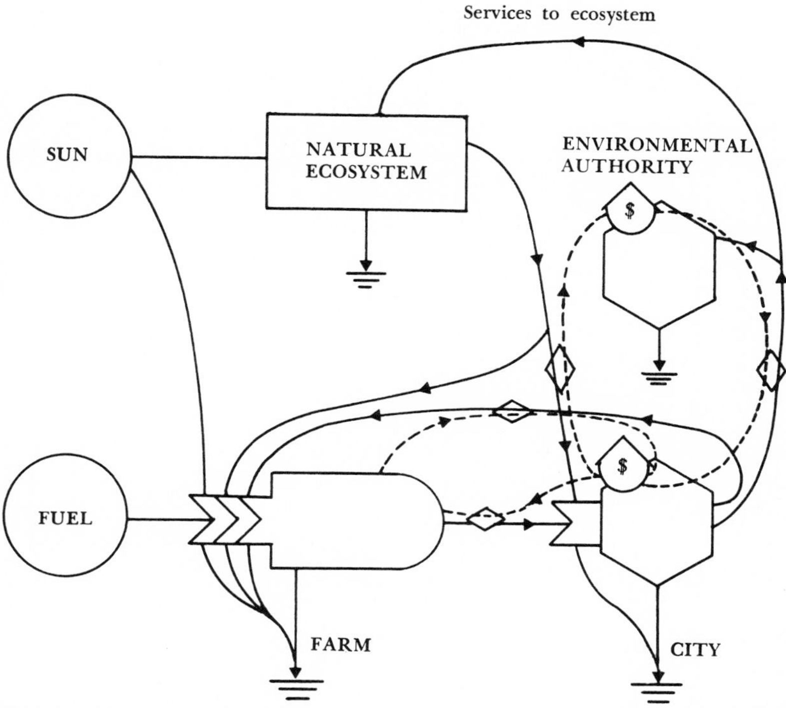

FIGURE 8. Provision for an environmental authority extending money coverage to include the life-support systems not now involved in systems of mixed energy and money.

taxed, but the moneys go into government uses rather than being obligated for the welfare of the natural sectors as corporate members.

Energy Cost-Benefit Analysis

The energy-economics model suggests means for doing cost-benefit studies where part of the value is ecological, with data in terms of energy, and part is the economic system of man, with data in dollar terms. Given in Figure 9 and in Table 1 is a very simple example in which the data aspects which are in money are converted to energies for inclusion and comparison with the work contributions of the parts of the system involving work without man, such as ecological productivity, wave work on beaches, stream-meandering work, etc. To make a rough conversion at least as a first approximation, we have used 10,000 kilocalories to the dollar as a rounded figure of dollar flow accompanying the average overall work in our economy (mainly by machines, power plants, etc.). An attempt is made to use this approximation to get at the energy being contributed by men and machines simply because the data are not usually in energy form. Errors that may accrue from this approximation are not inherent in the model but arise from having data in inappropriate form. In a recent report (7) we have attempted a more detailed evaluation of a region's energy value in a real situation, that of Naples, Florida. We made the energy value tabulations for the condition before man, for the present situation, and for two contingencies of extrapolated growth. The condition that leaves some of the natural land-use inputs with some of the inputs of urban development had higher values than either the primitive or the fully developed conditions.

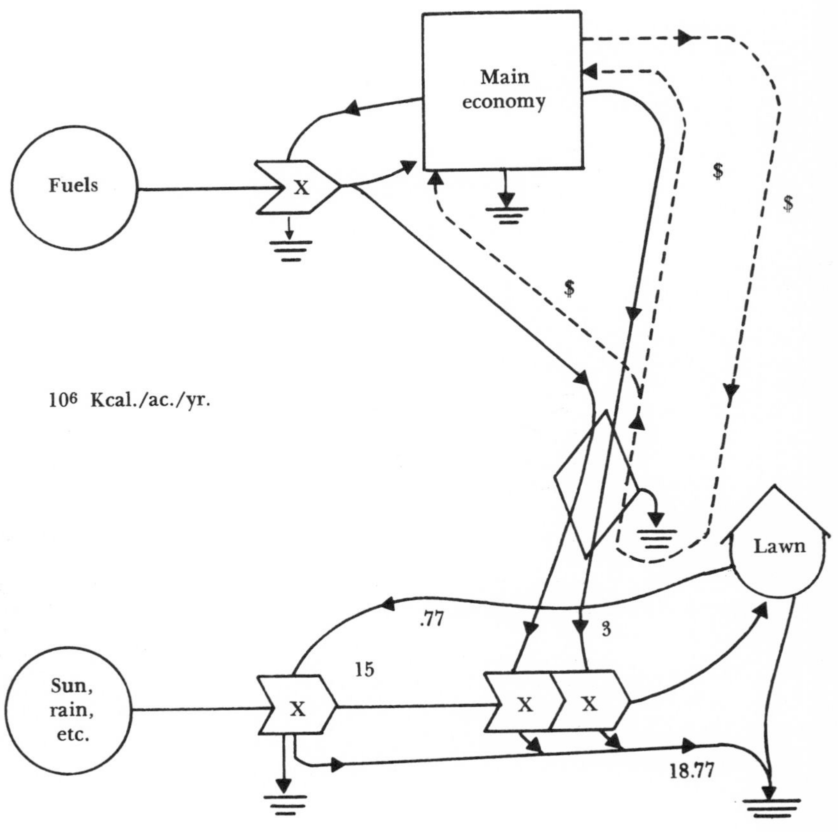

FIGURE 9. Energy diagram showing relationship of an acre of lawn to its energy sources and the general economy of man.

TABLE 1

A SIMPLIFIED EXAMPLE OF ENERGY COST-BENEFIT ANALYSIS FOR AN ACRE OF LAWN

	Annual Energy Flow (Million Kcal/Ac/Yr)	Dollars/Ac/Yr
1. Productivity from sun, wind, rain actions on grass; using 10 kcal/m²/day as grass production rate	15	1,500[a]
2. Purchased contributions of work and services done elsewhere toward this acre @ $300/yr[b]	3[b]	300
3. Work by fuels on the area @ 25 gallons of gasoline per year (water)	.77[c]	77
Annual total work	18.77	1,877

a. 365 days times 10 kcal/m²/day times 4.1×10^3m²/ac.
b. Using 10,000 kcal/$.
c. Using 25 gal/yr $\times$ 3.86 $\times$ 10^3ml/gal $\times$ density 0.8 gms/ml $\times$ 10 kcal/g.

REFERENCES

1. Anon. "The Energy Certificate." *Technocracy* (1937).
2. Gambel, A. B. "Energy R and D and National Progress." Office of Science and Technology, Office of the President, Washington, D.C., 1964.
3. Lotka, A. J. *Elements of Mathematical Biology.* New York: Dover Press, 1956.
4. Odum, H. T. "Work Circuits and System Stress." In *Primary Productivity and Mineral Cycling in Natural Ecosystems,* edited by H. E. Young. University of Maine, Orono, 1968.
5. Odum, H. T. *Environment, Power, and Society.* New York: John Wiley and Sons, 1971.
6. Odum, H. T. "An Energy Circuit Language for Ecological and Social Systems: Its Physical Basis." In *Systems Ecology,* edited by B. Patten. Vol. 2. New York: Academic Press, 1972.
7. Odum, H. T.; Littlejohn, C.; and Huber, W. "An Environmental Evaluation of the Gordon River of Naples, Florida, and the Impact of Developmental Plans." Report to Board of County Commissioners of Collier County, Florida, 1972.
8. Ricardo, D. *Principles of Political Economy and Taxation.* Everyman ed. New York: E. P. Dutton and Co., 1911.

Lewis and Clark College - Watzek Library
HC110.E5 C67
wmain
Conner, J. Richard/Economics and decisio
3 5209 00387 6196